BOOKS BY NICHOLAS CHRISTOPHER

Fiction
Veronica (1996)
The Soloist (1986)

Poetry
The Creation of the Night Sky (1998)
5° (1995)
In the Year of the Comet (1992)
Desperate Characters: A Novella in Verse &
Other Poems (1988)
A Short History of the Island
of Butterflies (1986)
On Tour With Rita (1982)

Nonfiction
Somewhere in the Night: Film Noir & the
American City (1997)

Anthologies (as editor)
Walk on the Wild Side: Urban American Poetry Since 1975 (1994)
Under 35: The New Generation of
American Poets (1989)

SOMEWHERE IN THE NIGHT

Film Noir and

the American

City

by NICHOLAS CHRISTOPHER

An Owl Book

Henry Holt and Company · New York

Henry Holt and Company, Inc.
Publishers since 1866
115 West 18th Street
New York, New York 10011

Henry Holt® is a registered
trademark of Henry Holt and Company, Inc.

Library of Congress Cataloging-in-Publication Data
Christopher, Nicholas
Somewhere in the night: film noir and the American city / by
Nicholas Christopher.—1st Owl Book ed.
p.   cm.
"An Owl book."
Originally published: New York, Free Press, 1997.
Filmography: p.
Includes bibliographical references and index.
1. Film noir—United States—History and criticism.   2. Cities and
towns in motion pictures.   I. Title.
PN1995.9.F54C54   1998   97-41597
791.43'655—dc21   CIP

ISBN 0-8050-5669-8

Henry Holt books are available for special promotions and
premiums. For details contact: Director, Special Markets.

First published in hardcover in 1997 by the Free Press

First Owl Books Edition 1998

Printed in the United States of America
All first editions are printed on acid-free paper.∞

10 9 8 7 6 5 4 3 2 1

Contents

Acknowledgments

I am most grateful to John Ashbery, Paul Vlachos, James Byerley, Robert Polito, and Monty Arnold for the often rare videocassettes, magazines, and books, not to mention the hot tips, which they generously passed on to me. And I would like to thank my wife, Constance Christopher, who over the years watched literally hundreds of films noirs with me—well beyond the call of duty—and offered insights and observations at every turn that have been of enormous help to me in writing this book.

Introduction

As a boy, I was never afraid of the dark. Shadows and light intrigued me. As far as I was permitted in those days of relatively safer streets, I liked to go for walks at night. My bicycle was fitted with both a strong headlamp and a red rear light, powered by a generator on the back tire, as well as assorted reflectors. I passed hours star-gazing on the roof. I even preferred attending night games at Yankee Stadium. A night owl then, as now, at one point I built my own shadow play theater—a crude but functional design—for which I concocted a series of one-act plays that were later performed with friends. My extracurricular reading before age twelve—often accomplished well after hours, with the help of a flashlight—consisted mostly of pulp mysteries and comic books, foremost among the latter the nocturnal, Gothic, subterranean Batman of the late 1950s and early 1960s. When it came to movies, my tastes ran to the B-variety: police thrillers, detective stories, and crime melodramas. Ditto the television fare that captured my attention; and in retrospect, early television shows like *Lineup, Dragnet,* and even *Perry Mason,* black and white in the starkly lit fashion of the day, intensely urban and nocturnal, *look* very dark, indeed.

I was born in February 1951 in New York City, in the dead of winter, at the height of the Korean War, the Cold War, and the McCarthy era. It was also the dawn of the Atomic era, and of the faceless, white-collar variety of organized crime, with its corporate structure—buying up banks and sometimes entire municipalities—but still relying on subcontractors of a gaudier sort, like Murder Incorporated, for raw street muscle. It was the heyday of labor unions and bebop jazz, and it was also the apex of the "classic" film noir era. In the month of my birth alone, my parents and their fellow moviegoers across America had the opportunity, at neighborhood theaters, to see the first runs of such seminal noir films as *Cause for Alarm, The Second Woman,* and *The Killer That Stalked New York,* as well as *The Enforcer* and *Cry Danger,* which premiered in New York just days before my birthday. Twenty more films noirs would be released by the major Hollywood studios before the end of 1951. Between January 1950 and December 1952, seventy-four such films appeared on American movie screens—a staggering number by today's standards.

My own connection, through relatives, to some of the 1951 phenomena to which I have alluded seems tenuous, blurred by the passage of time: for example, aside from the Strontium 90 in my bone marrow from the milk of 1950s cows exposed to atmospheric testing of atomic bombs, my most visceral link with the dawn of the Atomic Age would seem to be the fact that my father, fulfilling his wartime obligations, toiled in Chicago as a young engineer on the Manhattan Project; and my grandfather, it happens, stumbled onto the scene of one of Murder Incorporated's most infamous hits, seconds after it occurred, in the barbershop of a midtown hotel—an event he spoke of, with uncharacteristic amazement and fear, to the end of his life. How and to what extent the hysteria of the Cold War and the paranoia of the McCarthy witch hunts invaded my budding psyche I'll never know. What is available for me to see today, depicted with harsh clarity in the films noirs of those times, are the intricate surface textures and the submerged turmoil, the highly magnified inner and outer manifestations, of the urban life that surrounded me as a child. Unsafe, unsanitized, unaccommodating, film noir, now more than ever, appears to me to be the fugitive footage of postwar America. It is the negative from which all true prints would later be rendered, in which the conflation of the twin shocks (or ever-ramifying nightmares) of a near-apocalyptic world war and rapid-fire American urbanization would be captured and delineated, painfully and unswervingly, for all time.

I was twenty-two years old the first time I saw a film noir and knew it to be such. The film was *Out of the Past,* and I watched it in a theater in Paris, France, in the summer of 1973. This was a tumultuous time, not just in the United States, but also in France, where massive student and labor unrest had erupted that spring. Barricades blocked the steep streets near the Sorbonne, tear gas bit the air, and at particularly explosive city arteries, rubber bullets were being fired into crowds of demonstrators. Still, people were going to work, eating, drinking, making love, and attending the cinema. Footloose, zigzagging southward, fresh out of college, I was doing all of the former except working. The cinema was low on my list of activities, and it was quite by chance—as seems altogether appropriate now—that I found myself watching *Out of the Past* on a hot July night.

The theater was located on a narrow sidestreet off the Rue de Rennes in a working class district. Surrounded by tire shops, garages, and a sausage factory, it was improbably named The New Yorker, the letters glowing in indigo neon on the small, crooked marquee. Made in Hollywood and released in the United States in 1947, *Out of the Past* had been playing at The New Yorker for three weeks to standing-room-only houses as part of an ongoing "Festival du Film Noir Americain." It was directed by Jacques Tourneur (an American) and it starred Robert Mitchum, Kirk Douglas, and Jane Greer. A French friend who happened to be a medical student, and who had seen the film three times, advised me solemnly to smoke some opium before I attended a screening. Not a drug with which I had experience, I was nonetheless game, and he provided me with a sample (and his girlfriend's Pyrex pipe) that I shared with two other friends who immediately lost interest in going to the cinema and, after providing me with explicit, and bewildering, directions, instead drifted off to a party.

So I found myself alone on a hard seat in the rear of a packed, smoky theater (with posters of the Manhattan skyline in the lobby), where one could hear a pin drop—so reverential, so congregation-like, was this chain-smoking French audience—and watched *Out of the Past* in its original English, with French subtitles, and experienced the incredible and ghostly sensation of having entered someone else's dream for ninety-five minutes. An intensely vivid, seductive dream. Opium being renowned (De Quincey quotes Shelley in order to convey the drug's visual effects: ". . . as when some great painter dips/His pencil in the gloom of earthquake and eclipse") for inducing fantastic, symbolic, and terrifyingly "real" dreams, I sensed I had seen an unusual film, but ascribed my extraordinary exhilaration to the drug.

It was only a year later, when I was back in New York City, not so footloose, and saw *Out of the Past* again, *sans* stimuli of any kind, at a downtown revival house where it was playing for one night only. And, again, as I found myself entering that same vivid, darkly beautiful dream I remembered from Paris, I realized with astonishment that it had not been the opium which had engendered the dream, but the film.

I had seen films noirs before, with only the vaguest notion of what that term really signified (something dark and sinister?) and was attracted by their unique visual style, gritty, textured renderings of urban life, sharply drawn characters, and psychological complexity. In my early twenties, having become a committed city-dweller and devourer of literature and art that explored city life, I was attracted to the hard-edged but aesthetically arousing ethos these films projected. They seemed to me to be very tough and unblinking takes on the raw underside of the so-called American Dream. They seemed true. But perhaps because in my teens I had seen them through different eyes, none of them had ever hit me with the impact of *Out of the Past*. (To this day, maybe unfairly, I discount that pipeful of opium as a catalyst.)

Since that time, in mainstream movie theaters, art houses, and makeshift screening rooms, in Boston, Chicago, and New York, in a converted barn on Martha's Vineyard and a bakery storeroom on the Aegean island of Spetses, on clickety-clack home projectors and high-tech VCRs with freeze-frame and slow-down buttons and enhancement devices, I have viewed all of the 317 titles in the *Film Noir Encyclopedia* published in 1988, as well as about fifty other films I would classify as films noirs which are not included in that compendium.

But what was it about that film in Paris that not only overrode (or rode upon) the effects of the opium, but also managed to deposit me for a charged, magical stretch of time in the maze of downtown San Francisco on an ink-dark night, surrounded by menacing, jagged shadows, crystalline shafts of light, and men and women who were partly phantoms and partly larger-than-life (like people in a dream) shortly after the Second World War? And after that, started me off on a twenty-year odyssey and sometime obsession with an entire movement of film to which it belonged?

This book is offered as a response to those and other questions— one which, it is hoped, will carry the reader deep into the world of the films, as I was carried.

1. Into the Labyrinth

Picture first, flickering before you, impeccably photographed in rich tones of black and white, a sleek young woman with long dark hair, a cream-colored dress, low-cut and sashed, and a large, flat white hat that conceals her face. With a confident gait she is crossing a sunlit plaza in Acapulco in late afternoon toward a cool, dark cantina. This is our first glimpse of her.

It is also the hero's first glimpse, gazing out at her from the cantina where he has been sitting sleepy-eyed, sipping a beer. A onetime private detective, he has been sent to find her, for a sizeable fee, by another—truly dangerous—man, the urbane gangster, many steps removed from his crimes, who is her lover. After that first look at her, we know from his face that our hero will never take this woman back to the other man, dangerous or not. He knows it too. He is talking to us directly, by way of a voice-over, even as we are watching him, at a corner table, watching her. His voice is far away in time, distanced from the scene before us, reflecting back. Deep, smooth, and languorous, it is a voice with no future—only the past.

"And then I saw her," he says, pausing a beat, "coming out of the sun . . ."

Into the darkness that will be the prime element of their time together. A darkness inside and outside the two of them that will first enmesh, then (seemingly) liberate, and finally entrap them. The teeming, multifarious darkness of film noir. As her face becomes fully, clearly, defined in that shadowy cantina, we see just how beautiful she is.

Our hero does not speak to her, but they exchange glances, and that night he is sitting at the same table, waiting for her. "I even knew," he observes drily, "that she wouldn't come that first night."

But the next night she does come, and for two days he's had nothing to do but fill her out in his imagination. When she enters the cantina, his voice drops a notch.

"And then she walked in," he tells us, "out of the moonlight, smiling . . ."

And he keeps referring to her as emerging from various sorts of light. As a glowing, luminescent image. Almost otherwordly. Always striding into darkness. Always, after that first afternoon (the last afternoon of his life *before her*), at night.

The following night, on a deserted beach, surrounded by the nets of fishermen hung on poles to dry, our hero waits for her, not sure she will keep their assignation. He stands amid the nets like a netted fish himself. A fish she has netted. The surf rolling in behind him. The sand white as powder. Lunar. Wind whistles through the oarlocks of the upturned skiffs and rustles the sharp dune grass as he grows restless in a pool of shadows.

"And then suddenly she appeared," he says with a lift of anticipation, "walking through the moonlight, to me . . ."

To him.

Sitting under one of the nets together, he embraces her for the first time. And the net seems to thicken and close in on him, transformed into a spider's web. She the spider and he the fly. And who is really embracing whom?

When she begins to tell him of the danger they are running, the terrible vengeance that awaits him for betraying the man who has sent him (whom of course she herself has betrayed many times over), he cuts her off with a long kiss, murmuring, "Baby, I don't care."

With that, there is no turning back for him.

They make love in her beach house during a rainstorm. From the wicker door, opening and slamming in the wind, to the bedroom door, their discarded clothes are crumpled together. In the ensuing days, they become inseparable. He can't get enough of her. He sends misleading telegrams back to New York, to the man who sent him, his employer, saying he can't find her. With some cheek, he tells us,

"I sent him a telegram—*I wish you were here*—and then I went to meet her again." Then he sends no telegrams at all. The two of them decide to run away together, but on the day of their departure, the man they fear—and that fear has grown palpably now—arrives unexpectedly, en route elsewhere on gangland business, and nearly catches them together. He is having a drink with our hero when she enters the hotel lobby—out of the glaring sunlight—and he does not see her. And then he returns to New York.

The two lovers slip out of Acapulco that night, by ship, for San Francisco, where they live for a time anonymously. Fearfully, cocooned in blackness. In all their time together, they never feel safe. And as was inevitable, as they both knew would happen, the man who sent our hero to find her sends another man (our hero's former partner in New York) to find both of them.

The ex-partner runs into them at the racetrack. They try to give him the slip, separating and driving cars—each of them taking a different route—to a rendezvous at a cabin in the woods. Our hero is convinced he's not been tailed, and he waits for her on the porch of the cabin. She drives up and parks her car. And still she's coming to him in the darkness, striding out of the light. Not sunlight or moonlight this time.

"And then I saw her," he says, "walking up the dirt road in the headlights of her car . . ."

But another car pulls onto the dirt road from the highway, its headlights off, and snakes up through the trees. Something our hero had not counted on: his ex-partner has followed *her.*

The ex-partner confronts the two of them in the cabin, threatening blackmail. If they pay him off, he won't expose them. There is a fistfight between the two men during which she, effortlessly and unnecessarily, shoots the ex-partner dead. Stunned by her coldbloodedness, our hero looks at her as if for the first time. Then, in the ensuing confusion, she flees, leaving him to bury the dead man's body. And to take the fall for her.

Under cover, he remains on the West Coast, then changes his name and opens a gas station in a small rural town. Time passes. He lives simply and quietly. He gets engaged to a local schoolteacher with whom he likes to go fishing—in broad daylight, at a freshwater lake. With no nets in sight. Always in daylight, the sun shining so whitely as almost to blank out the terrain, making us wince. For as in many films noirs, it is the mundane, daylit world that seems unreal, while the night, complex, frictional, sensorially explosive, stimulating in its contrasts, envelops us with an exotic, often erotic, pleasure. "The night pleases us because it suppresses idle details, just as our memory does," Jorge Luis Borges writes in *Labyrinths*. Idle as in unexplosive, sensorially dull.

The extended prelude, like an elaborate mating dance, first in Mexico, then, especially, in San Francisco, sets up the true heart of the film: the hero's quest within the labyrinth of nocturnal San Francisco several years later. Discovered by chance in his new life by a minion of the man he fears, forced to leave behind his rural surroundings and his fiancée and to reassume his former identity for a single night, he is despatched on a bizarre, murky mission, to recover some incriminating tax documents that could put the man he fears into prison for life. It becomes a very long night indeed through which our hero plunges headlong—a night that can be seen as a microcosm of the many vast and varied, endless nights that backdrop all films noirs. In fact, among these films, *Out of the Past* is an oddity in that much of its narrative is constructed of nonurban flashbacks (Mexico, the desert, the small town) that frame the dense, purely urban sequence which is the film's crucible. What is not unusual is the jagged, fragmented mosaic in which these flashbacks are arrayed; like the voice-over, it is another distancing device that makes the action, and the orbit of the characters, that much more alienated, remote, and unstable.

When we first see him in San Francisco that frenzied night, our hero's rustic clothes have given way to the old trenchcoat and soft-brimmed fedora of his New York days; his mild, small-town manners have been swept aside by wisecracking and tough talk. A cigarette dangles from his lip. He squints out from behind its curl of smoke with a clenched jaw. Alert to danger, on his toes as we have not quite seen him before, he nevertheless has a look of doom in his eyes and seems to be carrying a dead weight on his shoulders. He is stepping back into the past, and instinctively he knows that means fulfilling the dynamics of the past, which have merely been suspended—like his true identity—during his years in hiding. He knows that just by being in that city under such circumstances, he has burned his bridges to his new life. That the circle of his fate, which had been left open for a time, is about to be closed, and there is nothing he can do about it. Though he tries.

Among the myriad people he encounters in the night is his former lover, who is now back living with the man he fears (who, she claims, is blackmailing her too). She also claims still to be in love with our hero. But this time he recoils. When he finds himself alone with her in a darkened room, his tone is no longer worshipful, and he's no longer talking about that ethereal light from which she was forever emerging, into his presence. In his mind, she has fallen miles since then, from shining angel to something considerably less.

"You're like a leaf," he tells her with disgust, "that blows from one gutter to another."

Often in film noir, men veer along a zigzag path with regard to the femme fatale, from reverence to loathing, in truth reflecting (and projecting) more than anything else their feelings about their own condition, their own entrapment, as the walls seem to close in around them. While many times serving as the agent of that entrapment, the femme fatale is always its dark mirror.

The downtown San Francisco in which our hero finds himself could not be more claustrophobic. It is a collapsing, involuted landscape, architecturally and emotionally. The walls that have not already closed in seem to be in the process of doing so before his (and our) eyes. The maze confronting him consists of rain-slicked streets and sidewalks canopied by iron trees; of caged catwalks, rattling fire escapes, dank basements, and twisting corridors; of after-hours office buildings, swank forbidding apartments cluttered with *objets d'art,* and a barren apartment containing only a corpse. Everywhere he goes, shadows are elongated, stairwells steep and winding, and elevators dimly lit; terraces are overhung with thick vines and vacant lots are surrounded by impenetrable foliage. And all the alleys are blind alleys. Our hero in his dark night of the soul has many stations through which he must pass (any one of which might be the terminus) and innumerable characters, on a broad demonic scale, who seek to impede or implicate him, or to grease the skids for his destruction.

There is the woman, his former lover, busily orchestrating his frame-up, casting illusions, manipulating and double-crossing others (truly she seems to have as many arms as a spider, working simultaneously), all the while professing her undying love for him. Is it a coincidence, or a subliminal association on the screenwriter's part, that the name of this archetypal spider woman is Kathie *Moffet*—a couple of vowels differentiating it from the celebrated nursery rhyme character, Miss *Muffit;* "when along came a spider and sat down beside her. . . ."

There is the second woman, a lesser agent of the man he fears— a sort of minor-league femme fatale—who attempts to seduce and distract our hero, even while maneuvering him deeper into trouble; but he rebuffs her. Her name, while we're at it, is Meta, a word whose definitions include "transformation" and "involving substitution"; for surely she is a disguised, temporary surrogate for the spider woman, who is otherwise occupied. In fact, the two women are explicitly linked when Kathie, making a telephone call within the sea of shadows that is Meta's apartment, pretends to be Meta, imitating her voice and even wearing her hair up (for the only time in the film) as Meta does.

And, streaming into our hero's path throughout, there is an infernal rabble that might have slipped en masse from one of the panels of Hieronymous Bosch's "Garden of Earthly Delights." Thieves, extortionists, and strong-arm men, bouncers and grifters, a diminutive embezzler, a pimp who's expert with a knife, a junky informer, and an icily professional hit man with an unnerving, unwavering smile plastered on his face.

But no cops anywhere to be seen. No pedestrians or bystanders— innocent or even neutral. Not a single uncomplicitous, untainted character except the mute cabbie who briefly shuttles our hero between several points along his dizzying path. Stores and businesses are closed. The absence of a general population is, by implication, a statement of contempt. That is, the great mass of citizens, faceless and oblivious, who will flood the streets at rush hour, en route to dead-end jobs, prisoners of the humdrum, are asleep, disconnected from the energy of the night, their windows sealed and curtained to the streets below. The city we see is the one they have blocked out, stripped of illusions: a jungle of tangled steel, oppressed by harsh weather, treacherously constructed, in which the only order is the unnatural order; the fittest, by necessity, are the most devious and most ruthless. The only motivation is the criminal one. The only law, survival.

Our hero does some maneuvering himself, punches and counter-punches, improvises with ingenuity, attempts a frame-up of his own, manages to kill the hit man in self-defense, and actually, futilely, gets his hands on those elusive tax documents, but he does not survive.

He lives on for a while, scrambling against the odds, but his death is foreordained. His circle has already closed. He entered the city on a dangerous, hazy errand (if it hadn't been those documents, it would have been something else) and wound up framed for murder, a hunted man, a fugitive whose "wanted" photo is on the front page of every newspaper in California, including his small town's gazette where his fiancée sees it. He's no longer merely a man with a preda-tory past and fabricated present, but one with no future. It is only a matter of hours before the other woman, the spider woman, has killed both her lovers: first, the dangerous man, shot in the back in his cavernous living room overlooking the desert, and then our hero, shot in the groin behind the wheel of his car, before she herself dies in a hail of police bullets. The three principals—three corners of a rotten triangle—are violently killed, unredeemed, in a chaotic, darkly duplicitous world, which if not within the confines of the in-ferno is surely within throwing distance.

While *Out of the Past* may have been my first model for, and threshold to, the film noir, a more precise abstract, or bare-bones for-mula (somewhat in the manner of a film treatment) of the genre, can be drawn. It might read like this:

It is night, always. The hero enters a labyrinth on a quest. He is alone and off-balance. He may be desperate, in flight, or coldly cal-culating, imagining he is the pursuer rather than the pursued.

A woman invariably joins him at a crucial juncture, when he is most vulnerable. In his eyes she may appear to be wreathed in light, beatific—a Beatrice—guiding and protecting him. Or duplicitous— a Circe—spinning webs of deceit and leading him directly to danger. Often she is a hybrid of the two, whose eventual betrayal of him (or herself) is as ambiguous as her feelings about him. Others seek overtly to thwart him, through brute force or subtler manipulation, or to deflect him into serving their ends. His antagonists are figures of authority, legal or criminal, that loom out of his reach, or else misfits and outcasts in thrall to the powerful. However random the obstacles in his path may seem, the forces behind them are always more powerful than he.

At the same time, the majority of people he encounters are powerless, and either indifferent to him, or terrified of being drawn into his orbit. When someone does extend him a helping hand, it is usually one of the most downtrodden—crippled, blind, destitute—who have little to lose, though for assisting him, they may pay with their lives. Crime as a constant, and vice and corruption, flourish in every stratum of society through which he passes. The farther he progresses, the more clearly his flaws come into focus. Whatever his surroundings, he remains isolated. The acts of nobility and high-mindedness we customarily associate with heroes in other forms are a luxury he can seldom afford.

He descends downward, into an underworld, on a spiral. The object of his quest is elusive, often an illusion. Usually he is destroyed in one of the labyrinth's innermost cells, by agents of a larger design of which he is only dimly aware.

On rare occasion—and here the woman may play the role of Ariadne in the myth of Theseus, leading him out as well as in—he reemerges into the light with infernal (but often unusable) tools to apply in the life he left behind. But scarred as well, and embittered, with no desire to return to the labyrinth, even were he equipped to do so. More likely, if he survives at all, he is a burnt-out case. And the woman, also like Ariadne, is certain to be abandoned, or destroyed in his place, sometimes sacrificing herself for him, in the end as ignorant as he of that larger design in which they were pawns.

From this classic model of the film noir, dozens of variations radiate. The hero is always an American between the ages of twenty-five and fifty. The labyrinth is an American city. The time is 1940 to the present, with a special concentration on the years 1945–1959.

In *Out of the Past,* the voice-over is essential to the film's overall impact. Narrative technique is particularly refined in film noir. Most of the films adhere to an investigative formula (in the broadest sense: psychological, oneiric, and dramatic) through which information is disclosed to the hero. The substance of this information—messages, conversations, thoughts, and raw data—itself comes to constitute a vast, invisible labyrinth that must be penetrated by our hero; inevitably it traps, not only him, but all those around him. The voice-over, on the simplest level, is the device by which the hero shares not only that information, but also his methods of absorbing, distilling, and even deflecting it. In other words, even while his actions reveal much about him, the voice-over shows us how his mind works. It is the oral mapmaking of his journey through the labyrinth.

Dead men tell no tales, the saying goes—but not in film noir, where the hero may narrate his own tale, fluently, from the grave. In *Out of the Past,* this nearly occurs, but, in fact, the voice-over disappears when the narrative arrives at the film's putative present—its coda, really—when Bailey stops relating his story to his fiancée and goes off to his final, fatal rendezvous with Kathie. There are other noir films in which it is clear from the first scene that the voice-over narration will be a posthumous one. The hero is clearly dead, and now he's going to tell us how he died. By way of imaginative voice-overs—alternately presenting facts, uncovering motives, probing his own psyche—the hero will guide us back into the labyrinth, retracing the path he followed to his destruction. He does so with varying doses of bravado, self-deprecation, and fear. His voice is usually an amalgam of many elements, at once knowing, sardonic, soothing, obtuse, arch, resigned. That it is invariably a streetwise voice is ironic, for the story he tells is one in which his street wisdom seems to have failed him on account of willfulness, arrogance, or a host of other character flaws which surfaced in the crucible that preceded, and precipitated, his entry to the labyrinth. This sort of voice-over becomes all the more poignant, and ghostly, when we realize that, as in classical mythology, it is a man's *soul* that has reentered the labyrinth. In effect, this serves to broaden the films' spiritual implications, bringing the totality of the hero's experience—including the manner of his death—into play in recreating and investigating the essence of his life. We come to see that the most "hard-boiled" noir narrator is the one who will most boil down the facts to achieve that essence.

As with most film noir protagonists, the posthumous narrator is possessed by what Leslie Fiedler, in asserting the primacy of the

Gothic influence on American literature since 1800, defines as "images of alienation, flight and abysmal fear." Speaking from the grave is a device Nathaniel Hawthorne and Edgar Allan Poe often employed. In film noir, in the context of a large city, this device has a particularly powerful distancing effect: the narrator is far removed from us—literally in the beyond—and from his corporeal self. It is as if he is gazing back into the maze of Los Angeles or New York from a distant mountaintop—or a remote planet—with an all-seeing telescope. He can offer us asides. Jump around in time. Send us up the wrong path. Or create a sudden detour. Most significantly, the very discrepancy between the time in which the action on screen is occurring and the time in which his voice is addressing us creates an element of tension, and coldly unsettling dislocation, even before the tensions of plot and characterization manifest themselves.

Take three such films that employ a hero's posthumous voice: *D.O.A.* (1950), directed by Rudolph Maté, and *Double Indemnity* (1944) and *Sunset Boulevard* (1950), both directed by Billy Wilder. All three are set in Los Angeles (except roughly one-third of *D.O.A.,* which is set in San Francisco). But it is a Los Angeles that is different in each of them—respectively bizarre, seedy, and fantastical. In plot, too, the three films could not be more dissimilar; nor could their heroes, occupationally: an accountant from the Arizona desert, a smooth-talking insurance salesman, and a washed-up, embittered screenwriter.

In *D.O.A.,* the hero has "already been murdered," he tells us. He doesn't know how, when, where, or by whom—the weapon is a slow-working poison—and he ends up being both the detective and victim of his own murder! Like *Double Indemnity* and *Sunset Boulevard,* this entire film is a flashback. (Actually, a set of extremely complex flashbacks within flashbacks, evocative of the jumbled, or mosaic, nature of time—its passages and elongations—in large cities.) In each of these films, the labyrinth symbolism is overpowering. In the opening of *D.O.A.,* the hero enters a police station (with a forbiddingly cavernous entrance) and proceeds with a determined stride along a maze of long, impersonal corridors, making a dizzying succession of ninety-degree turns, until he finds the small office that is his destination. It is here, speaking into a police captain's dictaphone, that he begins his narration, informing the police that he has been murdered; and it is in this office at film's end, as he completes his narration, that the poison finally takes full effect and the hero dies. Obtaining the solution to his own murder literally became the final labor of his life.

Double Indemnity also opens in an office, in downtown Los Angeles, with the hero speaking into a dictaphone. It is 5 A.M. He has been mortally wounded by a gunshot. His narration comes in the form of a confession, for unlike the hero of *D.O.A.*, this insurance salesman gone crooked is very much the instrument of his own destruction. In confessing, he attempts to untangle the skein of events that led him to this fateful point, not for purposes of expiation of sin (as in conventional films), but apparently so he can better understand exactly where he went wrong in his scheming. Again, we are presented with the absurdity of a dying man at the center of his own labyrinth seeking knowledge that can no longer be of any use to him. (A parable of absurdity to please the most doctrinaire existentialist.) And as in *D.O.A.*, the hero is in effect dying before our eyes for the duration of the film until, finally, in the last scene, he expires.

Sunset Boulevard, along the same lines, has the most dramatic opening of all—one of the most arresting in all of film. The narrator begins his story while we gaze from on high at a dead man floating face-down in a swimming pool. Several minutes into the narration, the film cuts to an underwater camera shooting upward from the bottom of the pool. We see the dead man's face. And at that instant the narrator tells us that *he* is the man in the pool. The film then folds back on itself, in a complex layering of flashbacks, only to end with his murder: narrating to the last moment, he's shot in the back, and staggers into the pool.

In another film, *Murder, My Sweet* (1944), based on the Raymond Chandler novel *Farewell, My Lovely* and directed by Edward Dmytryk, we find a hero, not dead, but as close as he might come to death, blind and battered after the zigzag journey through his particular labyrinth. As in *D.O.A.*, we begin in a police station. The hero, his eyes bandaged, is incongruously sitting in an interrogation room surrounded by police detectives who have turned glaring spotlights on him. He begins his narration, and it is not the confession we might expect, but rather an explanation of his innocence. Again, a complicated flashback structure follows, mirroring his tortured route through the labyrinth—for he is an oddly vulnerable hybrid of witness and investigator—which concludes with his having his "eyeballs scorched" by a revolver that was fired (at somone else) inches from his face. Having finally cleared himself with the police, his eyes bandaged, he is literally guided back into the night from the police station by the young woman (alternately a Beatrice/Circe figure) who variously led and misled him on his quest through the labyrinth of the city, where, metaphorically, he was blinded by the succession of duplicities and horrors he witnessed.

In each of these films, the hero's relationship to the city carries added poignancy and power because the posthumous eye (or post-mortem consciousness) he casts upon it is so devastating and all-encompassing. Here we have a tour guide to the labyrinth like no other, for the hero has actually traveled to the labyrinth's terrible center, where every street is a one-way street, and "died" to tell about it.

In film, as in the novel, a primary element must always be the manner in which a narrator, or a set of characters in concert, suspends and discloses information: this is what determines the element of suspense, which is the nervous system of the plot. In the whodunit we find one sort of nervous system, often rudimentary, occasionally—and more rewardingly—complex. But film noir relies on many varieties of suspense, with ingenuity and sophistication. In *The Dark Corner* (1946), for example, we are aware early on of all the information we shall need to solve the film's surface mystery; what involves us, suspends us, along a taut parabola from beginning to end, is watching as the hero—stumbling, fumbling, nearly self-destructing—attempts to discover information to which we, at every twist and turn, are already privy. The converse principle, at work in all films noirs with a voice-over—whether of the first or third person—is that the voice-over serves to seal off the action of the film. The disjunction between the voice-over, cool and calm, and the tangled, ongoing, present action of what we see, provides inherent, revelatory, sometimes unbearable, tension. The narrator distances us because he knows the outcome of the story.

While echoing myths that date back to the origins of the first cities (in fact, to the cave complexes of the earliest human habitations), the film noir is an utterly homegrown modern American form.

Its literary antecedents are eclectic: from Jacobean drama to Ibsen and Strindberg, Gothic fiction in Britain to the German Romanticism of Kleist and Buchner. It owes as much to Knut Hamsun's *Hunger,* Dostoevsky's *The Devils,* and Dickens' *Bleak House* as to the hard-boiled suspense stories that Dashiell Hammett, Horace McCoy, and Cornell Woolrich contributed to American pulp magazines such as *Black Mask* in the 1930s. In the United States its roots can be traced most directly to the work of Poe; our first poet of the industrialized, extended city, an avatar of the exotic and the macabre, he was also the inventor of the modern detective story. That he so powerfully influenced Charles Baudelaire, the greatest nineteenth-century urban poet—a specialist, like Rimbaud and Verlaine after him, in the sensual and psychological textures of the nocturnal metropolis—oddly mirrors the explosive impact that the so-called "black films" from America, nearly a century later, had upon the young French film directors of the *nouvelle vague,* or New Wave.

These directors—Francois Truffaut, Jean-Luc Godard, Claude Chabrol, Jean-Pierre Melville—in fact popularized the term *film noir* (coined in 1946 by the French critic Nino Frank) which then took some years to make its way back across the Atlantic. The incestuousness of the Franco-American connection ends there, however; by the time the French are shooting their own films noirs in the mid to late fifties, the classic American film noir cycle is nearly completed. The French at that point are fully cognizant of, and influenced by, the films noirs made in the United States, whereas the various American directors of films noirs from 1945 to 1955 have been blissfully unaware that, as a group, they were creating an entirely new genre of film. In fact, the term "film noir" in the 1940s and early 1950s was not at all a familiar one either to American filmmakers or their audiences. (Webster's lists its first English usage as 1958.) Had you told Billy Wilder in 1947 that you admired his latest film noir, he wouldn't have known what you were talking about.

The cinematic antecedents of the film noir comprise a rich stew. The German Expressionist films of the 1930s, and before them the "street films" of the 1920s, are the most powerful influence, in no small measure because many of the directors and assistant directors of those films emigrated to the United States on the eve of the Second World War, settled in Hollywood, and began making films in

English for the major studios. Immediately distinctive, these films utilized revolutionary techniques refined in Berlin and Vienna: moving cameras, severely angled shots, low-key photography, and innovative uses of light and shadow to frame backlot shooting, making the studio-simulated city streets, sidewalks, and rooftops appear more grittily realistic and forbidding than the real thing. Wilder, Maté, Josef von Sternberg, Robert Siodmak, Otto Preminger, Fritz Lang, Max Ophuls, Curtis Bernhardt, William Dieterle, and Charles Vidor are just some of the most prominent members of this group.

Another film noir antecedent is the so-called French poetic realism of the late thirties, especially in its depictions of metropolitan Paris and Marseilles, in the films of Julien Duvivier, Pierre Chenal, and Marcel Carné. It is seldom noted that a number of the German Expressionist directors—Siodmak, Lang, Wilder, Bernhardt, and Ophuls—traveled to Hollywood from Berlin via Paris, and were not only exposed to the poetic realism films, but directed a good many themselves, as did Jacques Tourneur, who made his directorial debut in France after serving his apprenticeship there in the early thirties. And Alfred Hitchcock, heavily indebted to the Germans (it's a little known fact that he directed his first two feature films at studios in Munich in 1925), also came to the United States in 1940, the same year that Orson Welles, with his brilliant Expressionist cinematographer, Gregg Toland, shot *Citizen Kane*. Stylistically and otherwise, with its chiaroscuro lighting, its reliance on a documentary-style, investigative voice-over, and its pioneering, deep-focus long shots, permitting objects in the camera's foreground to be simultaneously as sharply defined as objects in the far background, *Citizen Kane* was profoundly to shape all subsequent films noirs. "In one of G.K. Chesterton's stories," Borges writes, "the hero remarks that nothing is as terrifying as a labyrinth without a center. This film is that labyrinth." At the same time, there is the direct, though deceptive, influence on film noir of its not-so-close cousins, the detective and gangster films—so revered by Borges—which have reached their apex after bursting onto the American scene in the 1930s.

Yet another wellspring of the film noir is postwar Italian Neo-Realism—the naturalistic, dirt-under-your-nails, quasi-documentary films of Vittorio De Sica, Roberto Rosselini, and Luchino Visconti that demonstrated the heightened impact of dramatic material filmed in urban locales. This technique was often emulated films such as *Call Northside 777* in which the voice-over n solemnly announces that the film was shot at the "actual sites ᴏʀ ᴛʜᴇ events being depicted. Ironically, urban location shooting after 1945 became more popular and aesthetically effective because of photographic methods perfected during the war in effecting the aerial reconnaissance of cities that were to be bombed.

Lastly, there is the seminal contribution which the urban paintings of Charles Sheeler, Edward Hopper, Franz Kline, George Bellows, Martin Lewis, Reginald Marsh, John Sloan, and Georgia O'Keeffe made to the visual underpinnings of film noir: its intensely luminous detail, jagged perspectives, vertiginous heights, hallucinatory geometry, and bold compositional methods. Nicholas Ray's *Party Girl* opens with an actual painting behind the credits, a facsimile of the skyscraper in O'Keeffe's "Night City." And when Abraham Polonsky, the director of *Force of Evil,* was dissatisfied with the look his cinematographer, George Barnes, was getting, he took him to an exhibition of Hopper's paintings at a Greenwich Village gallery and said, "This is how I want the picture to look." And it did: full of black windows, looming shadows, and rich pools of light pouring from recessed doorways and steep stairwells.

Hopper was himself a lifetime moviegoer, constantly influenced by, and eventually, in turn, influencing, American films. Well aware of his symbiotic relationship to the movies, he was open in his admiration of their painterly ability to crystallize in a single flickering image the essence of an entire lifetime or of an epiphanic, otherwise ephemeral, moment frozen in time. These were exactly the sorts of images (and Hopper is one of the great masters of rendering urban light and shadow to the point of tactility, with exquisite textures) he conjured up on canvas throughout his career. One of Hopper's earliest jobs, in the years he supported himself as an illustrator, was to design posters for silent films—primarily gangster potboilers— which he was paid to watch and then interpret in a single graphic image. Later, his complex, resonant cityscapes provided an elemental grab bag for art directors and set designers, and in the summer of 1995, in conjunction with a show called "Edward Hopper and the American Imagination," the Whitney Museum in New York screened an extraordinary series of films "influenced by Hopper's work" entitled "Edward Hopper and the American Cinema," which included such classic films noirs as *Laura* and *Night and the City* and a number of European films, including *Masculin-Féminin* and *Blow-Up,* directed respectively by Godard and Michelangelo Antonioni, that draw heavily on American film noir.

But beyond these various influences, the startling and resonant elements of myth in which the film noir is steeped must be noted.

The city as labyrinth is key to entering the psychological and aesthetic framework of the film noir. As the German historian Oswald Spengler wrote in *The Decline of the West,* speaking of the megalopolis or "world-city" of the twentieth century: "The city is a world, is *the* world." He went on to characterize twentieth-century man as one who "is seized and possessed by his own creation, the City, and is made into its creation, its executive organ, and finally its victim." The city as a closed system. A beast with a life of its own, into whose guts the hero's quest is undertaken.

The city is a labyrinth of human construction, as intricate in its steel, glass, and stone as the millions of webs of human relationships suspended within its confines. It is a projection of the human imagination, and also a reflection of its inhabitants' inner lives; and this is a constant theme—really, a premise—of the film noir. In these films, the framing of the city, our visual progression through the labyrinth, is as significant an element as plot or characterization. The oblique lighting and camera-angling referred to, in both studio and location scenes (especially the night-for-night shoots), reinforce our implicit understanding that the characters' motives are furtive, ambiguous, and psychologically charged; that their innermost conflicts and desires are rooted in urban claustrophobia and stasis; and that they tread a shadowy borderline between repressed violence and outright vulnerability. Hence the obsessive emphasis on urban settings that are precarious and dangerous: rooftops, walkways on bridges, railroad tracks, high windows, ledges, towering public monuments (a Hitchcock favorite), unlit alleys, and industrial zones, not to mention moving trains and cars.

The dictionary's definitions of "labyrinth" all strike home for us: 1. a place constructed or full of intricate passageways and blind alleys; 2. a tortuous, entangled, or inextricable condition of things, events, ideas, etc.; an entanglement, a maze; 3. a tortuous anatomical structure. For the concept of the labyrinth operates on three corresponding and interlocking levels in the film noir.

First, the actual physical maze of the city: streets, sidewalks, bridges, automobile and subway tunnels, underpasses, docks and piers, airport runways and, in the postwar years, the expressways that crisscross (and ultimately fragment) the metropolis, and the highways that radiate from its noisy heart, like arteries, and disappear into the misty, silent, nonurban darkness. A maze of relatively few square miles, it is packed with millions of unique warrens: office buildings, apartment houses, department stores, and tenements; warehouses, hospitals, prisons, and parking garages; casinos, nightclubs, cafés, and bars; museums, theaters, concert halls, and galleries; train and bus terminals, stadiums, and even factories and refineries on the fringes of the city limits.

Second, the labyrinth that is, in the broadest terms, the human condition or situation in which the characters intersect and interact in the city, a labyrinth constructed of plot twists and stratagems, metaphysical conundrums, or bewildering and inscrutable enmeshments of time, space, and chance. A set of conditions that produces a*maze*ment.

And, finally, the labyrinth of the hero's inner workings—mental and physiological—subjected to brutal stresses and strains that mercilessly reveal his flaws. His anatomy is a kind of corollary to, and reflection of, the city's inner workings, in all their rich complexity. And when we speak of the workings of a city, the catalogue seems as if it must be endless. There is organized crime, social conditions at once fluctuating and polarized, the ebb and flow (and muck and mire) of politics and finance, ethnic clashes, cultural crosscurrents (and shocks), a Babel of languages and all their permutations (from street talk to salon niceties), and a psychic atmosphere in which nightmares and dreams, the fantastic and the mundane, collide at every turn. And, perhaps most elementally—organically—there is the way the city literally works, in terms of sewers, water mains, gas pipes, electrical and telephone cables (all subterranean), as well as the processes by which fuel, food, and other goods are supplied it from the outside, the other world, that cloaked, silent countryside beyond the suburbs that might as well be on another planet.

In film noir, the hero's penetration of the external labyrinth, the city, mirrors—often through a funhouse mirror—the transforming path he follows along his internal labyrinth. The farther outside himself he goes, the deeper he may find himself to be on the inside. Until inside and outside merge. If not his moment of epiphany, this certainly becomes ours, as witnesses.

"Labyrinth" derives from a pre-Hellenic, Lydian word, *labrys,* meaning "double-headed axe," which was an emblem of sovereignty in Minoan Crete, shaped like a waxing and waning moon fused together back to back and symbolizing the moon goddess' creative as well as destructive powers. In ancient Crete, as in Babylon (and other places as far-flung as Wales and Siberia), the labyrinth's maze and spiral configurations were directly associated with the internal organs of the human anatomy and the spiritual underworld, the one seen to be a microcosm of the other. The earliest labyrinths are associated, always, with the underworld, often called "The Land of the Dead."

In the labyrinth mythology of ancient Australia, a man must enter the maze to dance (paralleling the labyrinth at Knossus in Crete which was originally organized around a ritual dancing-pattern marked out in mosaic on the pavement, a line of girls leading a line of boys along a complicated series of spirals). The man's journey, undertaken at a critical point in his life, often as a spiritual test, is always related to death and rebirth. And the presiding personage at the labyrinth, who leads him into it, is always a woman, often veiled. The labyrinth consists of multiple spirals and concentric circles (resembling, among other things, both human intestines and the stellar swirls of the Milky Way) that serve *illusory* and *deceptive* functions. The latter adjectives, as becomes clear, are verbal touchstones of the film noir city. Also, as James Hillman has written of the ancient Greeks in *The Dream of the Underworld,* "'Entering the underworld' refers to a transition from the material to the psychical point of view. Three dimensions become two as the perspective of nature, flesh, and matter fall away, leaving an existence of immaterial, mirrorlike images, *eidola.*" Which could also serve as a definition of film.

Hillman stresses the "shadowy or shade aspect of the underworld." *Skia,* he says, "was another word the Greek imagination used for underworld figures. The persons there are shades. So, we must imagine a world without light in which shadows move." Perhaps surprisingly, yet another such word is "hero," for according to Hillman, "the hero was actually an underworld figure . . . even the term *heros* has been considered 'chthonian' . . . denoting a power of the lower world." He goes on to specify that the underworld is "the mythological style of describing a psychological cosmos. Put more bluntly: underworld is psyche. When we use the word *underworld,* we are referring to a wholly psychic perspective. . . . To know the psyche at its basic depths . . . one must go to the underworld. . . . It is in the light of the psyche that we must read all underworld descriptions." He writes that "underworld fantasies and anxieties" and "underworld images" are all to be seen as "movements towards this realm of death, whether they be fantasies of decay, images of sickness in dreams, repetitive compulsions, or suicidal impulses. . . ." And this could easily serve as a functioning definition of the film noir, in which the hero's descent into the labyrinth of the city inevitably parallels (indeed, *is*) a descent into the self.

On the Melanesian island of Malekula in the New Hebrides, near Fiji, a woman similar to the one in Australian mythology, known as a female guardian, draws an elaborate blueprint of the labyrinth in the sand before the cavernous entrance to the underworld. When the soul of the man who seeks to enter it arrives, the woman erases half of the blueprint and the man must know how to recreate it exactly with a stick or wand before she permits him entrance to the cavern. Similarly, at the cavern-entrance to the underworld in Virgil's *Aeneid,* Aeneas finds a diagram of the Cretan labyrinth engraved upon the rockface. According to the classicist W.F. Jackson Knight, who places "circular and labyrinthine movement" among the *Aeneid*'s most recurrent images, the very wanderings of heroes like Aeneas and Odysseus, emanating from Troy (whose name itself can mean "the wanderings of a maze") are symbolical labyrinths, projected onto a largely hostile world. Virgil also envisioned Rome as a twofold city, using the oddly grafted metaphors of beehive (the harmonious golden city) and labyrinth (the subterranean, unsymmetrical, shadow city). When specifically applied to the underworld, Knight goes on, Virgil's conception of the labyrinth is "the very picture of restraint, obstruction, and bewilderment" for the descending hero. Pliny the Elder, in writing of the oldest labyrinth in the West (fourth century B.C.) at Heracleopolis, paints a more terrifying picture of the labyrinth as a baffling, treacherous, nocturnal city in miniature, filled with dead-ends, fake doors, trap-passageways, and fierce images of gods and monsters, a place always in darkness, with halls so constructed that when their doors were opened, a spine-chilling rumble of thunder greeted the visitor. Mircea Eliade in turn has described the labyrinth of prehistoric times as "a theater of initi-ation"—a place where lost souls wander blindfolded in the company of a veiled woman in a phantom-life on the other side of the mirror of this life. In Hawaiian mythology, such souls are said to tumble from the tree of life and free-fall for many nights before they land in the great labyrinth that leads to the underworld.

In writing of maze symbolism, Knight observes that in the labyrinth "the overcoming of difficulties by the hero frequently pre-cedes union with some hidden princess." Labyrinths, as galleries of stone, are in fact still the staging grounds, as they have been since ancient times, for "a game or race in which boys compete to rescue a girl from the center of a maze." The film noir often takes these con-ditions and gives them an ironic spin, imposing destruction upon the hero rather than union, and allowing him to think he is rescuing a woman who in truth is not only in control of the situation, but is im-periling his own life. This hero, the film critic Richard Dyer writes, "has the double quest of the film noir—to solve the mystery of the villain and of the woman."

In every labyrinth, as in every film noir, a woman plays a critical role. When she is a Beatrice-type, she is almost too good to be true. Nurturing to a fault, loyal beyond the bounds of common sense, she is like the faithful guide who appears suddenly in a nightmare, or in the "dark wood" in which Dante found himself. As the Greek scholar E.R. Dodds points out, "The very word *oneiros* in Homer nearly al-ways means dream-figure, not dream-experience." When the chips are down, this Beatrice can be wily and ingenious, or so pure-minded as to be rendered nearly powerless in the Hobbesian moral grid of the film noir. For this, perversely, she often provokes us to anger, even contempt. When she is a Circe, or spider woman, on the other hand, we may find ourselves admiring her; for then she is indeed powerful, dangerously so from a male point of view. And her power and intelligence, though presented in terms of destructive potential, are always fueled by her sexuality. As in *Out of the Past,* sexuality is

an *active,* high-octane force—as active as a man's, if not more so—
and this is a revolutionary phenomenon in American cinema, a
bridge to the more liberated women of later films whose power, sexual and otherwise, is also presented in the service of nondestructive
urges.

So the spider woman of the film noir is a formidable personage.
Freud tells us that spiders can inspire a deep, primal (and castrating)
fear in men, and that the spiral web, in many cultures, is a fear-
releasing (and female) sign. Hillman writes that "spider images have
generally been woven into a great mother web of spinning illusions
(*Maya*), paranoid plots, poisonous gossip, and entrapping. . . ." The
spiral of the spider's web mimics the spiral of the labyrinth. The den-
sity of the web reflects the complex circumstances into which the
hero is plunged, and then manipulated. Is there a thread for every
labyrinth, tenuously laying out an escape route, like the thread Ariadne left for Theseus at Knossus?

That is one of the central questions at the heart of *Kiss Me Deadly*
(1955), which is perhaps the most perfectly realized film noir ever
made. Directed by Robert Aldrich, it is a symbol-laden, absolutely
pivotal film noir (the film encyclopedist Steven H. Scheuer has called
it "the apotheosis" of the classic noir cycle). Certainly it is the most
intricate textually. Produced just eight years after *Out of the Past,* it
feels light-years removed, and inevitably jolts first-time audiences,
including those who have seen a great many other films noirs.

Employing complementary elements of myth and plot with great
intensity and perhaps unrivaled technical brilliance (on this level
alone, it is one of the masterpieces of American cinema), it offers us
the most definitive statement of the noir ethos and the most delirious
depiction of the great American city in all of film noir. Now it is not
just a given city on a given night but an entire urban civilization that
seems to be unraveling faster than the mind can comprehend—a collective nervous breakdown observed at fast speed. A society at once
barbaric and overly refined devouring itself. Premeditated murder
has given way to spontaneous sadism; individual paranoia to general
anarchy; the prospect of a lifetime jail sentence to the numbing terror of nuclear holocaust. As in the San Francisco of *Out of the Past,*
the Los Angeles in *Kiss Me Deadly* is a city without pedestrians; instead, the newly constructed postwar freeways and the broad boule-

vards stream, night and day, with unending lines of moving cars, whose drivers and passengers, without exception, are in shadow, invisible to us throughout the film.

At the midpoint of *Kiss Me Deadly* there is a cryptic allusion to the labyrinth through which the hero is groping his way, made via a reference to the thread that has been left for him. One of the film's many psychological twists is that the Ariadne figure, named Christina, is dead. The posthumous thread she provided for the hero is composed of the most disparate and magical elements: from a scrap of verse by the nineteenth-century poet Christina Rossetti to a snatch of Schubert's "Unfinished Symphony" on the radio (actually, on numerous radios throughout the film, in shifting locales) to a gym locker in a private club, to a dead canary in its cage. And they all lead to a Pandora's box containing, not a cache of stolen gems or unmarked bills, and nothing so common as the incriminating tax documents of *Out of the Past,* but highly unstable nuclear material from the Los Alamos test site that is being peddled on the international black market! The labyrinth is the gorgeously ugly, topsy-turvy moral universe of postatomic Los Angeles, and the film's relentless subtext is nothing less than nuclear apocalypse. The latter is presented as not only inevitable, but perhaps desirable, given the vile, infernal world laid bare for us in the film—a world which will presumably be reduced to ashes.

The Pandora's box is indeed a simple black box—small, anonymous, and banal. Apocalypse in a box, shipped up from the desert. Except that unlike the box Pandora opened in the Greek myth of Epimetheus, from which the ills of Old Age, Labor, Sickness, and Insanity (among others) were released unto mankind, the black box in *Kiss Me Deadly* contains the single element that, ironically, will free men from those infirmities and all others—through annihilation. (Throughout the film, the dangerously fissionable nature of the atomic material parallels the fissionable nature of the characters, each in his or her own way verging on explosion or meltdown from the very first; the mechanic Nick, a kind of one-man Greek chorus, drives this point home—until he is crushed to death—with his signature greeting and constant refrain of *Va-va-voom!*) Unlike the heroes of other films, who might be grazed by a bullet or slashed by a knife, the hero of *Kiss Me Deadly* receives a radioactive burn across his wrist when he peers into the box for a split second. And the film concludes with a beach house outside Los Angeles turning into ground zero for an atomic explosion when the box is opened fully—its glowing, white-hot contents hissing and roaring like a living, malevolent being—setting off a ferocious conflagration and a chain reaction, into the city and beyond, that clearly will not be stoppable.

The hero is the sardonic, hard-bitten, quick-on-his-feet private detective Mike Hammer. Aldrich and the screenwriter, A.I. Bezzerides, have remodeled and considerably deepened Mickey Spillane's original creation—and added to the varnish of his cynicism a patina of sophistication and worldliness. He may be cold and callous, disdainful and physically brutal, but he maintains a well-appointed, even dapper, exterior. Rough-hewn within and polished without, Hammer is far more isolated and introverted than the hero of *Out of the Past;* he is in all ways a shadier yet more confident brand of detective, with a much less suppressed sadistic streak than his cinematic predecessors. He specializes in expensive divorce cases, often operating on the cusp of the law, playing both ends against the middle (for example, working for both a husband *and* wife, and framing one of them for adultery). With Hammer, we can forget the chivalrous codes of honor of the 1930s detective, and the rough-and-tumble, furnished-room, rumpled-raincoat persona of the 1940s private eye. Unlike Robert Mitchum's Jeff Bailey in *Out of the Past,* Hammer wouldn't be caught dead running a gas station; the mechanic Nick even makes house calls when Hammer requires his services. While every bit as good with his fists as the old private eyes, and no slouch as a street-fighter, Hammer comes off overall as a much more laid-back, materially oriented 1950s man, attached to his creature comforts and luxuries and happy to let surrogates do his dirty work when circumstances permit.

Speeding along a pitch-black ocean road late one night in his sports car convertible, Hammer nearly runs down a wild, barefoot woman wearing only a trenchcoat. Terrified, disheveled, she is running along the double line in the middle of the road and screaming for help. After swerving off the road, Hammer agrees, grudgingly, to give her a lift. They stop at a gas station, where she surreptitiously gives the attendant a letter to post. Then she and Hammer drive on until they come to a massive police roadblock. The cops are searching for a woman fitting her description who has escaped from an asylum. But Hammer covers for her, pretending she's his wife, and they're waved through. Minutes later, however, they are intercepted by a black limousine from which several men in dark suits (whom we only see from the waist down) emerge to overpower them. The woman, Christina, is tortured and murdered in Hammer's presence after he is beaten into semiconsciousness (at which point we only see *her* from the waist down, her legs twitching frantically as she suffers horrors we are left to imagine). Then she and Hammer are pushed over a cliff in his car, and he apparently escapes at the last instant, just before the car bursts into flames, incinerating her body.

Thus begins Hammer's quest, whose mantra is two words which Christina has both spoken to him and sent him posthumously (the contents of the posted letter): "Remember me." These are the words that begin Rossetti's poem "Remember": "Remember me when I am gone away,/Gone far away into the silent land." The silent land which is the wasteland—the postatomic city. It is only much later in the film that Hammer bothers to read the entire poem; in fact, maintaining his odd investigative passivity—a highly unusual trait in an investigator—he has someone read it to him. But after their brief ride together, marked by defensive silences, cryptic deflections, and verbal sparring, this is all Hammer has to go on with regard to Christina. (It is also curious—whether it is intended or not as yet another literary allusion—that in *Hamlet* the last words of his father's Ghost to Hamlet, spurring him on to vengeance, are also, "Remember me.")

The significant women in *Kiss Me Deadly* form a charged, uneasy triad. There is Christina. And Lily Carver, her roommate and seeming alter ego, who dupes and betrays Hammer and in the end shoots him at point-blank range (but does not kill him). And Velda Wakeman, Hammer's Girl Friday, who assists him—and does most of his legwork in the case—along his descent into the tangled netherworld from which Christina was a fugitive. Velda is Hammer's Beatrice and Lily is his Circe (undergoing effortless metamorphoses every time we encounter her, from waif to sex kitten to frightened innocent to cold-blooded killer). The two women alternate places at Hammer's side throughout the film, even to sharing his bed (or, usually, sleeping in it without him, for nocturnally he seems always to be roving), though he remains remote from them, cold, interested only in the information they can provide—in helter-skelter fashion—that might advance his quest.

In the end, it is Lily and Velda who are alone with Hammer in the beach house, but under very different circumstances. Velda, half-clothed, is imprisoned in a locked room, and down the hall Lily is holding a gun on Hammer. While doing so, out of stubborn curiosity and avarice, Lily opens the Pandora's box and, exposed to the nuclear material, is instantly ignited like a human torch. Velda is released from the locked room by the wounded Hammer, and the two of them try to stagger from the burning, imploding house, but they, too, are consumed in the fire. During the entire film, Lily and Velda never once share a scene together! The beach house finale is the only occasion in which we find them in the same place at the same time, though we never see them together. At the very moment Hammer releases Velda, Lily, a column of fire, dies screaming in the next room. (There is also a subtle echo here of the film's opening: for when Hammer "rescues" Christina on that ocean road, for all of a few minutes she too is scantily dressed and has just escaped from another sort of House of Bedlam—only to perish in flames.)

But rather than seeing Lily and Velda as split halves of the same woman—the all-important guide who accompanies Hammer into the labyrinth—it would be more accurate to understand them as thirds, with Christina as the missing, but ever-hovering, member of the triad. A ghost from The Land of the Dead ("the silent land") who never leaves Hammer's side. The perverse similarities between Lily and Christina are too blatant to be coincidental. Both enter Hammer's life barefoot and naked but for nearly identical clothing—Christina in her trenchcoat, Lily in a bathrobe (in Christina's apartment, lounging on her bed) of a similar shape and color and with a sash like a trenchcoat's. Both have fair hair cut short—choppy and extra short on the forehead. Both speak in oddly syncopated drawls—always with the implication that behind their words there are other words, carefully withheld. Both die by fire. Only at the very end do we learn that Lily's real name is Gabrielle; she murdered the real Lily, dumped her body in the river, and assumed her identity in order to ply information from Hammer on behalf of the smuggling ring that is trying to recover the nuclear material they stole and lost. So our triad of women takes on a phantom appendage—a fourth woman who is yet another ghost.

In a film in which elements of European high art such as abstract German paintings, Rodin sculptures, and Caruso's recordings of Puccini arias are constantly contrasted with the cultural barrenness of urban American life (where imported culture is a consumer good, on a par with the gleaming consumer items that Hammer enjoys, including an early-model portable television, an elaborate hi-fi set, and the three sports cars we see him drive which represent America's true culture) is the name "Gabrielle" a heavy-handed play on the fact that Christina Rossetti's brother was none other than the pre-Raphaelite poet, doyen of high art—and translator of Dante!—Dante Gabriel Rossetti? Certainly, whether Christina and Lily are mirror-images or dark psychological twins, they are much more inextricably, tortuously, linked than we have been led to believe by the shallow pretense of Lily/Gabrielle's posing as Christina's "roommate." So like the three sisters who are the Three Fates of Greek mythology, and the three witches in *Macbeth,* our triad is also one of interlocking identities and shifting perspectives, of ritualized incantations and portents of doom around, not a cauldron, but a deadly box. *Macbeth,* by the way, may also be seen as a direct literary ancestor of the film noir; on the cusp of Jacobean drama, utterly nocturnal, permeated with violence, blood, darkness, and guilt, when the play was adapted for the screen by none other than Orson Welles he shot it very much in the style of his films noirs.

The crucial scene in *Kiss Me Deadly* in which the labyrinth is alluded to directly occurs in Hammer's office, a sprawling, elaborate, impeccably decorated L-shaped room filled with futuristic furniture and art-deco bric-a-brac. It is nothing like the stock, sparsely furnished private-eye office with the clunky desk, swivel chair, dusty venetian blinds, and neon-lit window we associate with Sam Spade or Philip Marlowe. Across from Hammer's desk there is a sweeping picture window with billowing curtains that overlooks a wide boulevard on which the ubiquitous cars are streaming. Custom-designed to his persona, his office, too, feels remote and frigid, almost otherworldly. As does his gadgetry. For example, the state-of-the-art (1955-vintage) tape recorder/answering machine built into the wall through which he screens his calls (in 1990s fashion), only occasionally, and laconically, picking up to engage the caller in conversation. In a corner where the walls are mirrored from floor to ceiling, Velda is doing stretching exercises on a dance bar. Ballet music (yet another high-art touchstone) is playing on the hi-fi, and the floor beneath her is checkered with black and white tiles. She is wearing a striped black and white shirt and black tights. Hammer is leaning against the wall, sipping Scotch. (*Imported* whiskey—no private-eye rye for him.) They have been discussing the ins and outs of the case as it is taking shape, Velda doing most of the talking, as usual, letting Hammer know what she's discovered. Suddenly, twirling playfully around a black pole that also runs from floor to ceiling, she assumes a seductive voice and purrs, "First you find a little thread, the little thread leads you to a string, and the string leads you to a rope, and from the rope you hang by the neck. . . . What kind of girl was she, this friend of yours, Christina?"

Velda's wordplay around this reference to Ariadne's thread can be read as film noir's version of the inscription Dante affixed at the entrance to his Inferno: ABANDON ALL HOPE YOU WHO ENTER HERE. (And, as Hillman says, "To go deep into a dream requires abandoning hope.") The checkered tiles conjure up the obvious reminder that these characters are pieces being moved across a chessboard by larger forces; but they also refer to the labyrinth at Knossus in which the ritual dancing pattern was marked out in mosaic. That Velda is dressed as a dancer, and is ostensibly preparing to dance after her warmup, is yet another echo of the ancient link between the labyrinth and the dance; here, as in Minoan Crete, the hero and his female companion are compelled to perform such a ritual dance in negotiating the maze before them, whose corridors are every bit as intricate, delusory, and dangerous as those in a dream.

There is a small group of films noirs in which the hero is apparently killed at the outset before entering the labyrinth as a dead man—or as a ghost entering the underworld. *Point Blank* (1967) is the most notable of these: even at its climax we are not sure if the hero, who at the film's outset is trapped and shot point blank, in the seconds before his death has merely hallucinated the subsequent narrative in which he tracks down his antagonist—reducing the entire film to a dying man's epiphanic nightmare. *Kiss Me Deadly* may be one of these films, as well. When Hammer goes over the cliff with

Christina, we never do *see* him leap clear of the car before it slides into the darkness and explodes. We don't see anything, in fact: we just cut to Hammer regaining consciousness in a hospital bed days later, with Velda (and remember, her name is Wakeman, as, perhaps, in *Wake, man*) staring down at him. For the rest of the film, what with his icy demeanor, his strange admixture of aggressiveness and passivity, his bizarre hands-off approach to most of the actual investigating, and his utter lack of concern for the worldly (as in, *this* world, rather than the *under*world) losses he suffers during his odyssey—his detective's license, source of his livelihood, his cars, and ultimately, his most loyal confederates, Nick and Velda—Hammer might as well be a dead man on a posthumous journey. A man who has ventured into the silent land looking to unlock a riddle that will explain his own death.

In 1990, during a period in which the film noir (in vastly different, but also chaotic, potentially incendiary, cultural conditions) is resurgent, there is an eerily close echo of Velda's wordplay in the film *After Dark, My Sweet,* based on the 1955 Jim Thompson novel. At the film's most telling moment, having reached their fatal crossroads, the femme fatale (she isn't dancing, but she is standing on checkered tiles in her kitchen) turns to the hero and murmurs, "That door leads to a walk; at the end of the walk there's a lane; at the end of the lane there's a highway. . . ." The same highway from which he entered the maze that led him to her; the same highway, as she now indicates, that might lead him away from his fate, which of course is death. So archetypes that held up for four millennia—since the Cretan labyrinth was constructed—manage to hold up for yet another four decades in late twentieth-century America.

The Los Angeles of *Kiss Me Deadly* is by day a city of broad, sunblanked boulevards, of tree-lined streets with antiseptic lawns and boxy cars parked in pools of shade, of dusty vacuous office buildings with black windows, and flat nondescript smaller buildings, which turn out to be havens, by day, for nocturnal pursuits: dark bars, fortune-tellers' parlors, and windowless boxing gyms. By night, the city's downtown is a tableau of slashing white light, steep jet shadows, and richly luminous surfaces punctuated by the flashes of chrome and glass on parked cars, the mirrors on vending machines, and even the stainless steel cart of an all-night popcorn vendor, who would seem to have little prospect of making a sale on the utterly deserted streets. Those black office building windows at night seem to deepen a shade; when we are permitted a look into some building's interior, we inevitably see dappled Gothic hallways, jagged stairwells, galleries out of a de Chirico painting, or obliquely lit, repressive rooms. In fact, this tableau bears a strong resemblance to the nocturnal San Francisco of *Out of the Past.* But while Los Angeles in *Kiss Me Deadly* is a sprawling wasteland of endless, starkly white streets waiting for the flood of fire, the apocalypse of the Bomb, San Francisco in *Out of the Past* is a tight labyrinth which feels as if at any moment it might accordion in on its residents and engulf them in its blackness.

In eight years—during which the further darkening, enervating influences of the Korean War and the McCarthy era have taken their toll—the postwar city that seemed an insular netherworld of paranoia and dread has mushroomed into a full-blown Pandæmonium. The latter, in Milton's *Paradise Lost,* is the first City of Man, the capital of Hell, built by Cain under the tutelage of Satan. Its countless rooms, corridors, and galleries seem to proliferate without end, thronged with tens of thousands of fallen angels who embody, and take their names from, the vices of mankind. Shades of Virgil, Milton compares Pandæmonium to a beehive, its infernal spirits, in their evil-doing, as industrious as bees. Every film noir is the shadowland of a lost paradise, a fallen state. A silent land. And every film noir city traces its blueprint to some aspect of Pandæmonium.

By 1955, the film noir hero of *Kiss Me Deadly* is no longer merely a prisoner of his private hell: he is the tenant in a universal Hell, as boundaryless and unstoppable in its growth as the nuclear explosion that ends his life. The monstrous, hellish twist at the end of *Kiss Me Deadly*—when that Doomsday box, like a long-awaited, long-diverted Christmas present, is finally opened—is that its climax is really just the beginning of the end: the latter a popular phrase in the Atomic-Age lexicon. (There was even a 1946 film, *The Beginning or the End?,* a pseudo-documentary, jingoistic paean to the Manhattan Project and its godparent, the U.S. government, that extolled the Bomb's development as the crowning achievement of American scientific "know-how" and gumption; the film opened with a grandiose "dedication" scene in which a pompous narrator informs us that "a

print of the film you are about to see has been sealed in a time capsule, capable of withstanding even an atomic war," in order to edify
future generations!) Along with Hammer, and his companions and
antagonists in the labyrinth, we are to understand that the entire corrupt—and strangely static, not teeming—world of metropolitan Los
Angeles is about to be reduced to red-hot cinders. So when graphics
reading THE END zoom out the windows of the imploding beach
house toward the audience, I read it not as the usual passive, redun-
dant announcement that the film is over, but more as an urgent, existential postscript. And at the same time—the two messages needn't
be mutually exclusive—as a sardonic joke: play with fire, on a small
scale or a collective one, and you'll burn.

Hammer has projected himself into a nightmare not completely of
his own creation that overlaps, and feeds off of, countless other
nightmares. Every single major character around him, and most of
the minor ones, are killed violently. Incredible as it may seem, this is
not a startling fact in the film noir canon. In the urban universe of
these films, few characters survive, much less survive with any sort
of future on the horizon. *Out of the Past* is no exception. The promise
of apocalypse as a coda in *Kiss Me Deadly* makes it a spectacular example, but not a unique one. The specter of nuclear annihilation that
hovered over all American cities during the film noir era (especially
in its heyday) is clearly evoked by the unwavering fact that when
these films conclude with all their principals dead, it is usually for irrational, larger, supposedly deterministic reasons utterly beyond the
characters' control. A definition that could apply quite nicely to nuclear war.

The taut, nightmarish maze Hammer enters is wedged within a
second maze of gigantic proportions. Much of the tension in the
quick, slippery, descending arc he follows to his destruction lies in
the fact that the smaller maze is continually contracting while the
larger one is ever-expanding. The effect is dizzying. Like looking
through a microscope with one eye and a telescope with the other. It
is as if the claustrophobia of San Francisco in *Out of the Past* has
been magnified a hundred times. In *Kiss Me Deadly,* claustrophobia
has become a general condition, not just a specific symptom. That it
achieves this effect using that most sprawling of American cities, Los
Angeles, only adds to its impact.

Pervasive elements of myth inform film noir on the dee
The critic Northrop Frye's encapsulation of the solar m
span countless cultures certainly applies to the noir univer
hero travels perilously through a dark labyrinthine underw
of monsters between sunrise and sunset." The hero is amo   ᴗᴄ
monsters, out of the sun, until he reemerges—into the night. In all
films noirs, the respective labyrinths are as varied as the heroes who
must enter them. Which is to say that the depiction of the particular
city, its milieu, and its relationship to the hero on his quest within its
bowels is unique to each film. The city itself counterpoints and anticipates the hero's actions almost as another character would. In literature, we find this phenomenon in the Venice of Italo Calvino's
novel *Invisible Cities,* whose nameless, anonymous residents populate
a city at once monolithic and multifluid in its complexity, in the hallucinatory Paris of André Breton's *Nadja,* and the devouring, Gren-
del-like metropolis in the Russian futurist Andrei Biely's *St. Petersburg.*
The city-as-a-character in film noir is revealed to us incrementally, in
the way of a cubist construction, plane by plane, prism by prism, off
a multifaceted whole. (In a 1950 film, *Once a Thief,* the "City of Los
Angeles" is even listed among the characters in the credits.)

An astonishing number of films noirs begin with one of two images behind their opening credits: a cityscape at night, stationary or
panned by a moving camera; or a train or locomotive hurtling
through the night. The train we will discuss elsewhere, but the
cityscape is so prevalant as an opening for these films that it is mind-
boggling to contemplate how many different directors, producers,
and studio executives in the same city, during the same period, were
unaware (or unfazed by) the sheer repetitiveness of the device. In
these cityscapes we are often being introduced to the film's most significant element—the city—just as in other genres we more commonly see one of the characters enter a film's narrative frame (that
is, a specific locale or situation) behind the opening credits. In a film
noir, when the credits have run their course (and it's hard to resist
mentioning that in *Kiss Me Deadly,* alone among *any* films I've ever
encountered, the opening credits run *backward,* thus setting the
tone immediately for the film's upside-down moral universe), we
nearly always cut directly to its hero, somewhere within the enormous urban jungle we have been gazing at from afar.

He may be in a cramped room, crisscrossed by shadows, waiting apprehensively for a knock at the door; or sweating profusely, staring at his own reflection in a window while a telephone insistently rings; or behind the wheel of a car careering across a suspension bridge; or lighting a cigarette, glancing over his shoulder anxiously in the gloom of a public park; or struggling desperately against the flow of a rush-hour crowd; or kissing a woman on a rooftop, among the flapping sheets on clotheslines, while police sirens approach; or ducking from a nightclub in a rumpled coat and merging into the darkness of an alley; or huddled in a doorway in biting cold or blistering heat—for the weather in the noir city, like the human condition, fluctuates between harsh extremes.

From the first, the labyrinth in the film noir—the city-as-world—is made to appear implacable and unassailable, and the hero puny and vulnerable. The one, all stone and steel, will endure; the other will play out a short, transient role among millions of others as insignificant and interchangeable as he, and then disappear. For a brief interlude, he will be like a free-floating electron off the great mass of men. The hero of a film noir is not the hero as we find him elsewhere in film. Heroic he may appear on occasion, even recklessly so, and brave, and sympathetic despite his deep flaws, but when he comes into sharpest focus on one of those rain-washed, shadowy, starkly lit streets that is the *terra cognita* of the film noir, I see him (and have always identified with him) for what he really is: a victim.

2. Night and the City

When the French architect Le Corbusier first laid eyes on Manhattan, he exclaimed, "It is hot-jazz in stone!" It was November 1945, and he was approaching the city on a commercial airliner. His enthusiasm, not wholly a matter of professional admiration, was fanned by the fact that twelve hours before he had left behind a smoldering and war-torn Europe in which major cities like New York had been reduced to rubble. A Europe in which the cities that were still standing offered little jazz to be seen—or heard.

Invited to New York to participate in the design of the U.N. Secretariat Building, Le Corbusier had witnessed close-up the first modern war in which large cities and their civilian populations were systematically targeted for massive bombardments. In previous wars, cities had been subjected to sieges, occupations, sabotage, and artillery fire, but not until Hitler's *Blitzkrieg* overran Warsaw in 1939 had anyone seen a technologically advanced army and air force so singlemindedly encircle and decimate a nonmilitary target, full of innocent citizens, in order to extort a military surrender from their government. In our own higher-tech age, such a strategy (Hanoi/1969, Kabul/1979, Grozny/1995, and Sarajevo/1992–95) hardly raises eyebrows anymore. Why should it when a name like "Beirut" instantly conjures the spectacle of modern urban warfare in its most advanced (perhaps terminal) stage: the city itself as battlefield, imploding from within.

In 1939, this was still a faraway concept to Americans. While the cities on the U.S. mainland were untouched by the Second World War, their residents, sitting rapt before the stark newsreels presented (between the cartoon and the main feature) in their movie theaters, were themselves bombarded: with graphic images. The firebombing of London, the relentless pounding of Stalingrad and Nanking, the destruction of Rotterdam, and the carpet-bombings (one thousand tons of TNT a night) of Dresden, Hamburg, and Berlin. On the night of March 9–10, 1945, this sort of high-intensity bombing reached its apogee when 325 U.S. Army B-29s from the XXI Bomber Command dropped six tons of incendiaries over the heart of downtown Tokyo, creating a sixteen-square-mile inferno. The American crewmen, flying at an altitude of only five thousand feet, later said they could smell burning flesh, and their commanding general claimed that in those thirty minutes of bombing, more casualties were inflicted "than in any other military action in the history of the world." The raid left an estimated 97,000 dead, 125,000 wounded, and 1,200,000 homeless. Two months later, 800 B-29s literally scorched a 21-mile-long, two-mile-wide ribbon of fire from Yokohama to Tokyo.

Then, finally, a few months before Le Corbusier's plane circled over the glittering skyline of Manhattan Island, a single B-29 with a crew of ten dropped a clumsy, 200-pound spherical bomb officially code-named "Little Boy" on the commercial city of Hiroshima in southwest Japan, killing 80,000 men, women, and children in a matter of minutes and leveling ninety percent of the city's infrastructure—that is, nearly every building, bridge, train line, electrical tower, and telephone pole. At least 100,000 people were injured, and the number of official dead over the years, from radiation sickness and burns, would reach 187,000. For two days after Hiroshima, B-29s dropped propaganda leaflets over densely populated areas of Tokyo and Nagoya that began: *Evacuate your cities now!* Every day of added resistance will bring greater terror to you. Bombs will blast great holes in your cities." On the third day, 40,000 more people were killed and 60,000 injured when a bomb code-named "Fat Man," plutonium at the core surrounded by several tons of TNT, was dropped on the smaller industrial city of Nagasaki. Ironically, Hiroshima had never previously been bombed, conventionally or with incendiaries, because it was considered too insignificant in military terms. Thus Hiroshima and Nagasaki became the first cities of the Atomic Age. After the firebombing of Tokyo, the streets and rivers were clotted with corpses. But at the epicenters of the blasts that destroyed Hiroshima and Nagasaki there was barely even a scattering of rubble afterward, just blackened earth and hardened puddles of melted steel.

In the first newsreel rushed back to the United States for public consumption, the film itself seems to be crackling with radioactivity. First, the camera surveys the heaps of the dead and dying, then enters a clinic where a group of survivors—the grotesquely burned, the blinded, the maimed, and a dozen naked children in shock—have been lined up for inspection under harsh lamps. Then we're taken outdoors again, though the vista is so unreal it's difficult to grasp this at first. We're moving across a shadeless, dusty landscape—flat, blanched, and starkly lit as the desert—a necropolis where the city's central districts had once converged. Suddenly the camera stops before what looks like a man-shaped blot on a cement wall. The camera pans in closer and we realize that the blot is all that remains of someone who was utterly vaporized by the "fire wall," 50,000 degrees Fahrenheit at its core, that swept across the city (preceded by a tremendous shockwave, estimated at the force of five thousand locomotives traveling at 200 mph) and in this particular spot left behind only a two-dimensional impression, a charred shadow, with no evidence of bones, flesh, or clothing—nothing that will remotely testify to the human identity of the man who disappeared there.

It is from images of these foreign cities (ironically, transmitted through the medium of film) and their entrance into the dream-life of Americans, that the film noir springs. To the American in his neighborhood movie theater, in Chicago, Pittsburgh, or Miami, as well as smalltown U.S.A., the message is clear: the big city is now a place where a hundred thousand—no, even five million—people can be incinerated in the time it takes to boil an egg. Americans must deal literally and metaphysically with the hard fact that, like other city dwellers around the world, their lives and their civilization are now very much in other people's hands. The subliminal messages are far more complex, and insidious, and find expression—some of it in film—in all manner of human angst, alienation, and duplicity; in the simultaneous glorification of and disgust with violence, glamour, and power; and in the underlying belief that fear itself, planted deep in the collective bone marrow of the populace, can be a force as explosive and debilitating as that of any weapon of destruction.

Is it mere chance that the earliest surviving images of the city, on the pre-dynastic Egyptian pallettes, picture its destruction? Or that every advanced civilization in history has begun with a vital urban core—the polis—and ended in a graveyard of dust and bones, a city of the dead? Every American city is always a tale of two cities: the surface city, orderly and functional, imbued with customs and routine, and its shadow, the nether-city, rife with darker impulses and forbidden currents, a world of violence and chaos. The one superimposed uneasily over the other. Just as the sunlit polis and the sunless necropolis coexist uneasily, simultaneously, and are never mutually exclusive.

Noir has deep taproots in American urban culture. Certainly we find our first truly noir American writer, Edgar Allan Poe, surfacing with a voice like none before him and drifting through our large East Coast cities—Boston, New York, Baltimore—which he brings to life and redefines at the onset of the Industrial Revolution, just when those cities truly became modern. That is, they reached the point at which they would be recognizable to those of us alive today. The word, now a cognate, is French, but "noir" is an utterly homegrown, American phenomenon. Film noir is only the latest, most influential, and arguably the definitive manifestation of all things noir.

And what is noir, etymology aside? A state of mind, an aesthetic school, a philosophy, an ethos, a sensibility, an attitude, a symbolic system? Something undefinable—a kind of raw poetry, like the snatch of a ghost sonata one hears at the outskirts of the necropolis? Or is it, first and foremost, a *style?* It is all of these things and more. "Noir" has been used to describe everything from political movements and fads of dress to artistic trends and subversive impulses. Mercury-like, it slips easy definition. Using a simpler, maybe too simple, metaphor, we might say it is the dark mirror reflecting the dark underside of American urban life—the subterranean city— from which much crime, high and low culture, raw sexual energy and deviations, and other elemental, ambiguous forces that fuel the greater society often spring. Reflecting the infernal, complex lower depths of American urban life, which is composed in shifting parts of blood and cement, nightmares and iron.

One particular fragment of this mirror—like a touchstone to be returned to again and again—are the films noirs made in the United States since 1945. These films, which first reflected the urban landscape—physically and emotionally—eventually changed the way we looked at and felt about our cities, and in so doing, through their audience over the past fifty years and their considerable impact on the other arts and on popular styles, changed the cities themselves. However one tries to define or explain noir, the common denominator must always be the city. The two are inseparable. The great, sprawling American city, endlessly in flux, both spectacular and sordid, with all its amazing permutations of human and topographical growths, with its deeply textured nocturnal life that can be a seductive, almost otherworldly, labyrinth of dreams or a tawdry bazaar of lost souls: the city is the seedbed of noir.

In 1945, it is as if the war, and the social eruptions in its aftermath, unleashed demons that had been bottled up in the national psyche, not just since 1939, or the Great Depression (for the noir movement, as much as it is a collective shudder on the threshold of the Atomic Age, is also a delayed reaction—delayed by the war—to the Depression); demons lurking since the predawn of the Industrial Revolution and the breakneck consolidation of our large cities when Alexander Hamilton's vision of an urban, business-and-factory-oriented America prevailed once and for all over Thomas Jefferson's "democratic vista" of small towns and farms multiplying across the continent. Oswald Spengler, the visionary German historian, wrote on the eve of the First World War: "The rise of New York to the position of world-city during the Civil War of 1861–65 may perhaps prove to have been the most pregnant event of the nineteenth century." Certainly the American city as a large-scale enterprise is a recent phenomenon any way you look at it. Most of our enormous cities in the late 1940s had barely existed one hundred years earlier. Take Los Angeles: in 1830 a mission settlement on the fringes of the Spanish Empire, by 1945 it is a 500-square-mile sprawl. In 1830, Detroit was a trading post at a frontier crossroads. Houston a muddy cattle town called Harrisburg. San Francisco a hillside village which went by the name Yerba Buena. Chicago, which also boomed exponentially after 1865, had yet to be incorporated as a village. Denver and Seattle, of course, didn't even exist.

In historical terms, our urban culture has developed at hothouse speed, with all attendant hothouse permutations, glorious, freakish, stunted, and delirious. Gilded ages worthy of imperial Rome, and slums to rival Calcutta's. Quicksilver migrations, immigrations, and displacements. Brushfire wars and then two world wars fueled by the plants, factories, and small-bore industries of the cities. The second of these wars ends with a wildly unexpected plunge (the Manhattan Project was unknown to the public until the day Hiroshima was bombed) down a crossroad that no one had imagined. Journalists like Edward R. Murrow note without irony that the Allied victory is accompanied by a mood of uncertainty and fear far bleaker than at any time during the war, including Pearl Harbor. The war ends, but there is no closure. Another war—this one "cold"—begins immediately against a former ally that is suddenly an implacable foe, and dozens of potential Hiroshimas in the USSR and the U.S.A. are targeted for immediate and total annihilation at the commencement of "World War III." (*Time* magazine, government Civil Defense pamphlets, high school newspapers, and a slew of hysterical Cold War propaganda films all invoke the inevitably of the latter, with menace, and often an insane dash of religiosity.)

Forces are unleashed. Organized crime, street violence, political corruption, poverty—the popularly lamented ills of urban life in the 1930s—are amplified, and augmented, by the far more corrosive acids of despair, dread, and paranoia, even while the national economy, fueled by breakneck military spending after the war is won, booms. Like the conquistadors who brought untold diseases of the body to the New World in the sixteenth century, the G.I.s returning to the United States from Europe and the Pacific carry, not microbes, but lethal infirmities of the mind and spirit after four years of living day in and day out with brutality and violent death, and of surviving a war in which 1700 cities and townships were destroyed and 35 million people were killed. (During the war, a number of grisly espionage films, produced as exposés of Axis barbarism, are obvious precursors of film noir: *Secret Agent of Japan* and *Nazi Agent* in 1942, *Behind the Rising Sun* in 1943, and *First Yank into Tokyo* in 1945, all directed by future film noir directors and all depicting the sadistic treatment—floggings, beatings, graphic torture—that American soldiers suffered.) Shellshocked, cynical, and worn down, these returning veterans are either hypercharged and running on empty, or numb and cut off from themselves. At loose ends suddenly, they're under great pressure to reacclimate themselves. To turn off the black energy that enabled them to survive the war as if they are turning off a faucet. Many are debilitated physically and mentally in ways that render the medical profession of their day powerless. Psychotic lapses, insomnia, and amnesia are widespread afflictions. Among veterans, as compared to the population at large, the frequency of acute alcoholism increases exponentially. And drug abuse, which had markedly fallen off in the prewar, post-Prohibition thirties, runs rampant, with predictable results: many soldiers, just out of uniform, turn to serious crime, are drawn into syndicates in the multitiered, big-bucks underworld, and begin peddling the long line of illicit drugs that flourishes after 1945—heroin, cocaine, morphine, right up to crack, angel dust, and ecstasy in the present day—forever changing the face of our cities, large and small.

Violence breeds violence, and it is perfectly natural that soldiers returning from the battlefield would gravitate to the cities, where the action of the day, legal and illegal, was centered. Was smalltown America in any way prepared to grapple with the problems of such men in 1945? Lewis Mumford in *The City in History* writes: "No matter how many valuable functions the city has furthered, it has also served, throughout most of its history, as a container of organized violence." Certainly this is true of the American city, even in its nascent state, in the 1840s, when Alexis de Tocqueville observed: "Nevertheless, I regard the size of some American cities and especially the nature of their inhabitants as a real danger threatening the future of the democratic republics of the New World, and I should not hesitate to predict that it is through them that they will perish, unless their government succeeds in creating an armed force which, while remaining subject to the wishes of the national majority, is independent of the peoples of the towns and capable of suppressing their excesses." Tocqueville blithely calls for martial law in the cities, little supposing that Jefferson's rural vision will be rendered moot within a century, and that the soldiers he invokes as urban enforcers will, however valiant in foreign combat, be anything but immune to the "excesses" of the cities upon their return. And why on earth would they be?

Sexually these returning soldiers are at loose ends, as well, in 1945. Women, staffing labor-depleted factories and businesses to support the war effort, have entered the workforce in unprecedented numbers and after the war they are keeping their jobs. Many out of necessity: widows and wives who are supporting husbands who can't find work; and many others, having had a taste of financial independence and responsibility, who have no intention of relinquishing their footholds. Still others, "war widows," have taken up with other men in their husbands' absences, and the husbands have come back to find their homes broken. Without the all-consuming background of the war, men and women have to reinvent themselves in one another's eyes. Men transformed by violence return to women transformed in ways neither sex had previously imagined. The sexual energies of the country are like a severed wire throwing forth sparks. People are emotionally scalded. Scars aren't healing, and new wounds are festering. And it is the wounds—psychic, sexual, and physical—and the vast tensions, private and familial, that they generate, which are so glaringly amplified in film noir.

In writing of a country at war, which permits itself acts of violence that it would never allow the individual in civilian life, Freud stresses that this invidious paradox has a "seducing influence" on the morality of the citizenry at the war's conclusion. When a society bankrupted in this fashion can no longer credibly rebuke the individual citizen, he goes on, "there is an end of all suppression of the baser passions, and men perpetuate deeds of cruelty, fraud, treachery, and barbarity. . . ."

With this laundry list of vice, Freud could easily have been speaking of the film noir in its depiction of the postwar city. Consider that city not just in light of the idealized Renaissance concept of a human microcosm, but also within the bleak Gothic framework of the city-as-island, the self-contained, self-enclosing (and enclosed) moral universe divorced from the "natural world." Often with the atmosphere of a prison island, with blurred coordinates outside the safer channels of human intercourse, this city harbors a suffocating, utterly man-made (and artificial) atmosphere in which the extremes, and grotesques, of human behavior flourish. Between the economic poles of opulence and squalor, and the overlapping social codes of rapacious laissez-faire capitalism and organized crime, the indelible

motto of the postwar American city in the so-called boom years becomes "Anything Goes." In the early years of this century, Leo Tolstoy began his final (emphatically urban) novel, *Resurrection,* with
this passage, a kind of Zen distillation of the hardening moral isolation of the great cities: "Though men in their hundreds of thousands
had tried their hardest to disfigure that little corner of the earth
where they had crowded themselves together, paving the ground
with stones so that nothing could grow, weeding out every blade of
vegetation, filling the air with fumes of coal and gas, cutting down
the trees and driving away every beast and bird . . . grown-up people—adult men and women—never left off cheating and tormenting
themselves and one another. . . . What they considered sacred and
important were their own devices for wielding power over one another."

Power's inescapable twin is violence, and even by our standards in
the last, frayed decade of the century, when a serial killer can zigzag
through a city murdering a chain of victims with no better motive
than the number combinations on their license plates, or a thirteen-
year-old can gun down a schoolmate in order to steal his leather
jacket (careful to shoot him in the head so as not to damage the
jacket), the urban tableau of blood and guts in the noir universe is
still shocking. We're presented with graphic episodes of depravity
and sadism such as had never been seen before in American film.

A prison inmate wielding a blowtorch forces a rival inmate to back
into the maws of a giant industrial press where he is crushed to
death (*Brute Force*).

An undercover treasury agent is run over repeatedly and cut to
shreds by his antagonist—a smuggler of illegal immigrants—who is
at the controls of a huge plowing-machine combine (*Border Incident*).

A wiry prostitute rips off her wig, revealing herself to be bald, and
beats to death with a telephone receiver the pimp who is short-
changing her (*The Naked Kiss*).

A police detective, beaten and tied up in a chair, is forced to guzzle
hair tonic while a hearing aid, connected to a radio broadcasting a
frenetic drum solo at full blast, is stuck in his ear (*The Big Combo*).

Not one of these scenes involves a revolver, machine gun, or
knife—the weapons of choice in 1930s gangster films. Suddenly

those weapons seem almost primitive. Blowtorches, telephones, farm vehicles, the newly invented hearing aid: the wartime technological boom, with large-scale machines and gadgets esoteric and frighteningly domestic, makes itself felt not just in atomic doomsday scenarios, but also in one-on-one homicides and assaults where the weapon is clearly to be regarded as an extension of the assailant's fevered (and twisted) imagination. In film noir, even spontaneous acts of violence, when no weapon is readily at hand, can slide from the grotesque to the surreal; as in *Raw Deal* (1948) when a gangster, angered by a tipsy woman who has spilled a drink in his lap, hurls a platter of flaming crêpes suzette in her face.

The delirium of violence produces its own aesthetics, as a writer like the French novelist Louis-Ferdinand Céline—one of the godfathers of noir—demonstrates in his hallucinatory novels of urban apocalypse. A revolutionary stylist on the order of Joyce and Proust, Céline concluded his career with a trilogy chronicling his zigzag flight across Nazi Germany in the final days of the Second World War, with the Royal Canadian Air Force "raining white fire" from the skies and Céline heading, not for the border, but for the hellish center of that particular labyrinth: Berlin, a city of ashes, rubble, and outright savagery. Between the two world wars, Céline visited several American cities, notably the slums and factory districts not included in guidebooks, and recorded what he saw in his first novel, *Journey to the End of the Night,* as here about New York: "I again tried wandering about a bit in the principal streets of the neighborhood, an insipid carnival of vertiginous buildings. My lassitude deepened before a row of these elongated façades, this monotonous surfeit of streets, bricks, and endless windows, and business and more business, this chancre of promiscuous and pestilential advertising. A mass of grimy, senseless lies. Down by the river I came on other little streets, lots of them, which were more ordinary in size; I mean, for instance, that here all the windows of a single house opposite could have been broken just from where I was standing on the pavement." The downward spiral of his depression and rage while in our cities became increasingly severe, and it is ironic, from our point of view here, to note, in the same chapter of *Journey to the End of the Night,* the one outlet Céline found for himself: "I clung to the movies," he wrote, "with a fervor born of despair."

Céline would anticipate William S. Burroughs, Nathanael West, and Nelson Algren, among others, but before the Second World War there was no American novelist writing as Céline did about American cities. But, then, he had special credentials, and not just as a European whose cities were hit hard in wartime; as a wounded veteran of one world war and a buffeted (and ultimately wounded) urban refugee in another, Céline was able to dissect with ferocious precision the pathological effects of modern warfare upon the city and upon the individual psyches of the participants. (Detroit and Pittsburgh, to him, at the beginning of the Depression, resembled war zones.) In fact, Céline attributed the radical transformation of his writing style—the staccato, machine-gun bursts of prose, punctuated solely by ellipses—to his traumas as a trench soldier and as a victim thirty years later of the carpet-bombing of Berlin. Another former soldier, the Cubist painter Fernand Léger, put a more benign spin on the way in which the dehumanizing violence of war had refashioned his own method of seeing the world—especially the urban world—linking it, interestingly, to the impact of film upon his work. "The war had thrust me, as a soldier, into the heart of a mechanical atmosphere," he wrote. "Here I sensed a new reality in the detail of the machine, in the common object. I tried to find the plastic value of these fragments of our modern life. I rediscovered them on the cinema screen in the closeups of objects which impressed and influenced me."

The imaginative work of such artists and writers offers up telling clues about the mental landscapes of millions of other city-dwellers and ex-soldiers in the smoky aftermath of the war, as does the unique, and highly provocative, creative outpouring from the filmmakers of the time.

"A film is a dream," Orson Welles said, providing us with perhaps the profoundest, and simplest, definition we'll ever need. The film critic Barbara Deming elaborated on it: "It is not as mirrors reflect us, but rather, as our dreams do, that movies most truly reveal the times." If so, the broad cycle of films noirs that burst forth on the heels of the Second World War can be seen to comprise the complex mosaic of a single, thirteen-year urban dreamscape—often nightmarish, often fantastic and beautiful, always symbol-laden, and sometimes so starkly black-and-white (literally and figuratively) in its depiction of city life, and of the innermost conflicts and struggles of the human spirit in the city, that it shocks us into moments of recognition, and epiphany.

Imagine taking your dreams, especially the most frightening and recurrent ones, and affixing titles to them. Imagine using only single-word titles. First, adjectives: *Abandoned, Desperate, Cornered, Pursued, Notorious, Framed.* Then, single-word nouns: *Tension, Conflict, Fear, Crossfire, Whirlpool, Detour, Decoy, Crack-Up.* . . . You begin to get the idea. Every one of these is the title of a film noir, of course. Take the fourteen I've listed, rustle up some verbs and prepositions, and you might be able to write the story line for any number of other films noirs.

The nomenclature of the film noir canon could, in fact, keep a diligent cross-referencer (or semiotician) in clover for some time. The list of those films with the word "city" in the title is too long to catalog here; but consider a few: *Cry of the City, The Naked City, The Captive City, While the City Sleeps, The City That Never Sleeps.* Likewise, "street": *Side Street, One Way Street, The Street With No Name, Scarlet Street, Street of Chance.* And, of course, "night"—a list that seems never to end: *Nightmare, Nightfall, Night Editor, Night Has a Thousand Eyes, The Night Holds Terror, The Night Runner, Nocturne.* Then there are the very particularized subsets of titles. City addresses: *99 River Street* and *711 Ocean Drive;* and telephone numbers: *Call Northside 777* and *Southside 1-1000* (not to mention *Sorry, Wrong Number*). Names: *Laura, Gilda, Vicki, Mildred Pierce,* with a special category around the name "Johnny": *Johnny Eager, Johnny Angel, Johnny Apollo, Johnny O'Clock.* And the purely aesthetic, grisly-erotic, poeticized titles: *Force of Evil* and *Born to Kill,* with its own unique subset built around the word "kiss": *Kiss Me Deadly, Killer's Kiss, Kiss of Death,* and upping the ante to a level never quite surpassed, *Kiss the Blood off My Hands.*

These films share a stark, dark vision of American urban life. While they represent the apogee of black-and-white film making, with their stunning visual style and technical virtuosity, on the deepest level they are not concerned primarily with black and white—good and evil, as such—in moral terms, but with the grays, the subtler gradations (as in degrees of Hell) of a more pervasive evil. If the noir world is a fallen one, all its inhabitants are in a fallen state, differentiated only by the magnitude of their demons. Protagonist, antagonist, and every character in between, are on the same slippery slope (or ladder) into the netherworld—some higher, and some lower, than the others.

So when our two halves of the same city—surface and subterranean—are superimposed, the black and white blurs to gray and we inevitably find our urban inhabitants in a haze, moral and psychological, of ambiguity, mistaken identities, betrayals, and shifting allegiances. Everywhere—in the home, the office, the church, the nightclub—there are pitfalls, blind spots, booby traps. Tripwires that set off elaborate chain reactions. Jolts and shocks and boomerang effects of every variety.

Indeed, walking through a city like New York or Los Angeles is like walking through a dream—or nightmare. Corridors, stairwells, precipitate rooftops, towers and antennae, streets that can be shadowy and frozen in time or frenetic with flashing steel and chrome, forbidding doorways, gigantic windows that with a subtle change of light can become funhouse mirrors, not to mention the ever-changing, infinitely varied faces and grotesqueries—the city of dreams differs very little from the city of reality. On a city street, the eye shifts, the mind distills, the imagination refashions, but one is still overwhelmed by the sheer volume of incoming sensations. In film, as in other artistic media, these can, and must, be isolated and directed within a larger narrative context. The difference in film, as Marshall McLuhan points out, is that it has the power in an instant to present a scene—dense with landscape, figures, objects, weather—that would require many pages of prose to describe. An instant later, it repeats all of this visual information, and goes on doing so. As in a dream, much can be going on, many possibilities may appear to exist, but our unconscious leads us along a very particular path whose significance may only come clear when the dream is over. In an essay on the French poet and decidedly urban film director Jean Cocteau, Ezra Pound wrote, "The life of a village is narrative. . . . In a city the visual impressions succeed each other, overlap, overcross, they are 'cinematographic.'" So, to take the analogy a step further, walking through New York or Los Angeles is not simply like walking through a dream, it is like walking through a dream that is on film, flickering before us. For a human being, the city is a cinematographic experience even before it is put on film.

Perhaps, therefore, it is easy to understand why from the noir perspective the individual human mind and the collective urban psyche, the lone body and the body politic, often coincide. The psyche, especially, is explored in the noir films in the way earlier films, documentary and dramatic, dissected the inner workings of spy rings, big business, crime syndicates, and military operations. So at the same time that postwar traumas shape the lives of our cities, the craze—and quickening influence—of psychoanalysis hits our shores with a vengeance and for a while remains a peculiarly urban phenomenon.

In Hollywood, of all places, the obsession with psychoanalysis—as a cultural sensation, remember, not a medical advance—surfaces rapidly and is taken up with immediate enthusiasm by the film industry. Maybe this isn't so surprising: where if not the self-described dream factory of America should this be more likely to occur? Freud himself visited the famous "Dream Land" park at Coney Island in 1909. Newsreel footage records the moment for all time: a small, bearded man in a white panama hat and black suit standing bemused and curious among enormous totems, masks, and mysterious illuminated structures that might have tumbled out of a Piranesi sketch; had he lived into the 1940s, who is to say Freud might not have made a similar pilgrimage to the backlots of Paramount or RKO studios. At the latter, which produced dozens of important films noirs in a compressed period, he would have seen the nightshift of the dream factory—the nightmare division—operating at full tilt.

Violence, sex, and dreams: if there is a trinity of forces behind noir, that may be it. To which should be added glamour. For the film noir's multifaceted reflections of the American city are not restricted to the oneiric or the psychological, much less to the criminal, the sleazy, and the down-on-their-luck. It is not for nothing that "urban" and "urbane" derive from the same root, the Latin *urbanus*. The city has always been the locus for the worlds of fashion, style, art, commerce, entertainment, and information. The place where money and intellect, in complex combinations, reign supreme, anchored not to the cycles of nature but to those of so-called public opinion and taste. The place where violent spectacles, pageantry, sensationalism, and exhibitionism are daily staples. The metropolitan city, in its current, decadent, declining stage of the past fifty years is not just Vanity Fair, but a sort of continuous, 24-hour-a-day World's Fair, exhausting and exhaustive.

Sophistication, glamour, and cultural refinement are characteristics shared by many members of the noir population. Casinos and nightclubs, with names like The Blue Dahlia and Club Trinidad, full of sleek, elegantly attired patrons, are a fixture in the noir landscape. In such clubs there is invariably a steamy torch singer, a siren of the night in a clinging, shimmering evening gown who wails into a microphone under a spotlight. Across town somewhere, her opposite number, a smartly dressed, ambitious young professional woman is working overtime in her well-appointed office in a new steel-and-glass high-rise building. She may be hurtling to the top of the advertising heap (*Laura*) or running a publishing company (*The Lady in the Lake*). She lives in a townhouse flat decorated to the nines or an ultramodern, sky-high penthouse with a sweeping vista of the city. And just as the torch singer is often hopelessly entangled with the debonair, powerful, invariably corrupt proprietor of one of those hot nightspots (Eddie Mars in *The Big Sleep* sets the standard for this type), the professional woman may find herself mixed up with a suave art gallery owner (*Crack-Up*), a glossy magazine columnist (*Laura*), an avaricious magazine magnate obsessed with timepieces (*The Big Clock*), or a big-city political boss, still with one foot in the gutter yet always nattily dressed, with custom-made necktie and handmade Milanese shoes (*The Glass Key*)—all of these men sharp-elbowed members of a nouveau riche urban class that has risen up in the war-heated economy from the ashes of the Depression.

After the gasoline rationing, car-pooling, housing shortages, and dreary self-denial of the war years, people yearn for a glamour and recklessness that quickly becomes associated with personal freedom. If it's a fast buck or a dirty buck that gets them a table up close to the siren in one of those clubs, well, so be it. Add to this the tremendous postwar boom in consumer goods and luxury items—which first manifests itself, of course, in the cities—and the wildfire acquisitiveness and gaudy commercialism that accompanied it, and that "freedom-at-any-price" ethos takes on an even uglier tinge. Cinematically, we see it all take shape, up close.

The high-roofed, rectangular, black or gray coupe of the 1930s is supplanted by the long low convertible with curvy fenders, flashy chrome work, and six-inch whitewalls. Department store windows are packed with the latest innovations—manna for the increasingly restless, up-and-coming middle-class consumer—from two-piece bathing suits to electric shavers, deluxe vacuum cleaners, and air conditioners. There are automatic car washes. Drive-in restaurants and movies. Automated bowling alleys. Ten-story parking garages. Colossal toy stores. And the first self-service supermarkets. It is the age of the gimmick (still with us), the golden sunrise of mass-market advertising (that "promiscuous and pestilential" mass Céline referred to) and fast-and-loose public relations. Image is everything, and the urban consciousness is flooded with millions of images and messages a day, a cross-babble of hype and streetcorner lingo, from "powerbrakes" to "Iron Curtain" to "diamonds are forever." Alternately elegant and garish, with its stylized eroticism, noir provides us a luminous but hard-edged perspective on the high life, as lived by both low-lifes and swells and aspired to, in fantasy at the very least, by nearly everyone in between. It was shrewdly observed by one French critic that film noir is America's stylization of itself. This is a theme picked up on by the American writer and director Paul Schrader, who points out that noir is "not defined, as are the western and gangster genres, by conventions of setting and conflict, but rather by the more subtle qualities of tone and mood. . . . Like its protagonists, film noir is more interested in style than theme. . . . The theme hidden in the style."

As noir progresses into the 1950s, in films and in popular culture in general, elements of pop eccentricity and high funk—as well as unabashed surrealism—color it more powerfully. The nocturnal, bebop jazz of Charlie Parker and John Coltrane, the explosion of rock and roll—Elvis Presley and Little Richard—with its sexual electricity and Bacchic ritual, and the newly emergent blues (up from the Mississippi Delta, electrified, urbanized, already fusing with jazz and rock and transforming itself into an entirely new form of American music) provide the background roar as postwar melts into Cold War and the full aftereffects of the war hit America and her cities. Undoubtedly a pivotal moment comes when the Soviet Union—having used stolen blueprints from the Manhattan Project and Los Alamos—

tests its first atomic bomb in August 1949, four years nearly to the day after Hiroshima and Nagasaki.

Mumford points out that the original meaning of "civilization" is "the ability to live and thrive in cities." The modern city, especially its late-twentieth-century mutation, the megalopolis, is an increasingly "uncivilized" psychic battleground for both honest citizens and the wide array of subversive and destructive forces—from corrupt police and outright criminals to the agents of subtly insidious bureaucracies and rapacious speculators—all of them forever losing ground in a deteriorating situation, a hostile environment that has been shaped to a great degree, physically and spiritually, by one of history's most "uncivilized" acts: Hiroshima.

How grimly ironic—but somehow unsurprising—that the crew of the *Enola Gay* should have nicknamed the atomic bomb they dropped on that city after Rita Hayworth. One of them even stuck a 5×7 print of the famous G.I. pinup of Hayworth, crouched on a quilted bed in her satin negligée, thrusting out her breasts, to the bomb's underside. Picture that image spinning down through the hot air currents over Hiroshima for 31,600 feet (nearly six miles), falling for forty-three seconds before impact and incandescence at ground zero. The symbolism is dizzying. The "sex goddess" and "bombshell," the prototypical femme fatale of film noir—and supposed destroyer of men—as the mascot of the destroyer of cities.

Noir not only traces its roots to the dawn of the Atomic Age, but also displays an ongoing obsession with all things nuclear. And communist. The communists who are supposedly swarming our cities, raised to superhuman proportions in both the tabloid and mainstream press, have replaced the previously exotic, now mundane, gangsters and crime lords of the decades between the two world wars. In this context, we might, for example, consider Elisha Cook, Jr., one of the great character actors of film noir, whose career spanned the entire film noir era, from *Stranger on the Third Floor* in 1940 to neo–films noirs in the 1970s; in his obituary in the *New York Times* on May 21, 1995, Cook was described as the "hophead jazz drummer in *Phantom Lady* . . . Jonesy, the lovesick loser forced to drink poison in *The Big Sleep* . . . [and] the bedeviled race-track teller in . . . *The Killing*." But, most telling, here is what Cook is quoted as saying about himself: "I played rats, pimps, informers, hopheads, and communists." He was being honest: those were the roles for which he was typecast, and the transition from "rat" to "communist," public enemy (as in hoodlum) to public menace (as in subversive), was absolutely in keeping with the transitions of the times. Cook, labeled the "screen's lightest heavy" because of his small frame, was one of many noir heavies who made the transition from tommygun-toting gangster to microfilm-savvy communist agent.

After the war, almost all supposed communist activity in the American city related to the destabilization of the U.S. government and the destruction of the "American way of life." There are commie infiltrators, unionists, propagandists, and disinformation artists, commie hat-check girls and delicatessan owners, nurses and stenographers, even commie provocateurs fixing football games: they are everywhere suddenly, repopulating the noir underside of the big city and restoking the basic noir fuels of angst, alienation, and paranoia well into the 1950s. And what are they obsessed with night and day, above all else? What is it that drives them in their every move, large or small? The atom bomb. Supposedly they're working double-overtime to gain an edge in the never-ending arms race so that they might incinerate the very American cities in which they themselves live.

From penthouses to subbasements, factory locker rooms to subway token booths, the city is out of nowhere rife with atomic materials of every kind. There are clandestine blueprints, microfilms, aerial photographs, uranium samples, laboratory experiments, and life-or-death formulas scrawled on scraps of graph paper or—better yet—cocktail coasters. Scientists are in hiding, or sneaking through customs, or selling their souls. Smugglers, extortionists, and saboteurs are everywhere, their every move choreographed by grim commissars in the Kremlin. The three R's of the early Atomic Age might be Radioactivity, Red Menace, and Rearmament.

The films noirs woven of red menace/atomic angst themes (might we call them *rouge et noir?*) are varied and numerous, with a decidedly hyper-urgent, infernal take on urban life. Anticommunism, McCarthyism, and the Cold War take on a pathology of their own in film noir. Whenever things heat up with regard to the Cold War, we see a sharp resurgence of noir films: Korea, 1950; the McCarthy hearings, 1953; Berlin and the Bay of Pigs, 1961; Vietnam, 1965; and so on, into the neo-noir revival beginning in 1981 with the elevation of Ronald Reagan and his hot-button talk of "the Evil Empire." Once the communists replace the gangsters who dominated the decades between the two world wars as the bogeymen of the popular mind, "commies" and "Reds" are simultaneously vilified, scapegoated, and raised to superhuman status in the tabloids, the respectable press, much of academia, and certainly in the halls of government. In urban terms, commies are suddenly responsible for everything from political machines (which certainly predated Marx and Engels) to prostitution (which long predated the United States) to "the lack of student discipline in metropolitan high schools" as *Life* magazine solemnly reported in 1952! Communism, in short, became an all-purpose metaphor for decay, duplicity, moral disintegration, and the forces of darkness: all of them major elements in the noir city.

American cities in the postwar era had become gargantuan enterprises, with problems scaled accordingly. That the notion of a scapegoat, an outside agent with malevolent designs (from kamikaze sabotage to moral subversion) and a corrosive, subterranean influence on urban life, took hold should not surprise us. Viewing the cities as social experiments that demanded constant modifying and perfecting had become a quaint, utopian pipe dream in the popular mind—the stuff of do-gooders and effete think tanks. Instead, we increasingly began to see our cities as battlegrounds for conflicting, seemingly irreconcilable, differences—social, economic, racial, religious, and cultural. So while the United States couldn't do much militarily about communism abroad during the Cold War years (regional wars fought in that regard tended to end in stalemate or defeat), we could certainly deflect some of the heat emanating from our real problems by raising the straw man of infiltrators and collaborators. Thus the frenzied warnings to the public that saboteurs were besieging our great cities, brainwashed citizens bankrolled by Party coffers were securing strategic niches at all levels of society, and devious moles (the milkman, the mayor, the girl next door—*anyone* could be a Red) were becoming ubiquitous, skillfully exerting subversive influences. Only with the most exorcistic fervor, the exhortations went, could we hope to respond to such a threat—a threat *from within.*

Thus in film noir, scapegoats, betrayers, dangerous and mysterious strangers, people with double identities, mistaken identities, and those who simply, or subtly, aren't what they seem to be—in society, in organizations, even within families—are constants. As are, on the other side of the coin, McCarthyite elements representing blind authority, intimidation, biased inquisition, and intolerance. The comic book–style catchwords of the Cold War—"Red menace," "Redbaiting," "commie-hunter"—in all their permutations, make their way into noir films. But aside from the obvious Red-scare noir films, *Walk East on Beacon, The Whip Hand, I Was a Communist for the F.B.I., The Woman on Pier 13,* there are countless films noirs that make no overt reference to communism and are apolitical in theme and content, but nevertheless sharply evoke the political climate of the times in their obsession with, and cultivation of, these same characteristics of the noir city. The alienating, twin darknesses of paranoia and dread, spawned by communism and the nuclear threat, that so seized the collective consciousness of urban Americans during the Cold War are also the twin pillars that might be erected at the entrance to the noir city—the Cold War's true capital—whose apotheosis is no doubt the Atomic City.

Even before postwar communism offered itself up, the depiction of the Nazis in their last-gasp days provided a brief warmup act in this regard with a curious, documentary-style film, *The House on 92nd Street,* released just six weeks after Hiroshima. It was produced by Louis de Rochemont, the man who revolutionized American newsreels with his "March of Time" series, a smartly edited, dramatically arranged moviehouse staple, anchored by an authoritative, basso-profundo narrator, seen by millions in the thirties and forties. So one of the very first films noirs is not just inspired by the wartime newsreels, but appeared—in fact, was designed to appear—to its audiences as a direct continuation of the newsreel form. (Even down to the "March of Time" narrator, Reed Hadley, who would also lend his stentorian voice to such semi-documentary films noirs as *T-Men* and *Call Northside 777.*) Because the two atomic bombs were dropped on Japan during the final editing stage of *The House on 92nd*

Street, the film's plot was significantly altered by way of additional dialogue so that it suddenly centered around Nazi spies working frantically to obtain "Process 97, the secret ingredient of the atomic bomb." Even six weeks into the Atomic Age, a box-office maven (and ground-breaking journalist) like de Rochemont knew that this was a far more pulse-stopping plot hook than, say, the latest periscope design or the layout of a munitions plant—the standard espionage prizes of the war years. When the real-life stakes were raised, the dramatic ones had to follow. America's atomic appetite had been whetted, and would never quite be appeased.

Nuclear weapons are not just a manifestation of political impulses and supposed military imperatives: they are a product of our culture. As such, the emotional tidal wave they unleashed in the charged atmosphere of the late 1940s must be seen, too, as a self-inflicted phenomenon. The weapons were produced in carefully planned and funded government programs, with public and private manpower, and were specifically intended for urban targets. This whole process, politically and psychically, had the boomerang effect of poisoning the atmosphere of our own cities with dread and alienating fear. The simultaneous glorification of atomic power ("clean energy") by the U.S. government and the nuclear industry with their secret but not so subtle strategy of skewing American military policy almost exclusively to nuclear weaponry—bigger, more devastating, and ultimately more suicidal devices of destruction—proved to be especially insidious. For the ensuing psychological strains on a populace living under the spectre of a swift, irrational, and terrible death was tremendous—and certainly underestimated at the time. Dr. Johnson noted that the imminent arrival of the hangman focuses one's mind wonderfully. But what if the hangman were to lurk outside one's door—coughing, shuffling, occasionally peering in—for a year, ten years, twenty-five, at any moment, without warning, still likely to enter? Under the strain, one's mind might quickly grow numb, if it didn't burn out altogether.

Again, in considering the nuclear threat to Americans in cities, we are employing the terminology of noir: "numb," "strain," "burn out." Indeed, the language of noir is a highly familiar dialect in the Atomic City. Even temperate statesmen like Bernard Baruch (in 1946) and

George Kennan (in 1982) employed it in U.N. speeches; in speaking of the overkill targeting of major cities during the arms race, they used phrases like "the dark chasm on the brink of which we stand" and "like victims of hypnotism, like men in a dream, like lemmings headed for the sea" to discuss the residents of such cities.

Nuclear angst made itself felt in films of all genres after Hiroshima, with a notable infusion of hysteria after that 1949 Soviet test. There were spy thrillers and military melodramas, but most predominantly, horror and science-fiction films. In the latter, the angst was dealt with overtly, often in containable, physical terms. A dormant dinosaur is released from beneath the ocean floor (or the Arctic ice pack) by an atomic test and, instantly radioactive and hyperactive, stomps through a densely populated city until the military, aided by omniscient atomic scientists, can destroy him, usually with a nuclear-tipped missile or torpedo. The benign role of the scientists who developed the very weapons that were originally being tested was intended to counterbalance, with true-blue Cold War logic, any negative impressions we might formulate about atomic power, nuclear testing, or the harrowing fact that all our cities had become potential nuclear targets. In other words, the circular message was that although the mere testing of these weapons could cause a catastrophe, without them, we'd be done for. Dozens of variations on this theme were produced in the United States, Europe, and of course Japan, where movie audiences were coping less with incipient dread than with the lingering aftershock of having twice been a nuclear bull's-eye in reality. The great and highly significant difference between these sci-fi films and the film noir is that in film noir that same terrible nuclear angst is repressed, introverted, rechanneled, and not nearly so containable, much less resolvable, in the physical world. It finds easy conversion into psychoses and traumas far more devastating than the scaly, stiff-leggèd Tyrannosaurus Rex that can spit radioactive fire onto a skyscraper.

Orson Welles' *The Lady from Shanghai* (filmed in 1947, and also starring Rita Hayworth) pushes forth an insistent subtext of nuclear apocalypse and contains the definitive noir statement concerning the atomic bomb and the American city. The film's principal murder victim (there are many), a psychotic and double-dealing lawyer, manically foresees Armageddon at every turn, claiming he can "feel it." With dilated pupils, a face that won't stop sweating, and a shrill, singsong voice, he announces that he plans to escape to a remote Pacific island—a particularly acid joke on Welles' part since this was the very year the United States began testing atomic bombs at just such a place, the Bikini Atoll, "relocating" all the inhabitants and destroying the ecosystem. Later, on a boat in San Francisco Harbor, increasingly agitated, hours from his own death, still drenched in sweat, this man insists he wants to be "as far away as possible from *that* city—or any city—when they start dropping *those* bombs!" (By the time of Bikini, the erotic identification of Hayworth with the Bomb appears to have been institutionalized, with the blessing of the military brass: the first bomb dropped in the Pacific testing ground is named "Gilda" and has Hayworth's image, in provocative dress, painted directly on its casing—no snapshot taped on surreptitiously this time.)

Such films were merely mirroring, and focusing, the increasingly bizarre, frantic, and often contradictory statements regarding the American city and the Bomb that were surfacing in the news media, government agencies, universities, and among city planners and the new breed of self-styled Civil Defense experts who made a cottage industry of Cold War paranoia. The macabre notion of Civil Defense drills and escape routes, and the widespread construction of bomb shelters under streets and buildings in cities that could not be escaped or protected, would be fine examples of gallows humor were they not so cruel. For example, a less-than-full-scale nuclear attack on New York City in 1960 would have created a crater at least two miles deep; yet the average bomb shelter in the city was roughly 150 feet below street level. And it is interesting to note that in the two periods when film noir was most fertile—1945–58 and the mid-1980s—government officials were instructing citizens on what clothes to wear during a nuclear attack, how to drive their cars along special routes, and how to prepare for life after a nuclear war. One Reagan Administration official even went so far as to suggest that credit cards might be more useful than paper currency after such a war. Knowing the true consequences of such warfare, these officials, one must conclude, operated on a level of cynicism that boggles the mind. And it is exactly that sort of cynicism—and the pessimism, anger, and bitterness it must provoke—that found strong expression in film noir.

In fact, the whole Civil Defense craze (those little black and yellow signs, heavily rusted now, can still be found in forgotten nooks and crannies of big cities, pointing the way to bomb shelters) was part of a bigger, anesthetizing advertising and public relations campaign which attempted to convince the American public that nuclear war was survivable, winnable, and containable. At the same time, the public was being given another—completely contradictory—message in harsh doses. A *New York Times* article of the late 1940s, for example, addressed to the citizens of "New York, Chicago, and other big cities," spoke the typical language of the day on this subject: "If war is declared, you, your home, and your place of business will disappear in the next second." The climate was one of paranoia, apocalypse, and nightmarish fantasy; where else but in the realm of fantasy (and that includes books and films) can one contemplate a city's nuclear destruction, from vaporized humans to melted bridges? And the message—the big, overriding message—in the Atomic City was not just mixed, but schizophrenic.

A sampler of the public relations activities around this subject by various civic, governmental, and academic groups reads like the detritus of an opium dream, by way of a comic book. Most of the following are cited in the social scientist Paul Boyer's 1984 study of the period, *By the Bomb's Early Light.*

The city planners weighed in early on. For example, a respected urbanologist and president of the American Institute of Planners, a contributor of numerous articles between 1946 and 1953 to magazines like *American City* and the *Bulletin of the Atomic Scientists,* gave a speech in 1946 in which he argued that the threat of atomic annihilation might be the best thing that ever happened to American cities! Why? Because, with public interest so keen, long dormant city planners, ignoring urban blight since the turn of the century, might find "the threat of atom bombing a useful spur to jolt us forward."

The press managed to be both hysterical and erratic. Calling Washington, D.C., a "naked city" liable to be leveled at any moment,

Time magazine urged that federal agencies be relocated around the country. And in 1950, *Collier's* magazine published an article entitled "Hiroshima U.S.A.: Can Anything Be Done About It?" which vividly described a devastating hypothetical attack on New York. Then, within an eight-month period in 1950, in a wild bit of journalistic see-sawing, *Life* published one feature entitled "How U.S. Cities Can Prepare for Atomic War," discussing "the growing likelihood of World War III," and followed it up with an utterly pessimistic, apocalyptic piece which stated unequivocally that there was *no way* in which our cities could prepare for such a war and that Doomsday was virtually upon us. As David Bradley wrote in the *Saturday Evening Post* in 1951, the relationship between city-dwellers and the Bomb boiled down to "nightmares, hallucinations, and the convulsions" that would come of "a final global dementia."

The government, meanwhile, consistently followed the seesaw approach demonstrated by *Life:* on the one hand issuing Civil Defense pamphlets that instructed urban residents, in the event of nuclear attack, to "wear long-sleeved shirts that buttoned at the wrist, a hat with the brim down (to prevent facial burns), and, if possible, rubbers," and not to worry about corpses' being radioactive—"an impossibility, though the coins in their pockets might be temporarily heated"; and on the other hand publishing Pentagon white papers describing Soviet atomic weapons as capable of totally destroying "everything within an area of more than three hundred square miles . . . as an incinerator it would severely burn everything within an area of more than twelve hundred square miles."

No wonder that noir took such a strong hold on the national psyche during those years. Ambivalence, fear, anxiety, lunatic logic—all of these found their way into the popular culture of the times, especially in films. As Boyer points out, in those years, when discussing the state of the nation, even the usually arid tracts of sociologists, historians, and columnists are filled with lurid, often nihilistic "images of dreaming and nightmares" and a "dull sense of grim inevitability as humankind stumbled toward the nothingness that almost surely lay somewhere down the road." So staid a publication as the *Christian Century* declared in 1949 that in the years since Hiroshima the people in American cities "had reacted to the atomic threat as a sleepwalker would react to the edge of a roof toward which he was walking." (The latter metaphor is another that finds expression in several films noirs of the period.)

By the mid-1950s, the nuclear poker bluffing of the Korean War (another war, this one with a less than triumphant conclusion, that sent home a new wave of displaced, often embittered, veterans) and the cancerous aftereffects of the McCarthy era certainly rejuiced the fears and paranoias of 1945, but with far more cynical results. So that by 1955 the noir city of Los Angeles in *Kiss Me Deadly* has become nothing less than an apocalyptic playground.

Looking back now, with the Cold War over and the American city threatened more by *im*plosion than *ex*plosion, another quick, simple definition—like Welles' about film—comes to mind. "History," the historian Jakob Burckhardt wrote, "is what one age finds worthy of note in another." In late twentieth-century America, when several decades can feel like an age, it's not only that we can look back to the forties and fifties and appreciate the cutting-edge significance and power of the noir vision, but also that we can gaze into our national mirror today and discern all around us the dark tones and shock-waves of noir's resurgence. A resurgence that began in the mid-1980s, has yet to peak in the nineties, and was foreshadowed, briefly, in the late sixties. What we have found most worthy of note in another age, in other words, suddenly and inevitably applies to our own.

Quite simply, in times of stress—national stress, which is always most dramatically reflected in urban stress—noir since 1958 has resurfaced and reasserted itself with a vengeance. To begin with, there is the most noir film footage in all American history: the forty-seven seconds of Abraham Zapruder's home movie that captured President Kennedy's assassination in a motorcade (which, with the years, more resembles a funeral cortege, one black limousine after another, only the hearse missing) in Dallas in 1963. Within two years, our second—and most terrible—war of the post–World War era is raging out of control in Southeast Asia. Large-scale race riots have erupted in the major cities. Now we don't have to go to movie theaters to see newsreels of Dresden and Tokyo in flames: we can watch excruciating carnage on our televisions, over dinner, as the evening news carries us onto battlefields nine thousand miles away

or into streets less than a mile away. In 1965, federal troops are ordered into Los Angeles, which is burning as no American city
burned during the Second World War. (In May 1992, parts of L.A.
will burn again, under remarkably similar circumstances, and troops
will again be despatched to restore order.) And by Christmas 1968,
the United States will have dropped more tonnage of bombs on
North Vietnam than was dropped in all of the Second World War.

And what form does noir take in those explosive years? How exactly does it resurface? Luxury items and gadgetry now take on Roman proportions: cars are bigger, faster, and more wasteful, with
sharp fins, rocket-like bodies, and complex adornments of chrome;
high-speed jets thunder in and out of city airports, so that one might
easily breakfast in Seattle, lunch in New York, and go to sleep in Miami; and automation has transformed and further depersonalized
everyday life, from laundromats to drive-in banks. Styles of dress
take their cues less from Rome than Babylon: skirts of leather and
vinyl break six inches above the knee; shoes are pointy, stiletto-
heeled, and often painful to walk in; men are jangling jewelry and
growing heads of hair worthy of Restoration England. Decadence itself (the consumer variety) slowly becomes just another luxury
item—if not a virtue—available to millions. Drugs are taken up with
a vengeance by the middle class. Pornography goes mainstream.
And the stoic, uptight, antiseptically sexed screen hero of the 1950s
is supplanted overnight by the fictional likes of James Bond: "licensed to kill" (with insouciance, by the state), he drinks vintage
champagne, smokes exotic cigarettes, is "fluent in Oriental languages" (all of them?), careens down public streets with the abandon of a Grand Prix racer, and revels in casual, sometimes kinky,
sex, preferably one-night stands in deluxe hotel suites on his ex-
pense account (as a civil servant!). Next to the late forties, the mid-
1960s are Carnival under a full moon.

But it's a Carnival that is not all flash and glitter. There are noir
sideshows darker, and often more menacing, than those of earlier
decades. By now, noir has entered the cultural vocabulary; it is
aware, and imitative, of its own history; in ways, it is even feeding on
itself, on its own roots. There is a distinctly noir branch of rock and
roll: Lou Reed, The Velvet Underground, Captain Beefheart, The
Rolling Stones (who become an American band in the end, living and

recording in the U.S.A.), and of course Bob Dylan's *Blonde on Blonde*—recorded in seventy-two straight hours in 1966, fueled by heroin—the great breakthrough album of American rock, harsh, gritty, gorgeously textured, and noir to its bare bones. George Segal is producing his icy white papier-mâché sculptures of full-sized human figures (three-dimensional, blanched noir silhouettes) who inhabit vast, empty spaces until, later in the decade, fashionable suddenly, they are brought in from the cold to stand free-form in the living rooms of the rich. Before his death in 1965, Edward Hopper brings forth his final, fearful canvases of the New York streets. Likewise Charles Sheeler, who dies in the same year after his ability to work has been cut short by a crippling stroke. Lenny Bruce is delivering his scintillating and scabrous monologues at white heat in after-hours clubs in cities across America, monitored by vice squad detectives, until—hounded and broke—he O.D.s on a toilet shooting up speed. Then there are the angry, rambling urban sutras of Allen Ginsberg and the elegant black sonnets of John Berryman. Black Panther manifestoes. Marilyn Monroe as icon—and suicide. And Roy Lichtenstein's gaudy, gorgeous, imitation-comic-book portraits of rapacious femme fatales, spacy airline stewardesses, and forlorn, weeping heartthrobs straight out of film noir.

And what about film noir in the 1960s? The films, too, are propelled by higher-octane materials than their forties counterparts. And their vision has darkened considerably—and been densely involuted. *Brainstorm* (1965) and *Point Blank* (1967) are notable examples, populated by characters so cold-blooded, existentially blank, and alienated—sundered, actually, from the disintegrating society around them—that the metallic, splashily lit nightmare cities of steel and glass they wander seem most chilling for their matter-of-factness. They are presented, not as a heightened reality, but as the norm. Hyper, hallucinatory, ever unstable. As also in the 1961 film *Blast of Silence* in which a hired killer enters a labyrinth in Manhattan that is a veritable icebox morally and in which violence provides the only emotional relief.

The hero of *Brainstorm* is a brilliant research scientist who is literally, relentlessly, driven insane by everyone around him, from his employer, a sadistic industrialist, to his psychiatrist, a seductive older woman who, in the role of spider woman, leads him through webs of his own making, deeper and deeper into his derangement, before deserting him there. The hero of *Point Blank,* whether or not he is reenacting—post-mortem, a phantom of the isolation ward— his own murder, never behaves like anything but an ice man: no emotions, no doubts, no hesitation in avenging himself, one victim at a time, upon the long chain of betrayers—the entire hierarchy of an organized crime syndicate—who after swindling him led him to the violent end we witnessed at the film's opening.

The cities these heroes inhabit are offered up mosaic-style (mirroring the fact that linear time and space, on which cities operate, have been shattered), with telephoto zoom lenses and splintering kaleidoscopic images, as if a flashlight has been trained, unsteadily, down one of Pandæmonium's chaotic side-streets. That flashlight illuminates a world of amazingly casual and sudden violence and of fractured human relationships. Businessmen have become indistinguishable from gangsters, nervous breakdowns and emotional burnouts are depicted as commonplace, and all of it is backdropped by modish decors, automatic weapons, synthetic narcotics, and lethal pollution. The upbeat technological boom of the 1940s, mirroring the so-called peacetime use of the atom, has devolved into a toxic nightmare.

Dread is no longer a set of dark, threatening clouds that drifts in from somewhere else; it is the constant, unvarying weather that never leaves. If anything, after twenty years of Cold War posturing, fast-and-loose talk of Armageddon by reactionary politicians, big-time political scandals, the decay of the urban infrastructure, and an increasingly self-isolating, polarized society, the noir vision and the films it spawns quite naturally would be harsher and more unrelenting than its 1940s prototypes. The films push along a razor's edge, with a cruder, insistent emphasis on the urban experience as being *the* essential American experience. The pastoral, they insist, is not only quaintly self-indulgent, but also irrelevant in light of the *reality* (the word itself begins to carry a reproachful ring) around us. Even from a purely demographic standpoint, this is not surprising: Americans have become an overwhelmingly urban people, with predominantly urban fears and obsessions (and with sprawling suburbs whose problems, too, have been imported from the cities). Between 1945 and 1968 alone, twenty million Americans moved from rural areas into the cities; by 1968, seventy-one percent of the population lived in cities, on one percent of the land. By 1994, it was eighty-seven percent of the population. In 1990 it was recorded that fewer than sixteen million Americans—only one in sixteen—lived in towns with less than ten thousand people.

The arc that noir has followed, like a dark rainbow, over the evolving American city has begun to loom large again today for many reasons. Cities expanding so rapidly, beyond the point of no return, were bound to trigger social and cultural explosions over which they had little control. The 1990s are not like the late 1940s—or are they? There is no Hiroshima, and no World War winding down. But those same European cities that were leveled in 1945 are again sending ominous smoke clouds across the Atlantic. The Cold War is over, but violent neo-Nazis are on the rise in a reunited Germany. Sarajevo, where the bloody cycle of the world wars was first ignited, began the decade of the nineties witnessing horrors last seen in Europe in the heyday of Hitler and Stalin: concentration camps; mass rapes whose victims were forced to bear their rapists' children; torture on a grosteque scale; schools, mosques, and libraries torched in order to eradicate a people's religious and ethnic identity. Europe is overrun with desperate refugees. Strident nationalism and factionalism are boiling over, from Spain, where swastikas appear with alarming frequency on Madrid's walls, clear across the former Soviet Union, where breakaway republics, ethnic hatreds, and organized crime networks so powerful they control (echoes of noir) entire cities and provinces, and by 1997 have spread effectively—unbelievably, in the eight short years since the Berlin Wall came down—to American cities.

Back in the U.S.A. in the 1990s, we have our own homegrown terrorists and vigilantes promulgating their messages of violence and hatred. They may do it through the mails or on the Internet, with racial and ethnic venom, or they may do it in the streets with explosives. However safe our borders may be from the defunct Soviet Empire, a handful of vigilante terrorists are able to blow up a government building in Oklahoma City, at the center of the country's heartland, with a massive car bomb. And two years earlier, the tallest building in our largest city, at the center of the financial district, is bombed by foreign terrorists who had a wish list of targets that included the major tunnels and bridges leading in and out of New York. But it is the urban angst and economic fears that peak during the Reagan-Bush years, in what seems a silent conspiracy fostering urban decay and the brutal expansion of an economic underclass, which inflict less spectacular but far more lethal damage upon our cities. Years of conmen plying their trade from the pinnacles of government to the street corner, of soaring crime and an enfeebled justice system, of cities in which handguns are more readily available to children than library books, rekindle in Americans an appetite—a need—for film noir. Perhaps, as in the forties, these films seem absolutely realistic and true to life, and offer an emotional catharsis rooted very close to home; perhaps, too, they once again mirror with merciless clarity the collective dream-life of Americans. If so, the message coming through is that things are *worse* than they seem, and well out of our control, and as in a classic nightmare—or noir film—they can only get worse still.

While the numbers of 1950–1952 may not be matched in the foreseeable future, the jump in films noirs since 1986 (midway through the Reagan-Bush era) is amazing, and revelatory. Suddenly in that year the trickle of two or three films noirs produced yearly becomes a small flood. From mid-1986 to the end of 1987, fourteen neo–films noirs are produced, depicting cities as varied as New Orleans, Phoenix, and Honolulu. In ways that would have been inconceivable in 1950, these cities have become indistinguishable from the staple postwar noir cities of New York, Los Angeles, and San Francisco. From *Angel Heart* (1987) to *The Grifters* (1990), to outright remakes of classic films noirs like *Cape Fear* (1991) and *Night and the City* (1992), to a masterly and complex original like *The Usual Suspects* (1995), the neo-noirs, artfully shot in stark, tough color, have continued to crop up at a startling pace. Even a pop-gangster outgrowth like *Pulp Fiction* (1994) manages to fuse recognizable elements from a dozen noir films of the classic era; for example, the attaché case that floats through the film, purportedly containing an unknown, never-explained, glowing stash of contraband—gems? rare metals? atomic fuel?—is an echo of, and homage to, the Pandora's box in *Kiss Me Deadly*. Today, even in pulp, cartoonish renderings of the American city, such as comic books, dimestore thrillers, or even the mass-market *Batman* extravaganzas, the city is rendered as a noir grotesque: Batman's Gotham (as in *Gothic*) City and Superman's technicolor, chaotic Metropolis are quintessential noir cities, with all the trimmings—ever-nocturnal, crime-ridden, corrupt, economically polarized, and rife with demons. The modern noir city is a no-holds-barred playground for criminals, deviate types, vampires, and outright freaks (the Penguin, the Joker, Brainiac)—a Capital of the Night, where the forces of sex and death intertwine.

When the noir vision meshes with what we see in the streets, and in our hearts, it becomes not just topical, but necessary. Contemporary because it speaks to us directly, from the gut. The view of the French critics of the 1950s who insisted that noir was never a film genre at all, but *a way of seeing the world,* now seems more prescient than ever. In the "black" films inspired by the American city after the Second World War we can see the massive sea-change, and seismic aftereffects, that they reflect in our cultural history. The depiction of the cities of those years immediately after the war, vastly different from, yet vivid precursors of, the cities they have become, leads us across time—sometimes in a zigzag, sometimes along a beam of light, but always from a revealing angle—to the American city today, as we experience and reimagine it. Where the city of dreams leaves off and the city of steel and concrete begins becomes irrelevant in the end. In film noir, the actual and dream cities merge, are recorded fugitively, and transformed into myth—the most revealing mirror of all.

In the fall of 1925, twenty-one years nearly to the day before Le Corbusier caught his first glimpse of Manhattan, the Austrian film director Fritz Lang was a young man returning to Germany by ship after a whirlwind tour of New York and Los Angeles, where he had been observing motion picture techniques. Lang did not record what techniques he had gleaned, but he did say that while detained in New York Harbor the night of his departure, he gazed for several hours upon the twinkling lights of the Manhattan skyline and conceived the idea for his film *Metropolis,* which he would shoot in Berlin over the next three years.

Metropolis is a visionary film, of a futuristic, nightmare city in the year 2000. A dark city in which human beings are split collectively—as each of us is individually—between those who are all intellect and those who are all muscle. It is one of the German Expressionist films that most radically influenced the American film noir two decades later. That it was inspired by New York City and created by an artist who would later flee the nightmare city of Nazi Berlin to create a group of the most powerful and illuminating films noirs in the United States, many of them about New York—irony piled upon irony, as in many of those films—seems only appropriate. As we approach the year 2000, the quintessential American city that inspired *Metropolis* and the revolutionary American films that *Metropolis* in turn inspired, demand close scrutiny: how the past envisioned the future, and how the future fulfills the past, will after all tell us, as the film noir does, more about ourselves and our cities than we may want to know.

3. Postcards from the Ruins: Some Americans Abroad

Three distinctive films noirs were shot in European cities in the years just following the Second World War. Two were American productions, with American casts; in the third, the two central characters were archetypal Americans. Two of the films were set in cities utterly devastated by the war—Berlin, Frankfurt, and Vienna—and the third was set in London, a city that had been aerially terrorized. Though all three films are technically brilliant—one a masterpiece—they had little need of elaborate lighting, staging, or art direction. Even the finest on-location shooting requires an infusion of atmospherics. But not in these films. The decimated cities—bombed- and burned-out shells of buildings, mountains of rubble and debris, bomb craters filled with ashes, bridges that no longer led anywhere—provided all the atmosphere that was necessary. The cities spoke as loudly to American audiences as the stories that had been set in them.

However stylish their productions—for each of the films had a powerful and idiosyncratic director—these films, with American actors set down in the European cities that were a seminal part of the noir vision, reside in a special category: transplanted noir that at the same time is more raw than the American original.

The window of opportunity—an unfortunate phrase in this context, but true nonetheless—for such films to be made was necessarily brief: the Europeans, including the Germans, were with American assistance rebuilding their cities as rapidly as they could. All films are time capsules, but these three are especially poignant—and, in noir terms, invaluable.

Berlin Express, completed in November 1947, was the first American film to be shot in Germany after the war. In a credit, the producers note the cooperation of the "American, British, and Soviet Armies of Occupation." (But not the French, who for whatever reason, or out of contrariness, would not cooperate.) In Berlin, the principal location shooting occurred at the Reich chancellery, the Reichstag, the Brandenburg Gate—sites of enormous curiosity to Americans—and the Adlon Hotel; in Frankfurt, there were scenes filmed in at least two dozen different locations. And there were scenes set in Paris, which was not scarred by bombing, but was nevertheless emerging from the deep-freeze of a terrible occupation. The film was directed by Jacques Tourneur, who had completed his direction of my old touchstone, *Out of the Past,* ten months earlier. In fact, *Berlin Express* was his very next film.

Its plot is simple: a virulent group of Nazis who went underground at war's end are intent on preventing the unification of postwar Germany (and obviously can't foresee that the Cold War will do the job for them); on the train from Paris to Berlin, they attempt to assassinate an elder statesman who is the would-be architect of unification, fail, and kidnap him instead; his foreign—mostly American—colleagues then search for him, with the help of Occupation forces, through the tortuously complex ruins of Frankfurt; when they find him, it is purely by chance, and there is little hope—and, in fact, much pessimism—expressed as to any possibility of suppressing the neo-Nazis in future.

It is clear that the Europeans had bigger things to fear than the organized crime, drug rings, shellshocked former soldiers, and other subversive forces they shared with the noir cities of the United States. *Berlin Express* has an overriding theme: paranoia, pure but not simple. There is the paranoia engendered by the resurgent Nazis, and by the sheer magnitude of the nightmare landscape. And there is the even worse paranoia among the main characters, the kidnapped statesman's colleagues, among whom there is not a single relationship which does not become strained to the breaking point. They all know that one of their number is a traitor, a member of the Nazi organization, who has abetted the kidnapping. Where they are at that moment in time—combing endlessly through the rubble that is an unremitting and devastating reminder of war itself—is enough to poison the air completely. Even the exposure of the traitor does little to dispel that poison, and despite some surface niceties, the film ends as bleakly as it began.

For Tourneur, a director so subtle in his use of black and white that the variant grades of his blacks are discernible even to casual moviegoers, *Berlin Express* is an unusual departure. The delicately balanced, internalized fearfulness of *Out of the Past* and the even more modulated elements of fear in his other noteworthy films noirs differ markedly from *Berlin Express,* in which the entire landscape is fear made solid. Made visible. The four cult films on which Tourneur collaborated with the maverick (and pioneering) producer Val Lewton in a twenty-month span in 1942 and 1943—*during* the war—*Cat People, I Walked With a Zombie, The Seventh Victim,* and *The Leopard Man,* are famous for the fact that the nocturnal horrors at their respective centers remain *invisible,* menacing, detached while at the same time pushing at the envelope of our sensibilities from within. The tension, and the shocks, are heightened by restraint, and an ominous, unliftable sense of imminent danger. In *Berlin Express,* the sense of danger is anything but submerged, and the forces behind the extreme paranoia are never concealed.

Two destroyed cities, an express train linking them, and a set of the most fearful, suspicious passengers one could imagine—blasted of trust, each inhabiting his own cold sliver of a compartment: *Berlin Express* is a film reduced, or honed, to a noir skeleton that we can hear rattling throughout the film as surely as we hear the rattling of that train as it rolls through the wasteland.

Carol Reed, an Englishman, directed *The Third Man,* and another Englishman, Graham Greene, wrote it, but it is the two American actors, Orson Welles and Joseph Cotten, and the characters they portray, who lend it its significance as a film noir. Filmed on location in Vienna in 1948, it was released in 1949, and interestingly, in keeping with the great emphasis the film lays upon the four occupied zones of the city—American, British, Russian, and French (they cooperated on this one)—there are two versions of *The Third Man,* British and American. The former opens with a statement by the director, Reed, and the latter is built around a voice-over, in vintage noir style (much like the one in *Out of the Past*), delivered by Joseph Cotten.

The presence of Cotten and Welles gives the film an unmistakably strong American sensibility. Cotten acted in a number of memorable films noirs, most notably as the ladykiller (literally) on the lam from the city who visits his small-town relatives, for whom he can do no wrong, in Hitchcock's *Shadow of a Doubt* (1943). He also played the cuckolded, newlywed husband of Marilyn Monroe (he murders her and then dies going over the falls) in *Niagara* (1953). Welles directed and acted in two of the most dynamic and innovative films noirs ever, which, produced ten years apart, bookend the classic noir period: *The Lady from Shanghai* (1948) and *Touch of Evil* (1958). He also directed and acted in two noir curiosities. The first, *Mr. Arkadin* (1955), is a seedily baroque reprise of *Citizen Kane* and an over-the-top precursor to Federico Fellini's *La Dolce Vita*. Played by Welles, Gregory Arkadin, one of the world's richest men, a pioneer jet-setter, made his millions not in finance or commerce or even conventional crime, but in the white slave trade! At film's end, he leaps to his death from his private plane after learning that his daughter has discovered his true occupation. The other film, *The Stranger* (1946), is a curiosity only because, of all Welles' films, it does not distinctively hold a place in the great body of his work. Welles was notorious, by Hollywood standards, for marching completely to his own drummer once his films were in production; that is, he didn't care at all what the studio he was toiling for might think about his work. But in *The Stranger,* compliant with his studio for once, he turned out a linear, plot-driven film ("lead-footed," he called it). He did it for two reasons: ready cash, and the possibility of subsequent bankrolling by the studios; for despite having in his twenties directed two masterpieces, Welles was told he had to prove himself "marketable" to his Hollywood overlords. *The Stranger* flopped commercially and Welles was less marketable than ever. Afterwards, he would say: "I was ready never to act again." Fortunately, for us, he did.

Of course, both Welles and Cotten are best known for their superb work in *Citizen Kane,* a film without which we would not have film noir as we know it. Their personae in *The Third Man* are similar— with a twist—to those they displayed in *Citizen Kane;* in the latter Welles portrayed, extravagantly, a newspaper tycoon and heir to a mining fortune, while Cotten played his boon companion—prep school chum, college roommate (a whole string of colleges), and drinking buddy. Welles, who also wrote most of *Citizen Kane,* gave

Jedadiah

Cotten's character the name "~~Jessadiah~~"—a mock-Biblical, mock-prophetical name, with a grandiloquent ring, for someone who turns out to have scant ambition (certainly in relation to Kane) and whose few attempts at moral suasion with Kane badly fail. Later, when Kane is sliding daily between his roles as urban powerbroker, art collector, and raconteur—a decidedly gaudy and ruthless Don Quixote—Cotten becomes his Sancho Panza.

It is fascinating to note that Welles, to whom the adjective "quixotic" was often applied, began filming a version of Cervantes' *Don Quixote* in 1955. In his peripatetic style, he would tinker with the film for the next thirty years, until his death. Never completed, the film was structured like a labyrinth: one image leading to another, finding amplification but never resolution—or even continuity after a certain point. One of Welles' biographers, Barbara Leaming, described the fragments that made up the film as a puzzle which Welles was never able to assemble. He himself always referred to the ill-fated film as his "home movie."

In *The Third Man,* the circumstances are far different, but the Quixote/Panza link is not. Welles plays Harry Lime, an elusive, once again ruthless, kingpin in the thriving postwar black market. And, despite his coterie of sophisticated friends, loyal confederates, and a stunning Austrian actress who was his mistress, he turns out to be a rather loathsome blackmarketeer. Until late in the picture, despite his infrequent appearances, we have come to like, and even admire, Lime; he is certainly the most interesting character in the story. Then we learn that his specialty is not the usual contraband—gasoline, cigarettes, or identity papers—but penicillin, stolen from children's hospitals and replaced with a bastardized substitute that inflicts terrible deformities, or death, upon the unfortunate patients. When the Occupation military police get too close to him, Lime fakes his own death with the help of those confederates (neatly disposing of his inside-man at the hospital in the process) and—literally—goes underground.

Into all of this, quite awkwardly, drops Cotten-as-Panza, this time named Holly Martins, but if anything, less ambitious and even more ineffectual than Jessadiah in *Citizen Kane.* Martins is a down-on-his-luck, down-at-heels, hack writer of pulp westerns. "A drunken scribbler," the top military cop calls him. He's broke, cynical, and self-depracatory, and he's looking for his old friend Harry (yes, once again they've attended prep school and flunked out of college together), who has written to Martins, promising a job—presumably in the drug trade. But Martins knows nothing about Lime's illicit activities, and for most of the film he resists any suggestion that his pal might be a criminal. While trying to unravel the circumstances of Lime's faked death, Martins learns enough, however, to turn Judas (not mock-Biblical, but the real thing this time) and help the police trap Lime. For the latter, despite the odiousness of his crimes, one retains some faint sympathy to the end: it is hard, after all, to resist a character who, while several hundred feet above the city in a stalled ferris wheel, tries to explain his actions to Martins ("How could you, Harry?" the latter keeps badgering him) by making two observations. First, pointing to the milling crowds below, mere dots against the pavement, Lime asks Martins what he would do if someone were to give him (Martins) a thousand dollars for "every dot that stopped moving"—would he not accept it? Second, Lime observes that from Florence, with its incessant wars, political treachery, and "the Borgias," sprang forth the Renaissance—Dante, Michelangelo, and da Vinci—while Switzerland, "with ten centuries of peace and tranquillity, produced the cuckoo clock." A noir epigram, if there ever was one.

And where is all this occurring? The setting of this film differs markedly from the cosmopolitan opulence of *Citizen Kane.* The Vienna of 1948 that backdrops *The Third Man* is also quite different from the Vienna that existed between 1860 and 1941. This was the Vienna of the Ringstrasse: a vision of urban reconstruction on a grand scale that, when it came to fruition, transformed the city from a medieval capital into the birthplace of urban modernism. Two pioneers of modern urban thought, Camillo Sitte and Otto Wagner, produced their seminal works during the apex of the Ringstrasse epoch, honing their ideas about street-planning, architecture, vast public works projects, and magnificent, permanent installations of public art, from fantastic statuary to enormous obelisks and colonnades. Endearing himself to subsequent urban thinkers with a humanist bent—like Lewis Mumford, who cited him for his "passion for urban beauty"—Sitte, in his major work, *Der Stadtebau (City Building),* in 1889, railed against "the grid" school of thinking of one group of modernists and called for the cities of the future to employ more irregular streets and squares; he stated emphatically: "A city must be so constructed that it makes its citizens at once secure and happy. To realize the latter aim, city building must be not just a technical question but an aesthetic one in the highest sense." The Vienna of *The Third Man* is anything but secure and happy, and about the last thing on anybody's mind is aesthetics. The statuary, monuments, and many of the imposing buildings of the Ringstrasse are still in evidence, but many others have been reduced to the rubbled brick, jagged steel, and pulverized stone we saw in Frankfurt and Berlin in *Berlin Express.* But in this film Vienna is somehow more horrifying for the very reason that, rather than the near total rubble of Frankfurt, its ruins comprise a unique and eerie hybrid of a labyrinth that abuts various parts of the city—pockets of untouched buildings and clusters of unscarred streets—that escaped aerial bombardment and artillery fire in the closing months of the war. Most important to this labyrinth, however, is one of the public works projects that was a proud product of the Ringstrasse movement: the huge, labyrinth-unto-itself sewer system constructed in the 1860s that empties into the Danube River. "The blue Danube," one of the military cops sneers while trudging through pools of sewage during the elaborate manhunt for Harry Lime in the sewer tunnels.

Harry Lime becomes one of the first of the truly underground antiheroes in film noir, one whose labyrinth is figuratively and literally below the streets of a big city, when he takes to the sewer tunnels of Vienna. Mapping out in his head their byways, overpasses, minibridges, waterfalls, ladders, and stairwells, he manages to escape the tightening dragnet of the military police. The moral symbolism seems obvious enough: his mind is literally filled with the mechanics of sewage, reinforcing the notion that he is a sewer rat. Interestingly—is it a fascinating correspondence, or a coincidence?—in another film noir, *He Walked By Night,* set in Los Angeles and being filmed in 1948 at exactly the same time as *The Third Man,* another such criminal protagonist takes to the network of drain tunnels (constructed for flood runoff in a city of droughts) to elude a similar dragnet, and meets his end, shot while climbing a ladder to a sewer opening on the street—an opening that is by chance blocked—in exactly the same way as Lime.

At first, when he has been conducting his activities in the above-ground city, Lime has maintained his freedom by slipping from one Occupation zone to another, playing off the Russians against the British, bribing this official or that, but when things get too hot for him (in large part due to Martins' bumbling, but stubborn, attempt at playing detective in order to clear Lime's name) the sewers are his only recourse. In a sense, they liberate him: from his responsibilities to his accomplices; to his mistress, who truly loves him and believes he is really dead; to Martins, who has spent his last dime traveling to Vienna from the States. The sewers liberate Lime from his enemies, as well. He no longer has to deal with diplomatic maneuvering, fake passports, complex aliases, bribes, and all the rest. In the long run, or at least until he can plot an escape from the city proper, he is trapped. The maze of the sewers, to which he has access from every street in the city, is enormous, but finite, after all. In the short run, he is free. And without the unlikely assistance of Martins, the police would never, they readily admit, have trapped Lime in his labyrinth. Martins becomes the (ostensibly) unlikely agent of his destruction whom Lime himself, remember, very much in keeping with the laws of noir geometry, summoned to Venice.

In the postwar era, returning G.I.s are often portrayed in a negative light in film noir: unsuited for family life after years of battlefield brutality, mentally unstable, or even criminal. Lime and Martins saw no military service during the war—the one profiteered, a master criminal, and the other eked out a living churning out the trashy stories he himself disdained. They are extreme and perverse variations on the theme of the returning G.I.: still in Europe, among Europeans, in a devastated city, they remain darkly American to the core. In all their conversations together, they make reference to the United States and to their former lives there. These conversations come to resemble those of G.I.s in combat trenches who had known they would never return home from the war. But unlike the soldiers who liberated Europe, Lime is exploiting it. He is the flipside of the ingenious, upbeat, ever-resourceful American, a type we see often in film noir: the criminal mastermind, also ingenious and resourceful (and, in Lime's case, decidedly upbeat), the man who makes hay with a modicum of his own sweat and a river of other people's blood. (And note that the antihero of *He Walked By Night* is also a mastermind, but a solitary one who, unlike Lime, manipulates electronic gadgets better than he does people.)

Lime and Martins are, like other noir protagonists, post-mortem men: dead before they enter the labyrinth, and the ghosts of ghosts when they emerge from it, destined for the grave. Lime, who actually began the film as a dead man, in the end is finally placed inside his own dug-up coffin and lowered into his grave. Martins attends both of Lime's funerals—the sham and the real thing.

And in the film's closing scene, Martins is standing on the long, smoky white road out of the cemetery, the dust of Europe at his feet. Overhead, stretching away as far as we can see, there is a line of trees stripped of branches. Martins is deep in the silent land, waiting, hoping that Lime's former mistress, the beautiful actress, will stop for him as she leaves. During the course of his bizarre odyssey, Martins has fallen in love with her himself, but she remains devoted to Lime's memory. Even when she learns of his crimes, she does not turn on Lime. Because she has a fake passport (Lime's handiwork), she faces deportation and prison behind the Iron Curtain; but when Martins makes a deal with the military police—securing her freedom by betraying Lime—she brands him a traitor and refuses to speak to him again. So in the end, mistaken in her loyalties but still in love with Lime, she sees him to his grave. And with him dead, she is truly the only character left with any degree of vitality. Martins wants her badly. But as she leaves the cemetery, she won't even glance at him. She strides past Martins, out of the camera frame. Tossing away his cigarette, he stares down at his feet. And the film fades out—not to black, but white. A fade to white. Blank as the sterile road that stretches out before Martins, who has become both the ghost of himself and of Lime. A peculiarly American ghost, embodying the pale remains of both their thwarted ambitions.

In *Night and the City,* filmed early in 1949 and released the following year, there is another Harry who is an American con man—but a small-time one, energetic yet feeble beside Lime. Harry Fabian is his name and he is centered in a very different city—London—and an entirely different sort of labyrinth. He is played by Richard Widmark, who remains as powerful a noir icon as Robert Mitchum or Orson Welles; in fact, it is the face of Widmark, fearful, desperate, haunted, that filled the cover of the first, groundbreaking study of film noir ever written: the comprehensive *Panorama du Film Noir Américain (1941–1953)*, by Raymonde Borde and Etienne Chaumeton, published in Paris in 1955.

Night and the City was shot completely on location, and directed by Jules Dassin, an American. In a phenomenal creative burst, paralleling Jacques Tourneur's five years earlier, between April 1947 and December 1948 Dassin had directed three highly literate films noirs: *Brute Force, Thieves' Highway,* and *The Naked City.* Then he was blacklisted by the House Un-American Activities Committee (HUAC). Another important noir director, Edward Dmytryk, who as one of the "Hollywood Ten" had been blacklisted as a communist in 1947 and served one year in prison, in order to "purge" himself before the House committee provided incriminating testimony against several colleagues, of whom Dassin was one.

There was a certain irony to this. In the spirit of the times, Dmytryk, the son of Ukrainian immigrants to Canada, had been highly suspect to the fast-and-loose HUAC investigators, even before they knew a thing about his politics, because of his "Russian" extraction. And in that same year, 1947, Dmytryk had directed Hollywood's first serious exposé of anti-Semitism in the film noir *Crossfire.* The virulent, paranoid, eventually murderous anti-Semite depicted in the film was a returning G.I., no less, a plot element that took some courage to implement in those days. The G.I., played with chilling and ugly effectiveness by Robert Ryan, brutally beats to death a man for no other reason than the fact the man is a Jew. As the murderer is inexorably brought to justice, Dmytryk quietly turns the film into a stylized and highly effective morality tale. So, in retrospect, his shabby role in the blacklisting of Dassin seems all the more tragic. When he accused Dassin of being a communist, Dassin, who happened to be Jewish, denied the charge vehemently. He refused to cooperate with HUAC, who offered him a deal if he, too, fingered other filmmakers. He said he felt completely betrayed by Dmytryk's accusation, but was unable to refute it since it boiled down to his word against Dmytryk's. There was not a shred of evidence against Dassin—just Dmytryk's unfounded hearsay—but HUAC, undeterred by such Constitutional niceties, persecuted Dassin all the same.

The upshot of all this was that Dassin was forced into permanent

exile at age thirty-eight at the height of his creative powers. He was
just "gaining recognition as a director with something to say and an
interesting way of saying it," as the film historian Ephraim Katz has
noted. It is not surprising that the very next thing Dassin chose to
"say" should be *Night and the City,* a film about a man on the run
through a particularly odious labyrinth, paved with duplicity and
mendacity. Harry Fabian is an American in a foreign city, a man at
the end of his rope, whom another character sums up, memorably,
as "an artist without an art." And was not Dassin at that point in time
the very same thing: a director sharply attuned to the pulse of American city life who was unable to set foot in an American city. An artist
without a country. This film is both an idiosyncracy and a watershed
for that reason. On one level, Dassin was dealing by necessity, not
choice, with a European city; but in doing so, in the economically
straitened postwar years, he presented that city as the antithesis of a
great capital, the repository of a proud national culture. The London
he gives us, crime-ridden and hardscrabble, is recovering from
Hitler's bombardments and from years of terrible deprivation whose
aftereffects have lingered deep in its collective nervous system.

At the same time, for Dassin, London is a shadow-city, a stand-in
for the American city he has left behind. His previous film, *The
Naked City,* was a model of the semidocumentary variety of film noir,
in which New York City itself (photographed comprehensively in
over one hundred different locations) is the focal point. As the critic
Robert Ottoson points out, Dassin, who grew up in New York, exhibited in *The Naked City* an "exactitude in depicting New York's tenements, office buildings, police stations, docks, bridges, and
streets." Was it not the ghostly grid of this same city, a scant year
later, that Dassin superimposed on the London he discovered in exile? A London which he Americanized, not just with an American protagonist, a milieu of organized crime, a corrupted professional sport,
and a very American-style nightclub, but with a noir atmosphere—
American, by definition—that was sordid, claustrophobic, and ultimately terrifying. The film, not surprisingly, caused a scandal in
England, and within the British film industry, where, as Ottoson observes, "it ran contrary to the benign, tolerant, and eccentric qualities that the British presented to the world in the Ealing [Studio]
comedies." In its own genre, the film also ran against the grain of the

neatly sanitized British whodunits and the arch, police-inspector thrillers that are anything but noir in texture or substance. So *Night and the City* is a film that Dassin made while both off-balance and in his prime (a noir condition right there), at once an echo of his last three American films and the culmination—the crowning jewel—of his own abbreviated noir cycle.

As is made clear by the particulars of Dassin's personal history, and the politics of the time, *Night and the City* is a film that straddles the cusp between the films noirs of the immediate postwar years and the ones in the late forties that mirrored the gathering forces of the Cold War, with its culture of paranoia, dread, and overkill. In fact, the politics of the great film noir directors span the spectrum, from Sam Fuller, John Sturges, and Phil Karlson on the right to Abraham Polonsky, Robert Rossen, and Billy Wilder on the left; the noir movement, a revolutionary one artistically, defies pigeon-holing on that score. Fuller, for one, casts an eye every bit as scathing and subversive on American institutions, from medicine to the press, as Wilder ever did. Compare the latter's *The Big Carnival,* often called the most cynical movie ever made about the press, with Fuller's *Scandal Sheet,* which may be a close second. And for Fuller's dissection of the mental hospital in *Shock Corridor,* a vicious, infernal freak show which he portrays as a microcosm of America entering the 1960s, "subversive" may be too weak a word. Only in the overt red-menace noir films is a right-left polarization applicable; in the rest of film noir, the political subtext is far more subtle.

That said, Dassin's noir sensibility was clearly influenced by his blacklisting, and he may be seen now as a political casualty of that era who grafted the ramifications of his personal political history onto his final film noir. (In France, four years later, he would write, direct, and act in a terrific suspense caper involving a jewel heist, *Rififi,* but he would never make another film noir.) And it would surprise me, by the way, if the surname of the protagonist in *Night and the City,* "Fabian" (despite the fact that he is a decidedly apolitical hustler), was not a play—conscious or otherwise—on the British Socialist society of that name founded in 1884.

Night and the City begins with Harry Fabian running frantically through the streets and alleys of London, just as it ends with him running—right up to the moment of his death. In a city of informers and stoolies who would sell his life for the price of a drink, or just to get in good with his pursuers, Fabian can trust no one. In the end, holed up exhausted in a riverfront shack, he opens up for the first and only time, confessing to an indifferent old woman, a blackmarketeer: "All my life I've been running. From welfare offices, thugs, my father. . . ." From himself. The London through which he scrambles and skitters is a labyrinth of grotesques, of smoke and vapor snaking from sewers, of wind-whipped construction sites and vacant lots in which huddled figures warm their hands over oil drums dancing with flames, of rotting wharves and docks congested with the flotsam of both the sea and the city; most of all, it is a city of endless doors and passageways, through any one of which, and through all of which, death awaits Harry Fabian. His labyrinth is among the grimmest in film noir, for it is a maze in which every byway, and every possible combination of twists and turns, leads to his destruction. As in a Greek tragedy, this is inevitable and obvious from the first frame of the film to everyone around Fabian, and to us, but not to him. He is a con man, and the con man's signature trait is his firm belief that he can con anyone, and in a pinch, maybe even cheat fate for a little while. But the rub with Fabian is that because his abilities as a con man are so woefully meager he is able to hoodwink only a single person outside of himself: the film's oldest, most virtuous, and gullible character. With fate he hasn't a chance.

It is worth noting here, since this is the only time we will visit London through the lens of a film noir, that Sophocles' concept of "inevitability," of a man's fate being controlled by forces larger than himself, is a staple of the noir universe. London was, after all, the home of the Jacobean and Elizabethan playwrights steeped in the conventions of Greek and Roman tragedy: John Ford, John Webster, Thomas Middletown, Christopher Marlowe, Thomas Kyd, and of course Shakespeare. Their dramas, prominent in the genealogy of noir, are populated with ghosts, nightmare apparitions, and unholy spirits, and fueled by base elements like greed, treachery, depravity, and violence—and of course by murder, first and foremost. In his essay on Shakespeare and Seneca (whose five-act dramatic structure Shakespeare appropriated and refined), T. S. Eliot makes two salient points: that the Elizabethan period was one "of dissolution and chaos"; and that for the first time, the greater part of English literature emanated from a large, rapidly commercializing, wildly diversified city in London. In short, it had become an urban literature, which maintained a powerful noir undercurrent through succeeding generations, from the world-weary, urbanely cynical Restoration poets and playwrights like the Earl of Rochester, Sir Charles Sedley, and Sir George Etherege to Regency novelists like Daniel Defoe and Tobias Smollett (who more than de Sade, is Céline's great literary forebear), with their brutal, unflinching depictions of London's street life and its underworld, to the Gothic novelists Horace Walpole, Anne Radcliffe, and Mary Shelley, with their fantastical, rather than streetwise, veerings into violence and perversity, to Charles Dickens, with whom that dark undercurrent became a decidedly black river running into our own century. In short, the London of Harry Fabian is a city steeped in the noir sensibility, yet unique to the formal structure of the film noir.

There was one other noir film shot in London, a year before *Night and the City: Kiss the Blood off My Hands.* Its hero is an embittered American vet. But unlike *Night and the City,* there is no apparent rationale to the film's location, which could as well be in the United States It is interesting, though, that *Kiss the Blood off My Hands* opens with this epigraph: "The aftermath of war is rubble—the rubble of cities and of men. The cities can be rebuilt, but the wounds of men, whether of the mind or of the body, heal slowly." Such a description would apply to countless noir heroes, but not to any American city after the war. It would certainly apply to London, terrorized by Hitler's V-2 rockets and, in pockets, devastated like Frankfurt and Vienna. And isn't the use of the epigraph here revealing—like the "credit" and the "statement" that, respectively, begin *Berlin Express* and *The Third Man*—reinforcing the documentary-like slant of these films noirs set in Europe, firmly linking them to the wartime newsreels they succeeded by just a couple of years on movie screens.

As for Fabian, the expatriate hustler, with the hustler's universal and banal plaint of "I want to be someone," what has he done in London to set him off running for his life? Like a human pinball, little of substance, apparently, but much damage. For starters, he seems to have played no role in the recent war. At most, we can deduce he would have been a marginal errand boy to the likes of Harry Lime. And when we meet him, he is indeed a sort of errand boy—to a very small-time Harry Lime. Fabian is a tout who lures American tourists into a clip joint; this, tellingly, is the only use to which he puts his American identity. But he has aspirations to be a sports promoter—and they're eating at him. The premier promoter in London, another non-Englishman named Kristo, controls both professional boxing and wrestling, as well as a vast crime syndicate with which he oversees the other ventures in his ever-expanding portfolio. Kristo, a quintessential noir kingpin, feared by all and with no fear of his own—neither for the police, whom he also seems to control, nor for anyone else—is admired from afar by Fabian. While attending a wrestling match, Fabian falls in with Kristo's father and brother, visiting from abroad; the latter is a purely trained Greco-Roman wrestler, and the former, a legendary Olympic wrestling champion, is his trainer. It is clear that in establishing himself as a criminal, Kristo has debased his paternal legacy, for the wrestling he promotes—of the histrionic clown-show variety—is far removed from Greco-Roman.

In *Mythologies,* Roland Barthes has written, "Wrestling is not a sport, it is a spectacle, and . . . the public is completely uninterested in knowing whether the contest is rigged or not, and rightly so; it abandons itself to the primary virtue of the spectacle, which is to abolish all motives and all consequences: what matters is not what it thinks but what it sees. . . . Thus the function of the wrestler is not to win; it is to go through exactly the motions which are expected of him . . . in wrestling, a man who is down is exaggeratedly so, and completely fills the eyes of the spectators with the intolerable spectacle of his powerlessness." Which reads like yet another mini-definition of noir. For, along with boxing, wrestling is one of the unabashedly noir sports. Conducted in the "most squalid" urban arenas, Barthes goes on to say, it partakes "of the nature of the great solar spectacles, Greek drama and bullfights: in both, a light without shadow generates an emotion without reserve." In noir, the converse is true: a shadow without light can generate restraint, withdrawal, or outright paralysis, with no show of emotion.

With his unerring loser's instinct for water that is over his head, Harry Fabian becomes a man "exaggeratedly" down and "powerless" in a hurry. He dupes Kristo's strong-willed but guileless father into taking him on as his promoter, promising the old man, who is disgusted with his son's brand of wrestling, that the two of them will bring authentic Greco-Roman wrestling to London. Fabian's true intention is to use the old man and his good name to set up a rival wrestling network. Infuriated, Kristo looks on helplessly, unable to convince the old man that Fabian is a fraud. When Fabian signs a contract with the old man, he is in effect signing his own death warrant. Again, everyone around him knows it, and we know it: only Fabian, boastful, arrogant, and avaricious, is blind to the consequences. "You've got it all," the owner of the clip joint, his former employer Nosseross tells him, "but you're a dead man, Harry Fabian." (Nosseross is another of those names like "Jessadiah," in this film befitting the mock-Homeric, rather than biblical, subtext—Greco-Roman wrestling, Kristo's Greek heritage, frequent references to soothsayers.)

Overplaying his cards, swept up in a con that far exceeds his abilities, Fabian bungles things badly. What little control he believed he had over events evaporates rapidly when, despite his frantic machinations, he can't even raise the seed money with which to implement his scheme. Then he gets conned himself by Nosseross, from whom he is forced to borrow some of the cash. In desperation, he gets the additional money from Nosseross' wife, the steely co-proprietor of the clip joint, by securing her a (forged) liquor license with which she hopes to set up her own nightclub in order to break away from her husband. When the forgery is discovered, her plans fall through and she turns on Fabian with a vengeance, as does Nosseross, who believes (incorrectly) that Fabian is sleeping with his wife. Nosseross contacts Kristo and offers to help him get rid of Fabian. Using the money he's lent Fabian as a lever, Nosseross succeeds in sabotaging Fabian's plans—so well, in fact, that the sabotage itself spins out of control and Kristo's father is killed in the process. Kristo has Nosseross murdered. And then, offering an exorbitant bounty, he mobilizes the entire London underworld in a manhunt for Fabian.

We see Kristo, like Hades in his car gliding through the Underworld, driving around London in his open convertible personally putting out the word on Fabian. Fabian himself, his one attempt at the big-time stillborn, is on the run with nowhere to go. Completely exposed, he's a goner. Not just dead, but for all intents and purposes another of our post-mortem men. The ghost of a ghost in his labyrinth, which seems to have come alive beneath his feet, sucking him in. Everyone he runs to gives him the cold shoulder—or tries to detain him, in order to collect the bounty. He is betrayed high and low—at the lowest ebb by a man with a rag-and-bone shop who sells artificial limbs to beggars. As for the police, in the entire film we only see evidence of them twice: once when a rookie cop informs Mrs. Nosseross that her liquor license is a fake; and then when a police car (we don't see the cops themselves) pulls up at the end to pick up one of Kristo's wrestlers, "The Strangler," who has, indeed, just strangled Harry Fabian and dumped him off a bridge into the Thames. Kristo, who has watched—and certainly been an accessory to—the murder, pays no heed to the police; after tossing his cigarette butt into the river, to the spot where Fabian's body disappeared, Kristo ambles to his chauffeur-driven limousine, which is idling across the street. As in Shakespeare's tragedies, the man who, according to "the natural order of things," has the last word is the one who will be in control of whatever domain is specific to the play. In the case of Kristo, the domain is the underworld—both London's, and that other, noir underworld with the capital U.

At the conclusion of "The World of Wrestling," Barthes writes that "in America wrestling represents a sort of mythological fight between Good and Evil." But in a film noir set in Europe it seems that another sort of dynamics applies, again linked to the motifs of ancient Greece and Rome; this European variety of wrestling, according to Barthes, "presents man's suffering with all the amplification of tragic masks . . . for everyone must not only see that the man suffers, but also and above all understand why he suffers." And that we do with Harry Fabian, the American in a foreign city who fatally overreaches, wearing his mask of ignorance and conceit. He is a particularly stripped-down film noir hero, who achieves no real epiphany, unless it is his sole realization, finally, that he has no escape from death. Fabian's is a mask that goes blank in the end, blank as the whole of his life, in the same flat white light we see at the end of *The Third Man*. For it is dawn when Fabian emerges from his nocturnal labyrinth, at the bridge between this world and the next, and finds that Charon is a strangler and that the Styx is one with the Thames, its blacker-than-black water swallowing him and swirling on. The foreign city become familiar to us now. And the metamorphosis of the noir city complete: from the city of night to the city of death.

4. Office Buildings and Casinos

If there are indeed seven million stories in the naked city (when the city happens to be New York), there are at least that many structures in which human beings live and conduct their myriad activities. Add to that the number of structures that house the city's complex technology and machinery, store food and waste, manufacture goods and retail them, sit idle or are long abandoned. Multiply these buildings by the number of their individual rooms, corridors, closets, stairwells, elevators, basements, attics—all their cells large and small—and we would find ourselves talking in the billions. Are there any remotely definitive figures for the number of rooms, stories, even buildings, in cities like Los Angeles, Chicago, and New York? In the latter, that very query, made to four municipal agencies—Housing Preservation and Development; City Register: Recording Deeds and Mortgages; Environmental Protection; and General Services: Division of Public Structures—met with three polite "no's" and one abrupt expletive. Had the response been more positive, I would have ventured a follow-up query with regard to other fascinating statistics, like the number of windows, doors, and elevator shafts in the city; but, for better or worse, at the present time all such information must be left to the realm of the speculative—or the surreal.

Any city, of course, consists not just of its people and their wildly complex interrelationships, but its equally complex infrastructure and all physical manifestations therein, the mazes upon mazes—concentric, rectilinear, radial, even fourth-dimensional—with all the mutations one could imagine. For a moment, think of the modern city as a classical labyrinth of stone and metal made liquid; a liquid then brought to a boil, allowed to spread and layer itself incrementally like molten lava, before being frozen suddenly—then brought to a boil again, allowed to flow, and frozen again. On and on like that, indefinitely. Or not so indefinitely, as Mumford would have it when he insists that the rapid growth of the modern city sprawl, the megalopolis, which in this century has become the singular American urban form, is entering a terminal stage "in the classic cycle of [any] civilization, before its complete disruption and downfall." What we have seen occur in European cities is inevitable in our own, he argues, rooted as they are in a world culture evincing few signs of long-term stability, "a civilization that has," within a single thirty-year period, "undergone two world wars and prematurely terminated the lives of some sixty million people. . . . This metropolitan civilization contains within itself the explosive forces that will wipe out all traces of its existence." A credo implicit in the dynamics of the noir city which, organically, resembles the individual human being who carries within him at all times the seeds of his own destruction and death.

The noir city, in life and death, is never far from the metaphorical city-as-a-human-giant—an enormous supine form—that we find in the mythologies of William Blake and James Joyce, and in the musings of philosophers from Plotinus to Hobbes. Sprinkled among the conversations of the noir city's denizens are frequent references to the city's "heart," "eyes," "soul," "ears," "arteries," and so on. This anthropomorphic city "lives," "breathes," "bleeds," incurs cancers, poisons, and blemishes of all sorts, and even "dies" on occasion— but never for long. And if that inanimate metropolitan sprawl were ever to rise up and truly assume human form, with all the ills attendant upon it in a noir universe, it might most resemble one of those malevolent, malignant giants out of Grimm's *Fairy Tales* or *The Thousand and One Nights*—a figure enshrouded in black mist lurching toward suicide or hellbent on murder.

In the twentieth century, when technology and mechanical innovation have transformed political and social life in ways—and at speeds—unimaginable in the millennia preceding it, violence, as an accompanying force, has undergone its own fantastical transformations. "Under the peaceful surface and orderly routine of the metropolis," Mumford writes, "all the dimensions of violence had suddenly enlarged. As these forces developed, the metropolis became more and more a device for increasing the varieties of violent expression, and every citizen became a connoisseur in the arts of death."

In the explosive postwar American city of the film noir, violence becomes a delirious, everyday reality—a circus of horrors, from the child pushed onto a subway track by a drug addict to the crowded business office sprayed with gunfire by a disgruntled former spouse/employee/client—determined in no small part by the tremendous congestion of buildings, people, and vehicles. The realities of congestion are stupefying, but the possibilities—legally speaking—would be hilarious if they weren't so terrifying. For example, in 1949, under the zoning ordinances of the day, with no building over six hundred feet in height, the permitted, "acceptable" capacity of the residential districts of New York, according to the New York City Housing Authority, could have been 77,000,000 people, while the commercial districts could have provided for a working population of 344,000,000! (The so-called capacities today are even higher.) The social violence is connected symbiotically with the structural violence implicit in the ferocious ebb and flow—the internal tension—of the city's physical state.

In the postwar city, the pace of construction, demolition, and rebuilding is incredible. Whole neighborhoods rise, fall, and rise again at dizzying speed. Unlike the ancient or medieval city, the modern American city is one in which the chief architectural forms are based on abstract units of space, like the cubic foot. With few structural rearrangements, the hotel, department store, apartment house, and office building are *fully* convertible, one into the other. After 1945, this formula for urban chaos—barely a pretense of "city-planning" anymore—reaches a crisis point. Buildings are no longer designed for long-term use, but with the sole view of being wrecked and replaced by an even higher and more profitable structure, sometimes within a single generation. Add to this the destructive effects of those ineffectual zoning ordinances and the de facto nature of corrupt real estate maneuverings by the political and commercial class and you have a situation which can only deteriorate at an ever increasing pace. The menacing, consuming, internal chaos of the noir city becomes further reinforced by the institutionalized chaos of the physical city: a ravaged landscape, in other words, which in itself becomes a psychological burden.

"Nothing lasts"—one of noir's primary tenets—applies literally to the physical city, where mutability (and moral elasticity) rules, and nothing is fixed in time or space for long. Not the elements of the man-made landscape or the people who inhabit it, who come and go, devour and are in turn devoured by one another. Or by their surroundings, which come alive like the walls of a cave and, in an instant of terror, are revealed to be the guts of a beast. In the postwar era, all that perishes does so at many times the rate it once did. The noir city, forming and reforming itself endlessly, like a substance under a microscope, is inevitably on a road to dissolution, the knowledge of which ticks at every moment in the hearts of its inhabitants.

Much of film noir is concerned with people cut off not just from Nature, and from their own natures, but from one another and from any vital knowledge of the environment they themselves have created. Film noir represents "human solitude in a world of steel," according to Borde and Chaumeton. In this city of steel, electronic means of communication and high-powered vehicles often seem to keep people apart—to thwart, deflect, or pervert direct communication and straightforward movement. The postwar city-dweller is often so mobile, mentally, physically, and sensorially—that is, he enjoys the illusion of such mobility—that the inexorable fact of his being hemmed in, or paralyzed in some way, becomes all the more horrific when it comes clear to him.

In addition, all electronic forms—the telephone, radio, and television—have decentralized cities and made the so-called human scale obsolete. These devices heighten the already intense individual isolation and spiritual amputation of the noir city. The continual motion of cities, in machines of transportation and communication, in electronic impulses and cascades of words, is the foundation for much of the moral commotion in film noir. The rapid jumps in technologies of transportation and communication since 1945 have been a crucial factor in the intensified sense of alienation in the city, and in the noir films it is constantly reflected in the faster *pace*—of people and information—in the postwar life that they present. There is a clear correlation between technical and electronic "progress" and personal alienation and angst. A fear not so much that machines will replace us, but that they will fragment us, piece by piece, down to zero. For among the immutable laws in the physics of the noir universe, we will surely find the law of diminishing returns.

Since the Second World War, it is more the ethos of automation, rather than the industrial reality, that has contributed to the noir vision of the city as one vast, unified machine for creating wealth and delivering services—a hell in which, socially, politically, and economically, human and machine cogs are forever interlocked. The terrifying, mechanized city—the city as a beast with mechanical guts and a human nervous system—is a recurrent noir motif. One such example of this appears in the 1958 film *Party Girl,* directed by Nicholas Ray. Its hero, Tommy Fallon, is a cripple whose leg was chewed up by a drawbridge, in an accident, when he was twelve years old. When, later, he shows his lover the bridge and describes it as the place at which his life took a turning point, we see it as an actual, physical component of the city's machinery that has maimed him. Afterward, Fallon becomes bookish and attends law school. Hungry to acquire wealth and power as quickly as possible to compensate for his disability, he becomes the legal counsel to the city's corrupt political machine—a mouthpiece for crooked pols, punks, and killers. It is this second "machine" that truly cripples Fallon, chewing him up morally and spiritually. In this film the city, in both its physical body and its body political, is unambiguously presented as a destroyer of men, a furnace for human souls.

The fact that the Second World War was the most mechanized— and brutal—in history provided an inflammatory wellspring for these fears about the city as destroyer; today, such fears are fanned by the automation of warfare—guided missiles, "smart" bombs, computer-directed ballistic missiles—and the terror it inflicts upon urban civilians. What was only a nightmare a century ago—a world in which technology would spin clear of moral checks and balances and of the spiritual underpinnings of human society—is now reality. Following a self-destructive arc, the wheels of steel that power the modern city and its great human dynamos of ambition, fear, passion, greed, and lust must metamorphose into infernal, ultimately apocalyptic, wheels of fire as the metropolis devolves into necropolis.

From the first, we see an ongoing fascination in film noir with electronic devices, many of them developed during the war but only coming into their own—for legitimate or unscrupulous purposes—in the postwar city. A galaxy of new machines and luxury accoutrements became crucial items in the lives of the noir population. These included enormously improved office equipment, home-movie cameras, hi-fi phonographs, and inexpensive tape recorders. Electric shavers, tanning lamps, blow-dryers, and hair-curlers suddenly brought the beauty salon into the home. Other, more potent, electronic devices in the hands of both criminals and the police altered the urban landscape in ways that could be *heard* and *felt* rather than seen. Eavesdropping devices, phone taps, and zoom-lenses appear in *Laura, T-Men, White Heat,* and other films, finding their apotheosis in *711 Ocean Drive* (1950), in which the hero is a renegade telephone whiz, a master of technology eventually done in when the complexities of his own inventiveness boomerang on him.

The telephone whiz's immediate predecessor in film noir is the criminal in *He Walked By Night,* Roy Martin, who meets his end in the same fashion as Harry Lime, gunned down in the drainage tunnel system of Los Angeles which he has made into his private warren. Until he makes the mistake of shooting a policeman in a moment of panic, Martin has committed a string of unsolved robberies with impunity, victimizing electronics outfits whose machinery he modifies to his own purposes or resells to unsuspecting dealers. Martin is a war vet; when the cop he kills asks him for identification, such as a military discharge, Martin replies, "Sure, here's my discharge," and whips out a revolver, blazing away. He's also a former police lab technician, so he brings the technology of both of those worlds to his criminal activities. He is a nocturnal loner and a mechanical genius, as well, and with his full menu of postwar gadgetry, he is soon menacing the entire city. The film begins with a map of Los Angeles filling the screen, followed by a montage that introduces us to the various branches of the city's police department, accompanied by a full-throated documentary narration (it is this film upon which the *Dragnet* radio and television series were based). Finally, as in *White Heat* (a film in which the scientific wizard, played as in *711 Ocean Drive* by Edmund O'Brien, toils on the side of the law), released seven months later, we are propelled along through *He Walked By Night* wondering what sort of device—and each seems more lethal than the last—Martin will cook up next. In the end, the film becomes a kind of Atomic Age parable, which we see played out in other films preoccupied with mad bombers and saboteurs, and echoed, interestingly enough, in the present day, post–Cold War city where the single madman or fanatic with an explosive device has replaced the Soviet nuclear arsenal as a catalyst of mass fear. In keeping with this apocalyptic motif, we see the final credits of *He Walked By Night* roll over that map of Los Angeles which began the film, except now it is limned in flames that are licking inward, toward its center.

Also notable in film noir are the crucial uses to which the dictaphone recorder is put in *Double Indemnity* and *Phantom Lady,* the microfilm machine in *Pickup on South Street,* and the early fax-machine prototype in *Call Northside 777* which becomes the principal "character" in the film's climax (the camera almost never leaves it), transmitting between two cities an enlarged portion of a newspaper photo in order to save an innocent man from a life sentence in the penitentiary. And there are all the (then) novel surveillance devices employed in the films with Cold War plots, such as *Walk East on Beacon* (1952). Also, the ingenious technology used by bogus mediums and bunco artists—and even a few genuine clairvoyants—in films like *Nightmare Alley, The Spiritualist,* and *Night Has a Thousand Eyes,* all released within months of one another in 1947 and 1948 and concerned, not with communists and A-bomb blueprints, but with the far more ancient and mysterious lures of the occult and of those secrets which might lie beyond the grave.

Just as the development of the incandescent lightbulb by Thomas Edison in 1879 led to the introduction of the night shift in urban factories, and to the 24-hour-a-day city, the mass-produced electronic gadgets of the postwar era made urban man an information gatherer, a spiritual and mental nomad in his own home. (The pace at which those gadgets have evolved is truly dizzying: consider only that the technological capacities of the 11" × 9" laptop computer before me as I write this just two decades ago could only have been replicated by a mass of computers that would have filled a good-sized room.) The theme of the wanderer, the loner, the nightbird, the urban American isolated with and by his machines as the member (or piece) of an ever-fragmenting society, is very much a noir theme.

And no wonder that by 1995 in films like *The Net* we begin to see one variety of noir loner appearing, not on street corners or in bars, but in front of computers in darkened rooms, solitary hackers surfing through cyberspace.

Which brings us to the telephone, which from the 1940s on really is the ultimate noir machine. It's personal, and impersonal. It potentially connects everyone, and anyone, in the city, from loved ones to utter strangers, from the doctor and the policeman to the thief and the psychopath. As Marshall McLuhan has pointed out, the telephone has rendered certain notions of "distance" obsolete in metropolitan areas. In itself, the urban telephone system is an invisible labyrinth: of voices, disembodied emotions, projections, manipulations, and deflections, of connections and cross-connections as intimate—or impersonal—as one desires; and it is also a tangible labyrinth of lines, cables, and wires, above and below the city streets. Telephones can be used to make confessions or probe for facts, to inform or misinform, to persuade or be persuaded, to intimidate. Film noir is filled with telephones of all kinds: pay phones, office phones, bedside phones, restaurant and nightclub phones that are brought to one's table. Not surprisingly, telephones are often connected in the films to questions of privacy and secrets; they are emblematic of the *mystique* of communication in a world which is clamorous with sound and at the same time, at its deepest levels, eerily silent.

The American city owes its abstract grid layout to the railroad. The automobile went on to scramble the shape of the industrial town, mixing up its separated functions and wreaking havoc in a dozen ways. And airplanes, by so speeding up travel, made urban space as such almost irrelevant. But long before all of this, early in the nineteenth century, the city was already undergoing rapidfire transformations. The novelist Thomas Pynchon has written of Philadelphia at that time: "The city was becoming a kind of high-output machine, materials and labor going in, goods and services coming out, traffic inside flowing briskly about a grid of regular city blocks. The urban mazework of London, leading into ambiguities and indeed evils, was here all rectified, orthogonal. (Charles Dickens, visiting in 1842, remarked, 'After walking about in it for an hour or two, I felt that I would have given the world for a crooked street.')" As the physicist James Trefil points out, "Cities now grow in rings, with all the land at a given distance from the city center being used before land farther out is built up." Such growth was incremental "when individuals controlled their own travel by walking," but today the rate of "urban sprawl" has been increased exponentially. Or, as Trefil puts it, "There is no question that the modern suburb owes its existence and its organization to the internal combustion engine."

The automobile's effect on the postwar city is inestimable. It has transformed the city more profoundly—and negatively—in a more compressed period of time, than any other previous factor. To cite, for starters, a single ironical aside with regard to the automobile, the American city, and the notion of "progress": in 1907, horsedrawn vehicles in New York City moved at an average speed of 11.5 mph; today automobiles crawl at an average daytime rate of 6 mph—on good days! In Los Angeles, where mass transit has been allowed to atrophy, citizens since the Second World War have been encouraged to use private cars as much as possible, resulting in a city that has become a clotted mass of sprawling suburbs and helter-skelter expressways. Two-thirds of central L.A. is now occupied by freeways, parking lots, and garages. (Edging ever closer to Gertrude Stein's wry description of her hometown of Oakland: "There is no there there.")

Though by 1929 there were more automobiles in New York City than in the whole of Europe, in the first ten years after the Second World War American cities could still accommodate their traffic comfortably, despite a phenomenal boom in automobile sales, which were necessarily depressed during the war. (Just after 1945, there was one car per family in the United States, and in 1975, one car per worker; today, there are twenty percent more cars than total licensed drivers.) In the immediate postwar years, cars were modestly priced and offered freedom of movement to everyone from the soda jerk to the financier. America's decided ambivalence about the social and financial mobility implied in that statement is another matter altogether. In film noir, that ambivalence is certainly reflected in the unceasing portrayals of criminal entrepreneurs, returning G.I.s who "want a stake," and the scheming, climbing, hungry-to-get-ahead protagonists, who are ubiquitous in the city, from the tenement stoop to the penthouse.

The automobile, in fact, manifests itself as an important component of film noir in other respects, far less subtle. For one thing, the films reflect the automobile's use as a luxury item and status symbol and an instrument of power and control. It is a prominent vehicle for the police, who appear on film in the 1940s and 1950s more often in patrol cars than on foot. For all other citizens, cars are readily available in every shape and form, from taxi to getaway sedan, van and pickup to limousine, sporty convertible to the bulky family station wagon.

Add to those millions of rooms and cells that comprise a major city not only the interiors of buses, trucks, trains, and subways, but also the highly specialized, self-contained spaces, worlds unto themselves, of automobiles. Most significantly in film noir, the automble is yet another isolating urban device: solitary drivers, couples, whole families or even loose acquaintances are locked within a moving space, queued in traffic, their senses only fractionally connected to the surrounding city. In many films, crucial scenes occur inside cars. In *The Big Sleep* and *The Blue Dahlia,* for example, nearly all the romantic interplay—replete with sexual innuendo—between hero and heroine occurs in automobiles, which would seldom have been the case in the 1930s. The automobile turns up significantly in film noir not only within the confines of the city, but often *between* cities, usually at night. The passengers are traveling between two sets of existential or emotional situations—or two sets of trouble—often symbolized by the cities at either end of the journey. *Detour* (1945), *Gun Crazy* (1950), *The Devil Thumbs a Ride* (1948), and *The Hitch-Hiker* (1953) are all important—and very different—examples of such films, in which the automobile's interior can carry the same charged or claustrophobic atmosphere as the noir city itself. The automobile becomes an insulated version of the city in miniature, in transit.

Automobiles are also used to symbolize unbridled aggressiveness in film noir, and individual power run amok. Sometimes the car becomes a lethal instrument (the noir streets are the frequent scenes of hit-and-run homicides) or a suicidal one. In *Angel Face,* directed in 1953 by Otto Preminger, cars are a dominant image from beginning to end. The hero is an ambulance driver and washed-up race-car driver in Los Angeles. The heroine is a very fast driver. And the film boasts one of the most bizarre and startling climaxes in American cinema: the heroine takes the wheel of her sports car and as the hero slides into the passenger seat, popping open a bottle of champagne, she purposely throws the gears into reverse and backs off a high cliff. She has been an unbalanced character throughout the film, emerging from a major nervous breakdown, but her final act takes us—and the hero—very much by surprise.

As for trains, after 1945 the railroads which helped create the big cities took a backseat to the automobile. The "rapid transit" subway systems, built at the turn of the century, extended the dimensions of the city. They created not just a literal urban underworld, but as Trefil points out, the early elevated railways (still prominent in numerous noir films) turned "the streets themselves into tunnels, darkening the lives of thousands of people. For the fact is," he goes on, "that there can be only one upper level in any city. If that level is used for transportation, then the area under it will be dark and (usually) unpleasant. This, more than anything else, drove the move to subways."

In noir terms, trains and subways are also closed societies—not with one, two, or even six people, like an automobile, but with whole mini-populations. Trains and subways, too, become microcosms of the cities they are connecting, or affording internal transportation, and whose populations they are carrying. In film noir, extraordinary use is made of train interiors, and of train and subway stations as prime nerve centers of the city. Trains can figure prominently in noir narratives, or even encompass the entire narrative, as in the 1952 film *The Narrow Margin,* directed by Richard Fleischer. In utilizing the train's interior, Fleischer makes aesthetic decisions in the same way he would have had the location and interior shots been set in a big city. He makes ingenious cinematographic use of the compressed compartments, tiny lavatories, long lowlit corridors, dining, lounge, observation, and baggage cars, machinist's shop, engineer's quarters, and so on. The train's windows, mirrors, doors, and closets, which are integral to the action at every turn, are handled with incredible attention to detail. Fleischer makes a complete world of the train—alternately letting us forget we're on a train and allowing us to think of nothing else—as if it is a miniature city traveling between Chicago and Los Angeles; and he bookends the film with a brief prelude and an almost perfunctory postlude in the cities proper. The plot is deceptively simple: a detective is protecting a mob informer, a woman, en route to a murder trial; there is a contract out on her life and the detective is utterly in the dark as to who her potential assassin might be among the other passengers. It turns out that he is equally in the dark as to the woman's true identity. In fact, after a while, he is not even sure whom he should be protecting! The inherent claustrophobia of the story is enhanced by the overwhelming sense of physical compression, and the tight quarters in which the characters must operate: at times, it literally feels as if they have no room to think, or to digest information that is right under their noses. So what would be an oppressive environment in a city becomes a positively suffocating one onboard a train—a quintessential noir atmosphere.

Other films noirs use trains in equally self-reinforcing ways. For example, *Crack-Up* (1946), in which the title itself is a double-entendre which refers both to a train wreck and the protagonist's nervous breakdown. And *Union Station* (1950), which is set almost completely in the train terminal of that name in Chicago. Here the plot revolves around the kidnapping of a blind girl off a train. Again, the film is filled with trains and train motifs; in one of the few times that the action strays from the terminal, we witness a wonderfully harrowing scene on the elevated subway line. *Union Station* concludes in a subterranean tunnel *below* the underground track area of the terminal, on a long-abandoned, manually propelled shuttle car. Other films noirs with notable train presences are *The Seventh Victim* (1947), *Port of New York* (1949), and *Human Desire* (1953). The latter, directed by Fritz Lang and based on Emile Zola's *La Bete Humaine,* opens with a famous sequence in which we see innumerable train tracks running parallel to one another, then crossing, recrossing, and diverging several times—mimicking the lives of the ill-fated protagonists which the film is about to reveal to us—as a locomotive pulls into a huge train yard.

Trains and locomotives are a staple visual beneath the opening credits of countless films noirs. The sounds of trains, too, are a constant in the films. The whistle, roar, and clang of a passing train, the blur of its streaking lights, or its ominous shadowy bulk often correspond to violence or conflict within rooms in nearby buildings overlooking the tracks. In *Party Girl,* for example, in a union hall where the film's two most violent scenes occur, passing trains, seen from an odd angle through a high window, presage the onset of violence. And in *Sorry, Wrong Number* (1948), directed by Anatole Litvak, the trains with glittering lights passing on an elevated train track and a railroad bridge visible through a picture window are, literally, the only aspect of Manhattan with which the heroine, a wealthy invalid confined to her bedroom, is visually connected. The comings and goings of the trains she watches mirror the action of the narrative at crucial junctures, including, most significantly, the heroine's murder at film's end. Just as the trains, and the mechanized life of the city itself, are many steps removed from the invalid's highly circumscribed world, so too is the machinery of her murder, which she cannot stop even when she learns of it early in the film. This sort of Expressionist touch, using a significant and ongoing prop like the trains to amplify the resonance of a complex narrative, was one that Litvak was tutored in early on: as a young director, he served two apprenticeships: in Russian cinema, making Social Realist films, and at the UFA (Universum Film Aktien Gesellschaft) studios in Germany, where cinematic Expressionism was born.

After the war, the airplane and the new jet planes make all cities seem as one city, blurring boundaries of time and space. Today the air traveler in America might feel at times as if the entire country were urban. With urban points of departure and arrival, the vast countryside in between—the lakes, valleys, mountains, and forests previously *seen* by intercity train travelers—are now profoundly absent. The airplane urbanizes the American consciousness even before its passenger sets foot in a city. Still, the airport remains an entity outside the city proper and is rarely a backdrop in film noir; in fact, I can count on one hand the times I have seen it as such in the films. When the noir hero travels, he invariably gets in a car or boards a train.

But however revealing, and enriching, the role these vehicles—cars, trains, planes—play in the films, it remains a surrogate role. As the critic Robert Warshow has written, for the film noir hero "there is only the city; he must inhabit it in order to personify it: not only the real city, but that dangerous and sad city of the imagination which is so important, which is the modern world." The film noir hero, ranging widely in his various cities, from New Orleans to Reno to Detroit, tends nevertheless to gravitate to very specific sorts of buildings within the city. For food and shelter, unsurprisingly, hotels, boarding houses, and restaurants best serve his needs. But when it comes to doing his business, legitimate or illicit, financial or sexual, his choices usually boil down to the office building or the casino. As the protagonist of *The Unknown Man* (1951), the prominent lawyer who lapses into crime, observes of the noir city, "This is a city teeming with pride and corruption, where crime operates out of skyscrapers and plush hotels."

The office building—especially the skyscraper—is omnipresent and significant in film noir. Every city, Mumford tells us, from ancient times to the present, has been ruled by a god, and in the noir city that god is Money and his temple is the office building. A tower of dreams, a refuge in the clouds, high above the grime and ugliness below, the office building represents power, status, and an implicit sort of perspective; from the street or sidewalk of the labyrinthine city one can see far less of one's surroundings than from the thirtieth floor of a building. On the sidewalk, however, one does see those surroundings according to the scale of one's own body, with feet rooted to the ground; from high above, as we heard when Harry Lime was scanning the Viennese crowds from a ferris wheel's apogee, the noir protagonist may find that the godlike perspective dangerously reinforces his already well-developed antisocial proclivities. The wide panorama of an upper-story perspective can imply, however subliminally, an equally wide range of intellectual vision and emotional breadth, or—most commonly—a foundation of material security and worldly power; in film noir this is a frequent delusion, which segues into despair and destruction. Surely right here we have the three Ds of the film noir universe: delusion, despair, and destruction. The fourth D, the shadow into which these other three inevitably flow, is of course death.

The office buildings in the noir city share a number of root physical characteristics. For one thing, their enormous scale. The Chrysler Building (77 stories, reaching 1,048 feet) was completed in 1930, followed by the Empire State Building (102 stories, at 1,250 feet) a year later; but because of the Depression, the subsequent collapse of the real estate market, and the virtual strangulation of the construction industry, the real age of the skyscraper had to wait until after the war. The Empire State Building was constructed (60,000 tons of steel, 60 miles of water pipe, 6,500 windows, 73 elevators) at the breakneck pace of close to a floor a day. But, as the architectural critic Paul Goldberger has written in *The Skyscraper,* the Empire State Building at first "rented so slowly that for years it was referred to as the 'Empty State Building.' But unlike some kinds of skyscrapers," he continues, "it *could* make money once it was amply rented. A study for the American Institute of Steel Construction in 1929 reported that the optimum height for a building on a midtown Manhattan site would be about 63 stories. . . . The study showed diminishing returns at greater heights, until at 132 stories it projected that profits would disappear altogether." After 1945, many buildings in the 30- to 50-story range were erected helter-skelter, not only in New York, but in every major American city. And by 1950, the era of glass skyscrapers had taken hold with a vengeance, many of them packing tremendous visual and symbolic power in the postwar cityscape, comparable to the enormous structures erected in ancient Rome to celebrate military victories around the empire.

Ironically enough, Le Corbusier's U.N. Secretariat Building, erected as a center for peace and the prevention of war, is a prime example of this sort of postwar skyscraper: 39 stories, with long east and west walls of green glass, it embodied what Goldberger calls the first "idea of a tower that would appear to be sheathed only in glass." Had Le Corbusier had his way, there would have been many more such buildings—but larger—in New York and other cities. On that first visit of his to New York in 1945, he made another celebrated comment that has echoed down over the years: "The skyscrapers of New York are too small and there are too many of them." The city Le Corbusier envisioned more closely resembled the massive—beyond all human scale—futuristic, nightmare cities of some neo–films noirs of the 1980s like *Blade Runner* (1982) and *Black Rain* (1989); a city with a hundred World Trade Centers and Sears Towers in a concentrated grid of square blocks: cold, sunless, remote, imprisoning both physically and aesthetically, and for all intents and purposes nocturnal twenty-four hours a day. Truly noir.

The office towers that did go up after the war were severe enough, without reaching those hallucinatory levels of isolation. Mumford describes the new type of office building—with its roots back as far as the 1880s—as "symbolically a sort of vertical human filing case, with uniform windows, a uniform façade, uniform accommodations." Highly alienated, and alienating, the hive environments of these buildings—exquisitely bejeweled obelisks and rectangles when seen from a distance, as in those long pans of nocturnal skylines that open dozens of films noirs—experienced from within had a profoundly adverse effect on the individual and collective psyches of their denizens. For forty hours a week, these office workers were trapped by the time clock behind sealed windows, hierarchically regimented, pigeonholed and cubicled, held rigidly accountable for their actions, breathing recycled air (and, in those days, plenty of tobacco fumes) while bathed in the rays of fluorescent lights. Fresh air was kept out, sunlight was diluted by tinted panes, and the time of day—and even the seasons of the year, crudely marked by the alternation of central air conditioning and central heating—became an abstraction. In short, a general set of unnatural conditions came to prevail. Even the elevators, previously manned by walking, talking attendants, after the war become impersonal, high-speed, and increasingly sterile when automated models come into vogue. All of these social and environmental conditions are also—metaphysically and psychologically—crucial noir conditions: an unhealthy, even deadly, sense of confinement or entrapment; a sealed-in or claustrophobic situation; stark, overbearing lighting; widespread depersonalization and manipulation; tight control, invisibly exerted, from on high; individual isolation; and the illusion of time constricted, scrambled, or even erased, again by powerful forces unseen and untouchable.

A whirlwind tour of these buildings, in various films noirs, reveals all of these conditions at work, in varying ratios.

Force of Evil is a highly textured, allegorical 1948 film in which business offices, legitimate and otherwise, play a crucial symbolic role. Veiled beneath its exploration of the numbers racket, the film is one of the fiercest dissections of laissez-faire capitalism ever to come out of Hollywood. This sort of exposé (with the sheerest of "veils") was not an uncommon structural device in film noir. *The Big Knife,* for example, directed and independently produced—outside studio control—by Robert Aldrich in 1955, immediately after the release of *Kiss Me Deadly,* is as far as I know the most ferocious and sophisticated exposé of Hollywood itself ever made. Working from a script by Clifford Odets, Aldrich depicts all the movieland types—from the studio head played like Al Capone by Rod Steiger (who four years later was to play Capone himself), to the matinée star played by Jack Palance like a boxer in thrall to the mob (he even opens the film sparring in full ring regalia) to the assorted studio hacks, heavies, lackeys, and toadying P.R. types who resemble mob hirelings—as underworld types, presenting Hollywood, even as he dismantles it, as a vast, corrupt, and sinister netherworld, a mirror-image of organized crime. It is with a similar manipulation of "types" from the business world that Abraham Polonsky in *Force of Evil* anatomizes the complex organism of a metropolitan numbers racket, itself merely a single tentacle of a nationwide gambling syndicate. *Force of Evil* is a particularly beautifully constructed film, and I agree with Charles Higham and Joel Greenberg when they write in *Hollywood in the 40s* that its "dialogue, with its Joycean repetitions and elaborate unpunctuated paragraphing, is unique in the American cinema, and at times achieves a quality of Greek drama, a poetry of the modern city."

Joe Morse is a brash, but urbane, Wall Street lawyer on the make, who is brilliantly portrayed by John Garfield. Garfield, another victim of the HUAC blacklist—like Jules Dassin, for the crime of refusing to finger his friends falsely—is also like Dassin a product of the New York tenements, Jewish, involved in several pioneering films of the streetwise, socially aware variety (*Body and Soul, They Made Me a Criminal, Gentlemen's Agreement, He Ran All the Way*). While Left-leaning—Garfield insisted that he never traveled any farther to the left than the liberal wing of the Democratic Party—he was certainly not a communist. More importantly, before Marlon Brando and James Dean, Garfield was Hollywood's first smoldering antihero, sexy, up-from-the-streets, brash and dangerous—but sensitive. Whether playing a boxer, a drifter, a revolutionary, or even a violinist, Garfield brought these qualities to all his roles.

In Joe Morse, Garfield created a character of unalloyed ambition and a greed so forthright that it seems almost refreshing at times. Joe is retained by a man named Ben Tucker, who made a fortune as a Prohibition-era gangster, to organize a takeover—neatly, cleanly, with all the trappings of "legality"—of the New York numbers racket. This crucial transition in film, from the violent gangsterism of 1930s crime to the white-collar, high-rise, criminal syndicates of the postwar era, is evinced in near textbook fashion in *Force of Evil.* As Colin McArthur notes in *Underworld U.S.A.,* his study of American gangster films and thrillers: "Large-scale general labour racketeering was smashed in 1943 and the criminal organizations then vied for control of the racing wire and other gambling operations. . . . *Force of Evil* deals with one aspect of gambling . . . and it faithfully reflects the quasi-respectability of the Forties racketeer. . . . The leading gangster figure in Jacques Tourneur's *Out of the Past* is presented as a gambler, and the prominence of gambling in racketeering in the Forties may help to explain the ubiquitousness of the night-club owner, operating crooked wheels and marked decks, as a villain in the films noirs of the period." McArthur goes on to cite such characters, and the films they inhabit, along with "jazz and the anarchic comedy of the Marx Brothers as an unusual rejection, within popular art, of the optimism of American culture." Or as Robert Warshow succinctly concludes: "The gangster is the 'no' to that great American 'yes' which is stamped so big over our official culture and yet has so little to do with the way we really feel about our lives."

Joe Morse's world, dominated by the numbers racket, is so absurdly determinist that at one point a regular patron at one of his betting parlors, who is nearly run down by a speeding car, barely heaves a breath of relief before telling Joe excitedly that he will immediately bet the first three numbers on the license plate of the car, certain the near hit-and-run was both an omen and a stroke of good luck. "What a good day this is for me," he exclaims, though he came within a hair of violent death. Joe, who has listened to him with cynical aplomb, turns away deadpan and mutters, "It's always a good day when you don't get killed." Which might easily serve as his credo.

While there are nightclubs galore—significant in themselves—in *Force of Evil,* it is the sleek office building with the expansive view of New York Harbor and the plush, stylish, top-floor suite from which Joe Morse operates that is central to the film from the first. Joe's older brother Leo is a small-time numbers operator, who will at first resist, and then be smashed by, the takeover Joe is engineering for Tucker. When Leo is introduced to us, he is operating out of a tenement, far from his brother's place of business on Wall Street—"still in the slums," as Joe himself reproaches him. Clearly traveling in ritzier circles, Joe hasn't seen his brother in years. Leo talks about his numbers operations as if it were a mom-and-pop candy store, an asset to the neighborhood that performs a neighborhood "service," as indispensable in its way as the local grocery, laundry, and liquor store. Knowing that Leo, prideful and stubborn, will resist (like the small-scale entrepreneur resisting monopolists) the syndicate takeover of his operation, Joe takes a taxi up to his former neighborhood and confronts his brother, in his seedy, rundown office, with these words: "Leo, let me take you out of this airshaft and get you a real office, in a real building—an office in the clouds." "Real," but also in the "clouds"—a paradox to which Joe seems oblivious. And it is that obliviousness, and his hubris while standing on the most impermanent of ground, that leads to his inevitable downfall. But not to his death; it is Leo who dies at the end of this tragedy, abducted at gunpoint by hoodlums while dining in a cheap spaghetti joint, in a scene reminiscent of a Prohibition-era gangland film—a reflex reversion to gangsterism by Joe's overlord when all Joe's legal arm-twisting, double-talk, and oily inducements have failed to sway Leo. Leo dies and Joe lives on, but on the descent now—far from his placid harbor view where the boats, bridges, and smokestacks are like a child's toys, far from his gleaming mahogany desk with the leather accoutrements and the swivel chair in which he leaned back puffing cigars while wheeling and dealing on the telephone—descending deep into the inferno.

It is under one of those bridges—one of the seventy-three that connect Manhattan Island to the rest of the world—that Leo's bullet-ridden body has been dumped by his murderers. No longer one of the safe and remote fixtures adorning a picture window, no longer a toy-sized illusion, the bridge is now something Joe must see up close, without obstruction, in all its enormity—like the rackets syndicate—dwarfing everything human. Polonsky and his cinematographer George Barnes (the one he took to the Hopper exhibition to reinforce his sense of noir textures and composition) create a spectacular montage, rapid looming shots of the bridge and the jagged, dangerous rocks beneath it, from above and below, that backdrops Joe as he descends by a long spiraling stairway from Riverside Drive to the riverbank below. He sees his brother's body sprawled lifeless on the rocks, "like rubbish," and after vowing aloud that he will dedicate himself, even if it means his own death, to breaking up the rackets, he announces—this his moment of epiphany, if not quite redemption—that "I killed my brother." Going down that long stairway, round and round—labyrinth-style—Joe muses on the voice-over, "I just kept going down and down, it felt like I was going down to the bottom of the world, to find my brother." His dead brother, broken and bloodied on the rocks that are smeared with the filth of the gulls, the flotsam and jetsam of the river ebbing around him, and the dirty, opaque water licking at his feet.

And we could not be farther from his suite of law offices with the tasteful masculine bric-a-brac than we are at that moment when Joe pulls Leo away from the water and kneels down beside him, knowing he must leave him there for the time being; knowing that while he may be Cain flooded with remorse, he is certainly not Orpheus, who could bargain with Death, or Hercules, who could wrestle him for the privilege of carrying one of his charges from the depths of the underworld to the light of day.

The Big Clock, another film released in 1948, and directed by the often underrated John Farrow, is dominated by a modern office building in which nearly all the action occurs. Here the noir universe *is* the office building. The corporate (*corpus,* "the body") world—a city within a city—as seen from within the bowels of its own labyrinth. The hero, George Stroud, is played by that most urbane Everyman, Ray Milland. Despite, or perhaps because of, his finely edged veneer of ambivalence—which devolves into outright reluctance about his roles as *wunderkind* magazine editor and adoring but perpetually absentee husband and father—Stroud is every bit the ambitious, workaholic, corporate climber that we saw in Joe Morse.

Because of his job, Stroud has yet to go on his honeymoon; after five years of marriage, it's become a bad running joke between him and his wife. Even Stroud's and Morse's respective corporations—bodies whose corruption begins at the top, with the head—appear interchangeable as we get to know them. As usual in film noir—where, as with every other aspect of society, the moral and ethical pretensions of big business are entirely suspect—there is implicit irony in the fact that Stroud's job (running a trendy magazine called *Crimeways* within a gargantuan publishing empire) is tinted for us with the same colors of corruption, cynicism, and deception as Morse's position as a "legal mouthpiece" for the rackets. Both men, despite their obvious intelligence, differing but manifest charm, and breezy air of independence, are subservient to autocrats who allow their lieutenants as little real breathing room as the working stiffs who do the drudge work that keeps every empire going. Indeed, Stroud's employer, the monomaniacal magazine tycoon Earl Janoth—a man obsessed by *time* (with the pun fully intended, which did not make the film popular with the magazines in Henry Luce's empire)—is portrayed more as a criminal mastermind and totalitarian dictator than a global businessman.

Charles Laughton plays Janoth as a mannered psychopath, insane, domineering, manipulative, and utterly ruthless—with facial tics, rolling eyes, and a small, twitching moustache whose strong resemblance to Adolph Hitler's would not have been lost on film audiences in 1948. In fact, Laughton's Janoth comes off as an out-of-control child, dangerous, demented, engaged in a rather lethal slapstick. This portrayal of Hitler himself was common in films of the time, both during and after the war, from Charlie Chaplin's grotesque caricature in *The Great Dictator* (1940) to the ridiculing, low-budget programmer, *Hitler—Dead or Alive* (1943), which more resembles a Three Stooges romp than a wartime action flick. Higham and Greenberg write that Laughton plays Janoth like "a psychotic old baby." He speaks, almost without variance, in a mechanical, monotonous voice—clocklike to a fault—a daunting feat, even for a great actor like Laughton. It is not the numbers rackets across the United States that Janoth controls, but the long and, in his case, insidious, reach of the journalistic word. From every indication, what he most relishes about his power is not his ability to influence public opinion—for which he seems to have little interest—as a communications czar, and certainly not any appetite for pursuing "the truth" in order to better, or even alter, the nature of American society, but his sheer lust for sales. The bottom line. Cash, and the power into which it translates. In fact, in the noir newsroom we seldom find the crusading fervor or egalitarian impulse that are typically ascribed to publishers and editors in American film. Joe Morse would have felt very comfortable—maybe more comfortable than George Stroud—in Janoth's executive suites.

The petty tyrant ruling a vast empire, Janoth's only crusade is for control, on what seems a relatively small scale. To him, political moving-and-shaking and the clout of his empire in the bigger scheme of things—like the daily life of the U.S.A.—are apparently a necessary nuisance. Though he wants his magazines "to reach every home in America," and manically hires and fires editors strictly according to the circulation numbers they post, Janoth finds his keenest satisfaction close to home, personally tormenting his employees. He docks the pay of a janitor who has left a closet lightbulb burning; dismisses the security guard who let his (Janoth's) mistress into the great man's private elevator; and threatens to blackball any writer or editor who wants to leave the company for a rival magazine. Janoth's sole intimates are his mute, armed bodyguard—again fashioned after the monochromatic goons who cater to the whims of crime bosses in gangster films—and his vivacious and mercenary mistress whom he takes especial pleasure in tormenting. Janoth taunts her with charges of infidelity (despite his own infidelities), manipulates her with his niggardliness, and unleashes on her the brunt of his toxic compulsivity; for example, he is unyielding in his insistence that she adhere to his tortuous personal timetable ("I'll get in from Washington at 4:43 P.M., so expect me at your place at 5:22 sharp.").

In *Love's Body* Norman O. Brown writes: "The urban revolution in the Ancient Near East was to make a world fit for kings to perform in, the city of the great king; a city and a tower that would reach unto heaven." And in his previous book, *Life Against Death,* he argues, "The city is a deposit of accumulated guilt. The temple buildings which dominate the first cities are monuments of accumulated guilt and expiation. . . . Hence a city is itself, like money, crystallized guilt. . . . And guilt is time." And in the city, Mumford writes, "time becomes visible." Brown then cites Frank Lloyd Wright, whose observations about the city are as sharp as—and certainly more sharp-elbowed than—Le Corbusier's: "To look at the plan of a great city," Wright says, "is to look at something like the cross-section of a fibrous tumor." If guilt is time, rendered solid, frozen indefinitely, in the buildings of the noir city, then the Janoth Building in *The Big*

Clock is the quintessential tower to a king, however petty, who is, after all, obsessed with time and guilty of murder—the primal crime—
and whose mantra, uttered *sotto voce* like a despairing exhalation in
his worst moments of stress, is *time.*

But this tower is also—and we are never for a moment allowed to
forget it—a functioning office building in which hundreds of people
around the clock are putting out a half dozen glossy magazines with
subject matter that covers the spectrum: *Newsways, Styleways, Air-
ways* . . . we see their logos from within an ascending elevator whose
doors open at various floors. Some of these people are secondary
characters—a handful with speaking lines—but the vast majority are
extras who come and go, milling in the lobby, packing the elevators,
hurrying along the corridors, shuffling papers, juggling telephone
receivers, but seldom, in Janoth's domain, congregating around the
water fountains. As in most films noirs, they seem absolutely authentic, for they are no different than the "extras" who surround us
in our own lives in large cities, especially those in our neighborhoods or places of work who, while remaining nameless, become
familiar to us by way of their looks, gestures, or even a single distin-
guishing quirk. In the Janoth Building, in addition to the abused jan-
itors and security guards, there are pert elevator operators, ushers
in crisp uniforms, stylishly coiffed executive secretaries, energetic
typists, buttoned-up clerks and stenographers, harried editors, and
laconic reporters. Nearly every scene occurs in an office, a conference room, a corridor, stairwell, or elevator, and—when things get
most interesting—in the building's lower depths: the basement and
subbasements, and most revealingly, the complex guts of the enormous electronic clock that dominates the main lobby. This clock is
Janoth's pride and joy, to which *all* the clocks in his far-flung empire,
dozens of American cities large and small and forty-three foreign bu-
reaus, are synchronized. It is also a tourist attraction. "The most accurate and the most unique privately owned clock in the world," one
of the building's tour guides intones to a group of rapt visitors, "built
at a cost of six hundred thousand dollars. It's set so you can tell the
time anywhere on the earth: London, Chicago, Honolulu. . . ."

It is near the subterranean entrance to the clock's interior, at the
film's opening, that we discover George Stroud darting around a corner to avoid a security guard and squeezing into an alcove for con-

cealment. First, the camera has panned over the city's dark—not glittering—skyline, just a few windows lit up here and there, and zoomed in on the Janoth Building, entering one of its lower, unlighted windows and depositing us, precipitously, into its shadowy recesses (again, the labyrinth within the labyrinth) near the clock. Stroud is wearing an expensive, well-tailored business suit, but his tie is pulled down, his hair is mussed, and he's perspiring freely as he slips into the bowels of the great clock and ascends a spiraling, iron stairway to the main control board. The board is flashing with dials, gauges, and tiny lights. Through the slats of steel blinds Stroud can peer out at the building's main lobby where security guards and employees with flashlights are hurrying back and forth in search parties. Searching for him. He's frightened and his voice is strained, anxious, as in a voice-over he begins to address us. "How did I get into this rat race, anyway?" he asks himself. "Just thirty-six hours ago I was down there, crossing that lobby on my way to work. A guy with a good job, a wife, and a kid. A respected member of the community. Just thirty-six hours ago, by the big clock."

Note his odd use of "rat race" before he provides us with that capsule bio. Ostensibly he is referring to the cat-and-mouse game he is playing with his pursuers. But "rat race" is a term which had entered the language just eight years before this film was produced, in 1939, at the dawn of the modern business era; it had already become a cliché for the plight of the urban office worker, hustling and scrambling through his frantic, often mind-numbing forty-hour-a-week job, competing intensely for higher wages, bonuses, and, most of all, enhanced status in the ever-shifting hierarchy of the corporate pyramid. I would emphasize here the word "competing," as in "competition," which Webster's cites as a "strenuous, wearisome, and competitive activity." Many feelings would undoubtedly churn through me if I were to find myself suddenly the object of a vigilante dragnet for a crime I did not commit, but thinking I was "competing" at something (except in the vaguest sense, eluding capture seems a very different sort of activity) would likely not be one of them.

I dwell on this because it seems clear as the film progresses that Stroud, a skilled editor and a man who chooses his words carefully even while under fierce pressure, is alluding here, not so much to the exhausting cat-and-mouse game in which he has been engaged for several hours, but to the long years of his professional life under Janoth's iron fist. Years in which, serving as one of the "favored" courtiers in an unhealthily driven court, Stroud has abandoned even the illusion of a workable family life. This is a man, chipper and loquacious at the office when we see him in flashback, who claims to be miserable for having allowed Janoth to talk him out of ever, in all those years, taking his wife, not just on a vacation, but on their honeymoon. Who has thrived in—and on—rat-race terms while in Janoth's employ, even while lamenting, rather lamely, that he should never have given up his low-paying job at a small-town newspaper in West Virginia when Janoth seduced him into running a glitzy national magazine. "And I had more money in the bank then than I do now!" Stroud declares unconvincingly, for by then we have glimpsed his wife and son at ease in an enormous, luxuriously appointed, duplex apartment, the height of 1940s urban chic, which he would have been hard-pressed to find in rural West Virginia.

How George Stroud has ended up in the workings of Earl Janoth's monstrous world-clock, implicated in the murder of Janoth's mistress, is secondary to the arduous inner journey he is forced to undertake in search of his true—or is it his false?—self. During that journey, there are many wondrous and bizarre elements that come into play and reveal themselves to us: the fact that Stroud, disgusted with himself for lingering in a bar, commiserating with Janoth's put-upon mistress, and missing (he gets the *time* wrong) the train on which his wife and son have left on the Strouds' final stab at a "honeymoon," he goes on to carouse and bar-hop the night away with Janoth's mistress rather than find some other means of transportation; the fact that Janoth, the man obsessed with timepieces, in a fit of rage has himself killed his mistress with a sundial (!) which she and Stroud picked up in a bar while on their bender; and the fact that Janoth, once he is truly a criminal, a first-degree murderer (and not just an odious autocrat reflecting the attributes and attitudes of the master-criminal), behaves no differently, and is perceived no differently by others. Without missing a beat, he continues to be ruthless, devious, duplicitous, and impatient with others: ready and willing to do *anything* to further his own interests, just as he has always been in his business dealings. Except that now he is covering up a murder.

And therein lies the most wondrous and bizarre plot twist of all, for Janoth designates George Stroud as the man in charge of finding the supposed murderer of his mistress, utilizing the vaunted reportorial machinery of *Crimeways* magazine. Unknown to Janoth, it is Stroud himself, under the absurd alias Jefferson Randolph (a name he drunkenly used in one of the bars he lurched through), who has become the prime suspect. So Stroud is transformed into one of the most absurd of noir heroes, a man hunting himself; eventually, when one of the witnesses from a bar spots "Jefferson Randolph" in the Janoth Building, and Janoth has the building completely sealed up, Stroud, as the film critic Foster Hirsch has pointed out, finds himself "superintending a fake search for himself, an investigation that becomes a search into the self . . . into the heart of darkness."

There are several conventional films of the late forties that purport to examine "the man in the gray flannel suit," including the film of that title. And there is another notable film noir, also released in 1948, *Pitfall,* whose hero, a middle-class insurance salesman with a far duller lifestyle than George Stroud, declares dourly to his wife: "Sometimes I get to feeling like a wheel within a wheel within a wheel." More than any of those films, though, *The Big Clock,* through Stroud's forced self-investigation, unflinchingly dissects one such corporate man—not only his job, but his marriage, his friendships, his emotional grid, and his deepest fears. Ultimately, the film examines the way Stroud—the keenest of observers as an editor, but until now blind to the realities of his own life—finally begins to look on himself, and how this may change him, if he survives.

In the end, Stroud's place of work becomes the nightmare labyrinth in which he is both hunter and hunted, until finally he ends up inside the big clock, a state akin to being inside the brain of Janoth himself. The beginning of the end for Janoth comes when Stroud inadvertently shuts down the clock, thus causing every clock in the building to stop. This unnerves Janoth even more than the murder he has committed. "It can't have stopped," he sputters, shaking and banging one of the clocks in his private office, "it's not possible." For the first time, we see him catch a whiff of his own mortality. So invested is he in that clock, the nerve center of his building, that in his mind its demise is synonymous with his own.

Janoth despatches his bodyguard, with shoot-to-kill orders, to the big clock. Outwitting the bodyguard, Stroud manages to trap him between floors in Janoth's private elevator. Soon afterward, Janoth panics, and cornering Stroud in his office, tries to shoot him himself. He misses, and rushing through the jammed elevator door, plunges down the deep shaftway to his death atop the roof of the elevator in which the bodyguard is frantically hitting the buttons. Janoth is sprawled dead after running from a man who just moments before had been running from him—dead in the darkness within the innermost depths of the Janoth Building. His "fall," in true noir fashion, comes not in the form of scandal, ruin, a humiliating trial, and prison; instead, all of that is condensed into a literal plunge. In this labyrinth, in a sudden reversal (when Stroud is most vulnerable), it is Minos, the king, who is destroyed.

There is a strong parallel here to the climactic scene in *Force of Evil,* in which the executive suite in the office building also becomes—and manages to feel quite natural as—a setting for gunplay. Actually, for an all-out shootout. Tucker, the white-collar numbers syndicate kingpin, Fico, his bodyguard/enforcer, and our other corporation-man-on-the-make (at least until that moment), Joe Morse, reach an impasse that no words can breach when Joe, raw but energized after finding his brother's dead body, informs Tucker that he's going to get even with him by busting the rackets wide open. Joe, the lawyer, for the first time in the film has armed himself before this meeting. So when Fico draws his revolver, and Tucker follows with a pistol from his desk drawer, Joe is ready for them. They all fire away, the one lamp is hit, and in the darkness the three men hit the floor, still firing. The plumes of flame from their pistol barrels occasionally flare their faces to life in a tableau which is otherwise solidly black. Sometimes, for five or six seconds—an eternity on film—we see only black. And we hear only the rustling of the men's clothes and the sandpapery sound of their breathing as they crawl for angles and advantage on the wall-to-wall carpeting amid furniture, curtains, office equipment, and fallen objects.

Tucker's opulent office has become an infernal cell—a hell, like Janoth's elevator shaft—at the very center of the building which he owned and ruled over just minutes before. Each bodyguard figures prominently in his respective boss' death: while Janoth plunges onto the elevator in which his bodyguard has been rendered impotent, Tucker, making a desperate break for the door of his office, is shot in the back by Fico, who thinks he is shooting Joe. In the shaft of light that streams in from the corridor, Joe spots Fico and in turn shoots him. Tucker and Fico lie dead in the darkness and Joe—like George Stroud, who finally gets to "leave the office," striding out of the Janoth Building—walks out of Tucker's office, closing the door behind him.

Though not with the all-inclusiveness of *The Big Clock,* there are numerous other films noirs in which office buildings figure prominently, and are richly evoked. *Double Indemnity* (1944), directed by Billy Wilder, is certainly one of the most literate and elegantly constructed of all noir films, with a screenplay by Raymond Chandler and Wilder from the novel by James M. Cain.

Double Indemnity has a deceptively simple plot: a smart, maybe too smart, sharp-tongued insurance salesman, Walter Neff, is seduced by Phyllis Dietrichson, the wife of a well-to-do oil wildcatter. Neff is drawn both into her bed and into her plot to murder her husband in order to collect on a substantial life insurance policy. There is plenty of steamy interplay between Neff and Phyllis as they climb a slippery ladder of lust, sex, and betrayal. The setting is Los Angeles in midsummer, and Neff's lyrical voice-over ebbs and flows with recurring motifs, fugue-like, throughout the film, first and foremost associating the cloying, sex-drenched scent of honeysuckle in and around the Dietrichson house with murder. (Neff's voice-over recalls the best of Philip Marlowe's interior monologues in Chandler novels like *The High Window* and *The Big Sleep,* but leavened mightily with the acid worldliness of Wilder.) The film also devotes a good deal of time to the insurance business, as a business. The dialogue and the voice-over are filled with talk of premiums, actuarial tables, sales strategies, claims fraudulent and otherwise, and of course, insurance policies, their arcane language and myriad clauses, including the double indemnity clause (in which the beneficiary collects double the policy amount if the insured dies in an accident) that gives the film its title.

Some of this insurance talk takes place in the Dietrichson home, where Neff makes his sales pitch to Phyllis and her husband; but most of it occurs at Neff's office in the central city, where the film begins and ends. In fact, nearly the entire film is presented as an extended flashback, a mosaic of complex time jumps, narrated by Neff into his office dictaphone. As in *The Big Clock,* the film opens with Neff arriving at his office—except that he arrives in the predawn in a speeding sedan with a gunshot wound in his shoulder. Then he nearly bleeds to death while making his confession, spilling his guts literally and metaphorically, into the dictaphone. At the end of the film, not knowing that a janitor has phoned the police, Neff, just this side of consciousness, indeed tries to "leave the office" (for the Mexican border, no less), but is not as successful in doing so as Joe Morse and George Stroud were. He collapses outside the glass door that leads from the agents' individual offices to the mezzanine and its elevator bank, and it is made clear that the only destination left to Neff is the gas chamber at San Quentin. (Wilder originally shot a final scene in which we watch Neff walk into the gas chamber months later, then cut it and reshot the office building scene.)

The glass door leading out of the offices is an interesting touch. Reminiscent of the underground workers' area in Lang's *Metropolis,* the offices of Neff's insurance company are a modernistic, highly impersonal warren of cubicles and shared spaces—two or three desks to a small room—behind a wall of glass. There is little privacy. (The one time Neff wants to speak alone with someone, he must ask his office mate to step outside.) And there is also, one imagines, little dawdling, gossip, or banter by the coffee wagon. The different floors, with their mezzanine structure and their identically sized and spaced offices, comprise a classic beehive structure. Within this space, work appears to proceed mechanistically, neatly, by the numbers—just like the policies that are being underwritten, amended, approved, filed away, or investigated. And the latter only occurs when things get messy; that is, when avarice, greed, or lust, as they are wont to do, overtake the numbers, nullify the policies, subvert the organization, and lead a strayed organization man like Walter Neff to his demise, bleeding on those highly buffed, antiseptic tiled floors.

Or maybe not so strayed. In the end, after all, Neff goes to the office to die. It takes him a while to dictate the entire story of his transgression—a narrative, incidentally, which he directs, not to the police or the world at large, but specifically to his boss. Certainly had he foresworn his confession while he still had the strength, there would have been time enough for him to have gotten some medical attention before fleeing to Mexico. True, Neff is a noir hero of the most abject variety, dealt a far tougher hand than George Stroud, or even the unfortunate Joe Morse, whose brother's blood is on his hands. Stroud meets a Circe, Janoth's mistress, who tries to interest him in a blackmail scheme (he isn't interested) against Janoth because of which she ends up murdered; the Circe Walter Neff encounters, proposes a partnership (and he is interested) that will climax in the murder of her husband, and she also ends up dead, "executed" by Neff, but not before she has shot him too, deep in the labyrinth into which she has led him and which he can no longer exit—just as he can no longer exit his office building. At the same time—in a closing irony typical of Wilder's noir vision—we are to understand that, good insurance man that Neff is, in his mind if not his heart, he feels compelled to file his final report, "closing the Dietrichson case," even if the report doubles as a confession of two murders, one of them cold-blooded and premeditated, which ensures that he'll get the death penalty.

The Blue Gardenia (1953), directed by Fritz Lang during his Hollywood years, is another newsroom-centered film in a Los Angeles office building. The film takes its title from a restaurant—not a nightclub, as in *The Blue Dahlia.* Also, the song "Blue Gardenia," sung by Nat King Cole, is heard on a phonograph at a critical juncture in the film. Plotwise, the film is a kind of inverse, a crucially altered mirror-image of *The Big Clock:* a woman goes on a blind date with a ladies' man, a cocky commercial artist who has come by to pick up one of her roommates on a dinner date that has gone awry. There are three lookalike, nearly indistinguishable, blondes sharing the same apartment (Lang, like Hitchcock, had a perversely dry sense of humor), and the one who was supposed to dine with the artist is out somewhere else. So the woman who is home goes out with him. He gets her drunk at his apartment, begins to force himself upon her, and before she passes out cold the last thing she remembers is grabbing the poker from the fireplace and striking out at him. Emerging from an alcoholic blackout (similar to George Stroud's), she assumes the next morning, when she hears of the artist's murder, that she committed it.

At the building where her roommate—the artist's intended date—is a telephone switchboard operator, a newspaper columnist begins a manhunt for the killer, by way of his column. After ascertaining that the victim was seen shortly before the murder at the Blue Gardenia restaurant with a young woman, he dubs the murderer the "Blue Gardenia girl" and is immediately flooded with phone calls—first, people claiming to have seen this mystery woman, and then dozens of young women who, yearning for the allure of the "Blue Gardenia girl," "confess" to being the killer. So, here again, as in *The Big Clock,* we have a wrongly accused person who is honest, but also gullible and careless, and an extralegal search for the killer that emanates from the offices of a newspaper, under the direction of a powerful journalist. The significant difference is that in *The Blue Gardenia* the purpose of the search is to exonerate the wrongly accused person, while in *The Big Clock* Janoth is searching for an innocent man whom he is framing.

Again, the unceasing life of the office building—the office building as a compressed, complex, tautly wired microcosm of the city at large—is central to the narrative. We see not only the intimate workings of the newspaper, but also the elevator operators, security guards, shoeshine boys, and flower sellers, the tobacconist and kiosk clerk, the doormen and porters who tend the milling cosmopolitan lobby, and even the mechanics and attendants who run the building's underground garage, maintaining the news trucks and looking after the employees' cars.

Once again, the film opens with someone coming to his office, but this time it is the film's most empowered character, the newspaper columnist—no crippled George Stroud or fatally flawed Walter Neff—and it is not night, but a clear, sunny morning. He arrives at the office in his new car, which is exactly how he leaves it in the end, confident and full of himself. This despite the fact that, even with the true murderer arrested (despite the glamorous Blue Gardenia monicker, she turns out to be a shabby, pathetic young woman whom the murdered man seduced and impregnated months before), the film's conclusion is anything but uplifting. It is, as the critic Douglas Pye asserts, "as bleak a 'happy ending' as one can find in film. All the characters remain trapped within repressive attitudes and practices that the film has exposed as grotesquely destructive and they appear to accept their situations complacently." Which is a definition that might be applied to the rarefied group of films noirs in which the principals survive—unlike the more typical *Double Indemnity* or *Out of the Past* in which they are all destroyed—but with little hope for redemption, much less renewal. Fritz Lang, for one, emphasizes in all his noir films that there is a heavy price to be paid, always, by those who live on beyond the formal perimeters of the noir labyrinth, leaving the inferno, not for purgatory, but limbo.

Johnny Eager, the hero of the film of that title, is one of those who does not survive. One of the earliest films noirs, *Johnny Eager* (1942) is a curiosity in many ways. Foremost among them is the fact that its hero, a powerful gangster, maintains a difficult alias, as a taxi driver, to camouflage his true activities. When we meet him, he is behind the wheel of his taxi, wearing a crisp uniform, en route to his regular meeting with his probation officer, before whom he is in every way the reformed felon: polite, recalcitrant, praising the virtues of his new life on the straight and narrow. Then he's back in his taxi, negotiating the busy streets, but not picking up any fares. His next stop seems an unlikely one: an elaborate dog-racing track—including a park, a man-made lake, restaurants, and imposing arcades—that is still under construction. Parking the taxi, he enters an unmarked door in the track's main building, which has already been completed. Proceeding along a dizzying succession of corridors and byways, he finally passes through a concealed door to a secret room and boards a small elevator (in terms of privacy outdoing even Earl Janoth) to a lavish suite of offices, which, of course, are also secret. He is still wearing his taxi driver's leather jacket, khaki shirt, bow tie, and modest cap with the taxi company's insignia over the brim. But not for long. With disdain creeping into his previously genial features, he sheds his workingman's garb for a smart smoking jacket, combs his hair back, and rubs his face with both hands, a brilliant pantomime in which we can feel—in a rush—his tremendous relief as he removes the invisible and onerous mask of civic virtue in which he has clothed himself. All mannered iciness now, he takes a cigarette from the carved ebony box on the desk and lights it with an engraved silver lighter—a far cry from the matchbook he fumbled with at the probation office to light a cigarette that had been stuck behind his ear. A man comes into the office with a sheaf of papers and addresses him with deference, at which point the humble taxi driver sits down authoritatively in the padded chair behind the opulent desk, prepared to do business, his transformation complete. He is Johnny Eager, once and future crime lord, calculating and efficient to a fault, and this is his office, at the heart of the gambling complex he is building with the happy acquiescence of a coterie of politicos he has bribed. (In typical noir fashion, the lowly probation officer who diligently monitors Johnny the cabbie remains absurdly ignorant of his true activities, which are common knowledge among the city's top officials—the probation officer's superiors, none of whom is ever brought to justice.) Later that day, Johnny Eager's next stop is the nightclub where, outside the realm of his calculations, he chances on the unlikely young woman who, unwittingly and reluctantly, proves to be the pivotal figure in his downfall. The name of the nightclub is The Black Cat.

In *Pitfall,* that other unhappy insurance man, John Forbes, rebellious cog spinning within the maddening machinery of his office bureaucracy, is disgruntled in marriage and work. But he discovers that the twin poles between which his life is being torn apart are no longer—as they were for years—his dull suburban home and his arid office, but his office and the cocktail lounge to which he has begun to gravitate in the company of an attractive model. Originally he encountered her as a minor figure in a case he was investigating. But soon enough he is playing hooky from the office at midday, trysting with her at the cocktail lounge and tooling around the harbor in her flashy motorboat as their flirtation blossoms into a full-blown affair. The model still has criminal connections, and as Forbes is drawn farther into her orbit, his own life predictably begins to unravel. She is a classic femme fatale, leading him into a labyrinth so unfamiliar, and pitch-dark, that he is virtually transformed into a blind man when it comes to discerning the exigencies of his own fate, trapped long before he is aware of it. Like the fishermen's nets in *Out of the Past* that shadow the face of Jeff Bailey on that beach in Acapulco, venetian blinds cast imprisoning bars of shadows onto the face of John Forbes. This is not an uncommon image among film noir protagonists. What is unusual in Forbes' case is that the shadows seem to follow him everywhere, because from the first he is everywhere trapped: sitting at the unadorned desk in his office; visiting the model's apartment for the first time; but, especially, sliding into the plush leather booth beside her at the cocktail lounge. And as the shadows cross his face, she gives him her take on the ethos of the cocktail lounge (another name for "nightclub"), delivered in a husky, silk-lined voice through the curling smoke of her cigarette: "This is the life. Have you ever noticed? If for some reason you want to feel completely out of step with the rest of the world, the only thing to do is sit around a cocktail lounge in the afternoon. . . . You sit around in the gloom, figure some things out . . . then you go out and the sun hits you . . . and you feel like you're coming out of a hole in the ground. . . ." The name of the cocktail lounge is The Tropicana.

In *The Dark Corner* (1946), a heavyset man in a startlingly white suit is pushed from an upper-story window in a high-rise office building in midtown Manhattan. He is standing in the shadows at the end of a corridor, near an elevator bank, with his back to an open window. His companion, a wealthy art gallery owner whom he is blackmailing, a slight, dapper man in a three-piece suit, a homburg, and spats, pushes him through the window with his hand-carved, ivory-knobbed walking stick. Just a quick thrust to the man's solar plexus, then a shove, and he is gone. And we cut to a shot of him falling and falling, spreadeagled against the busy street below, where cars and buses, taxis and trucks, are whizzing by, and pedestrians are swarming. His mouth is open in a scream we never hear. And his eyes are wide, terrified, gazing up toward the summit of the building which, minutes before, he ascended in an elevator with his murderer. We cut to the latter, readjusting his hat, gazing at the tip of his walking stick as he might admire a golf club or tennis racket (though he is anything but the sporting type), glancing at his watch, and waiting for the elevator to arrive. When it does, he calmly enters, tips his hat to a pair of well-dressed women, and calmly stands beside them as the elevator descends. He remains composed and self-contained, never once looking at the bar of flickering numerals that light up as they sail down past one floor after another. And he steps into the lobby long after the heavyset man in the white suit has completed the same descent, at a slightly greater velocity, and, to the sound of screeching tires, horns, and horrified cries, drawn a widening crowd of pedestrians, taxi drivers, and finally policemen.

Later, a private detective, just out of jail after having been framed by his partner, trying to get back on his feet, is framed again, by the dapper art-gallery owner. This time he is framed for the murder of his partner, who is having an affair with the gallery owner's spoiled and sexually starved young wife. ("He loves me," she laments, speaking of her husband, "and gives me everything a man can give a woman—but still it isn't enough.") The private detective, knocked out in a cheap furnished room that is crisscrossed with heavy shadows, wakes up with a poker in his hand beside the body of his partner, who has been bludgeoned to death. Jazz is playing loudly on a radio. In fact, jazz is playing in the background during nearly all of the film's crucial scenes—but especially on radios—just as Schubert's "Unfinished Symphony" is playing in *Kiss Me Deadly*. At one point, the music is played "live" by a jazz band, in a nightclub to which the private detective retires at his darkest hour with his loyal and indefatigable Girl Friday, to whom, while gripping a highball glass, he intones an epigram which could also be his epitaph: "I can be framed easier than Whistler's mother." The band picks up the tempo, and the jazz grows more frenzied. "Music like that does something to me," his secretary purrs, leaning back into the darkness.

Eventually the frame falls apart and the detective is cleared when the gallery owner's wife, grieving for her dead lover, overhears a confrontation between her husband and the detective. From the head of the steep stairway that leads down to the gallery's vault, she shoots her husband with the revolver she took from his desk. For years, even while declaring at cocktail parties that "love is a disease," he has kept her on a pedestal, and now she shoots him from a pedestal height. A great height, for his pedestal was one which grew over the course of their unhappy marriage. It is nearly as great a height, relatively speaking, as that office building from which the gallery owner pushed the man in the white suit. That building, photographed majestically from afar, before and after the murder, is the Grant Building, newly constructed at the time. And the name of the nightclub is The High Hat Club.

The pivotal moment in *The Big Clock* occurs in the nightclub where George Stroud meets, and has drinks with, Janoth's mistress, thus changing the course of his life. Along with the mistress' murder in her apartment, it is the single most significant scene in the film that takes place outside of the Janoth Building.

In *Force of Evil,* Joe Morse is a man obsessed with secrecy. In the film's opening, in his office, we see him open his wall safe and then unlock the desk drawer in which he keeps his private telephone. An instrument essential to someone at the nerve center of a numbers racket—a business conducted almost exclusively over the phone wires. When he finds out the phone is tapped later on, his boss Tucker's wife taunts him with these words: "You might spend the rest of your life trying to remember what you shouldn't have said." Later, in a nightclub with a young woman who worked for his brother and who wants Joe to break from the rackets, Joe lets slip his prized reserve and gets drunk. Methodically he falls to pieces while a jazz band plays in the background—but still, always, remains the man of secrets. When he decides to confide in the young woman, and despite the fact the music is clearly covering up anything he might say at their table, he calls the floor captain over and, slapping some money in his palm, gestures toward the band. "Tell them to play louder," Joe growls, "I have something private to tell the lady. Something private from the whole world." This, too, is a pivotal scene, barely preceding his discovery of Joe's brother's body under the bridge, and the only time we ever see him open up to anyone. And certainly the nightclub is the film's most significant locale outside of his brother's office in the slums and the totemic office building where Joe himself does business.

In both *The Big Clock* and *Force of Evil,* the respective nightclubs are unnamed, visited only once.

But that is not the case in many other films noirs in which nightclubs and casinos also play an integral, but more central, part. There was a boom of such clubs in American cities after the war, emblematic of the new night life—stylish, flashy, often frenzied. And more often than not, paradoxical: in the noir city, the nightclub can serve as a glittering, silvery-black mirror reflecting the after-hours diversions of the postwar economic boom, and at the same time can appear to be no more than a sordid, gloomy watering hole for life's losers. A place which the noir hero must enter for various reasons during his quest—usually with disdain. The nightclub can be the center of a duplicitous moral or criminal web, run by a man whose interests radiate outward from the club itself.

These nightclub proprietors form a bridge between the gangland bosses of the twenties and thirties and the white-collar criminals of the fifties and sixties. They operate as "legitimate" members of society, with clientele drawn from all corners of the urban elite: politics, business, entertainment, the arts. They have lavish in-house offices and usually patrol their domains in black tie and white tuxedo jacket. They meet payrolls and pay their taxes—or at least the taxes on one of the sets of books they keep. Some have families living in the best parts of town, and some indulge in philanthropy on the side—for cosmetic reasons, or to keep their wives busy—which would have been a leap for their 1930s counterparts, whose primary business machine was the tommy gun. At the same time, these nightclub owners are connected, without exception, to organized crime, or head crime rings of their own. For every waiter, busboy, and big-band musician in their employ, there is also an informer, a grafter, and a torpedo to do unto his enemies as they would do unto him. The nightclub owner walks, and sometimes pirouettes, the cutting edge between the city's daylit business world and its criminal underground; in fact, he is often an intermediary between the two, and his establishment in the 1940s is the place where the city's many currents and undercurrents—commercial, political, sexual—merge after nightfall. The champion boxer, the corrupt alderman, the debutante, the syndicate lawyer, the young publicist on the make, the dissolute playboy, and the financier and his wife may all be rubbing elbows at the bar; or, with introductions arranged by their host, the sharp-eyed proprietor, they may even be sharing the same table. Often amazingly elaborate worlds-unto-themselves, these nightclubs and casinos in some cases form the core of an entire film noir.

While its roots extend far back in the history of urban civilization—both Athens and Rome had their nocturnal dives, of course, as did Chaucer's London—"nightclub" enters English usage in 1894, on the heels of the so-called Gilded Age and the economic crash of the previous year: a historical progression that offers up an eerie but unsurprising mirror-image of the dynamics by which the Roaring Twenties were followed by the Great Depression three decades later. (While we're at it, note that the word "breadline" comes into existence in 1900, not 1930.) During the depression of the 1890s, William McKinley is elected president. Precursor to Herbert Hoover, and surely the Ronald Reagan of his day, McKinley was referred to by the journalist William Allen White as "on the whole decent, on the whole dumb . . . [he] . . . walked among men like a bronze statue determinedly looking for a pedestal" and once declared that he hoped to "civilize and Christianize" the Filipinos, unaware, it seems, that they were already Christian. It is during the McKinley administration that we most clearly see the foundation stones of twentieth-century urban America being laid: spectacular wealth and opulence on a lopsided seesaw with abject poverty and rampant slums; runaway robber barons and the first large-scale urban street gangs; sweatshops and the rise of the labor unions. In neighborhoods just blocks apart, there are people with money to burn and families getting by on five dollars a week. New industries are cropping up, with expanding offices, growing staffs, and streamlined business practices at the same time that legions of unemployed workers, including migrants from the hard-hit farming states, take to the streets to protest, and on occasion to riot. And, of course, for all of these people, rich and poor, in the rapidly expanding cities, there is nightlife—a concept that means many things in many places.

In Manhattan, for example, the spectrum of nightlife is wide and the quality varies wildly: from the dank, darkly lit bars of the Lower East Side, where draft beer is ten cents a pint and the entertainment might consist of a single man hunched over the keys of an upright piano in a cloud of smoke, to the swank new clubs on Fourteenth Street where magnums of French champagne are served up in fine crystal while showgirls who bathe in milk and don feathered wings, like angels, descend from the ceiling in gold cages. The turn of the century is the period in which the nightclub is established in the American consciousness, but as the years pass, the word takes on grander connotations. Today there are still seedy clubs, of course, but "nightclub" retains a surface gloss that "bar" and "tavern" can never boast in the first place. For a hundred years now, a nightclub is less a place where one would go exclusively to drink (though, of course, for many it serves that solitary function) than to be entertained, to socialize, and even to eat, as one would seldom expect to do any of those things in a bar.

It is during the Great Depression, in 1936, just on the threshold of the noir era, that "nightclub" enters the language as a verb, as well. In Webster's, "to nightclub" is an intransitive verb meaning "to patronize nightclubs" (accompanied by the new noun, "nightclubber"), a verb which in the 1980s, during the Reagan era, is shortened, as in "to go clubbing." Certainly by the late 1940s the nightclub embodies the postwar hunger for luxury, glamour, and personal freedom. And it emerges accordingly in the film noir, employing surreal and oneiric elements and providing an exterior landscape that reflects the interior workings of noir protagonists. But there is more—on the surface and below—to the noir nightclub than that. From the first, it is not just an aesthetic but an economic emblem in these films.

On its surface, after all, the nightclub represents leisure, luxury, and self-indulgence. Stimulation and excitation are provided, through liquor, entertainment, and social—ideally, sexual—encounters. How many patrons enter nightclubs in search of sobriety or meditative peace? In *The Theory of the Leisure Class,* Thorstein Veblen writes that "conspicuous consumption of valuable goods is a means of reputability to the gentleman of leisure. As wealth accumulates on his hands, his own unaided effort will not avail to sufficiently put his opulence in evidence by this method. The aid of friends and competitors is therefore brought in by resorting to the giving of valuable presents and expensive feasts and entertainments . . . [and] his consumption also undergoes a specialisation as regards the quality of the goods consumed. He consumes freely and of the best, in food, drink, narcotics, shelter, services, ornaments, apparel, weapons and accoutrements, amusements, amulets. . . . He becomes a connoisseur. . . ." The proprietor of the noir nightclub, though frequently an outright criminal or shady entrepreneur, often affects—at least on the floor of his club—the manners of a gentleman. He may display better manners and be capable of more polished speech than many of his patrons. Although in his private offices he may address his minions and henchmen in the dialects of the slums from which he sprang, in the plush and mirrored public arena of his club he is fluent in the language of the monied classes—the judges, businessmen, and society swells with whom he banters easily. He moves with equal composure among their wives, daughters, and mistresses, whose furs, jewelry, and gowns, after all, are purchased at the fine stores he himself patronizes—in company with, or on behalf of, *his* wife, mistress, and daughters. In short, the nightclub owner—the shrewd and hard-boiled former gangster who has risen—aspires to further evolution, to becoming no less than Veblen's gentleman of leisure while retaining the underpinnings of his street smarts and street savvy.

He is a man above it all. Wearing the finest clothes. Impeccably groomed. Expensively accessorized, from his tie pins to his automobiles. Never soiling his hands. Or punching a clock. Or answering to anyone. He keeps his own hours—by definition, at night—on his own terms. And of course he does it on his own turf, which happens to be luxuriously appointed, filled with glittering company, maintained by employees who (in livery and otherwise) could double for a gentleman's servants, and stocked with all the leisure items a gentleman could require, from costly beverages and rare victuals to elaborate entertainments and available women across the social scale. The film gangsters of the Prohibition era certainly frequented the speakeasies which they owned (while avoiding their own bootleg liquor), but they wouldn't have been caught dead spouting philosophy (the nightclub owner Martinelli in *Dead Reckoning* quotes Nietzsche not once but twice) or discussing a charitable theater benefit with a society matron (Marko in *Black Angel*). And when the oldtime gangsters did venture into the no-man's land of "high society," as did James Cagney in *Public Enemy* and Edward G. Robinson in *Little Caesar,* they were treated as loutish, even comic, figures—gaudily dressed, clumsy with the accoutrements of their sudden wealth— and quickly slapped down. Not so in film noir. For example, both Eddie Mars, in *The Big Sleep,* and Slim Dundee, in *Criss Cross,* with their easy manners, sharp English tailoring, clean-shaven good looks, and slicked-back fair hair, look as if they have just stepped out of a photograph of Oxford graduates at a class reunion. Their brand of nightclub owner often ends up leading a life with more leisure pursuits—including horse breeding, extended ocean cruises, European vacations, and elaborate country houses—than the monied classes who patronize their clubs but still work by day and, for the most part, sleep by night, like the working stiffs of the lower and middle classes.

So the noir nightclub is rife with ironies. It becomes the beacon whereby the boy of the streets, who has risen with his fists and a gun, can attain not only great wealth but instant polish. "Respectability" is a word that crops up again and again with these nouveau riche gangsters. Gradually they become not just aspirants to, but the perverse custodians of, an ethos of glamour and leisure in the postwar years—trendsetters in their own way. Having avoided military service in the war and quietly, ruthlessly accumulated their fortunes, by 1945 they are the de facto upper crust of the criminal world: they sleep on silk sheets, invest in legitimate businesses, marry, or see that their offspring marry, into the "respectable" world even while they themselves remain plugged into the dangerous currents of the nightlife. They are perched a good many rungs up the ladder from the legions of fast-buck artists and hustlers that emerge from the armed forces—including the lower-strata members of organized crime who could not avoid the draft—to make their way in the ferment of the big cities after the war. These nightclub owners have it both ways: running their nocturnal empires and dutifully subscribing to a season at the opera house.

To a great degree, it is the nightclub owner as arbiter who determines the dynamics of the nightclub's sociology and etiquette in the noir city: table placement, hierarchies of preferential treatment, the sophisticated uses and abuses of alcohol and drugs, the sexual mores of dancing, dating, and picking people up, and the broad composition of the social scene, from criminals to glitterati, star performers to prostitutes. The nightclub owner can be a kind of social chemist—forever manipulating and reformulating—with the club as his laboratory, and the effects of his actions rippling out into the greater society.

Which may be why, in this area, it is not a social scientist or gossip columnist, but a former nightclub proprietor who provides us with a particularly succinct and knowing take on the psychopathology of nightclubs. Ian Schrager, in the 1990s a successful hotelier, is the former owner of Studio 54, the Manhattan club which in the late 1970s and early 1980s reigned as a premier nightspot. (Things went sour when Schrager and his partner were convicted of income tax evasion.) In its heyday, at peak hours, bouncers let patrons into Studio 54 one at a time, according to their celebrity and/or pocketbooks. The club was famous for its enormous dancefloor, strobe-lit, thundering with disco music, and packed with crowds from nightfall to dawn that looked as if they had drifted in from a Mardi Gras parade. Though the clientele included well-known politicos, mayors, and congressmen, as well as the wives and daughters of presidents (an unthinkable possibility in the moralistic nineties), the club's restrooms, unrestricted as to gender, were often jammed with patrons snorting cocaine off their wrists. It was a place every bit as risqué—or what passes for risqué at any given moment in the tundra of popular fads—in its time as the racier postwar nightspots that cropped up fifty years ago. So Schrager bears solid credentials when he comes forward to proclaim to *New York Magazine* that "a nightclub reflects the collective consciousness. It manifests the moment." Including that urban moment which we see frozen for all time in the film noir nightclub. By 1953, in fact, late in the "classic" noir cycle, so pervasive is the association in the "collective consciousness" between noir and the nightclub that even in an airy episode of a television sitcom of the day, *Topper,* at a time when such fare was a far more sanitized barometer of cultural phenomena, there is a club (employing a stripper with whom the straitlaced banker Topper becomes enmeshed) called the *Noir Café.* Italicized, still, because the association continues to cling to its French (as in sinful) roots.

If the noir universe can be seen to operate around the action of various complex institutional wheels—enmeshed like gears and, on occasion, spinning eccentrically—the nightclub in many films emerges as the most unambiguously powerful (and visible) wheel. From its hub radiate power (financial and political), sexuality (raw and stylistic), and secrecy (private and official). This is even the case in films in which much of the real action ostensibly occurs elsewhere. *Dead Reckoning* (1947) and *Criss Cross* (1949) are two such films. Plotwise, the former is built around a returning, and highly decorated, soldier's disappearance and murder and the noir hero's affair with the soldier's fiancée (who turns out to be the ex-wife of the murderer, a crooked nightclub owner!); the latter is centered around an armored car heist and the noir hero's affair with the wife of the heist's primary beneficiary, a crooked nightclub owner.

Dead Reckoning is set in a southern city, which is unusual for a 1940s noir. It's in the Deep South, apparently, for the city is called Gulf City, and its torrid climate—geographically and sexually—is a recurring motif in the film. As with New Orleans in *Panic in the Streets* several years later, much is made of the southernness of Gulf City's netherworld—in the same vein that the netherworld aspects peculiar to Chicago or New York are highlighted in other films. So in the opening pan of *Dead Reckoning* we see a neon sign atop a hotel roof describing Gulf City as the "Tropical Paradise of the South." At the same time, our hero Rip Murdock, played by Humphrey Bogart at his most hard-bitten and cynical, tells us early on that Gulf City is "a city I'd never heard of." This is curious, because throughout the film Gulf City is portrayed as a large city, not a backwater. Has he not heard of it because it is infernal? A city that is not to be found in the conventional atlas, but only on the noir map, deep in the labyrinth.

At once steamy, seamy, Gothic, and elegant, Gulf City is a particularly fantastical urban labyrinth. The fact that for us its name is a fictional concoction is enough to set it apart from the majority of film noir cities, which are wholly unambiguous about the fact—reinforced by on-location shooting—that they are very much the "real" cities they purport to represent, and in which we live. And as the film progresses, we don't miss the fact that it is not conventionally set in Miami or New Orleans; in fact, we find that Gulf City's possibilities as a dream city, a place the hero has never heard of previously, are enhanced by the fact that the filming is restricted to studio sets, with no recognizable exterior backdrops. Populated by phantoms and demons, full of fire symbolism and fire itself, Gulf City is also a place where rain arrives warm—sometimes hot—in sudden squalls; where black vines thick and mobile as serpents climb the sides of buildings; and where the air seems literally to be choking the inhabitants, who cough, hack, and mop their brows throughout the film.

Murdock is a former Army paratrooper who says he doesn't "trust anybody, especially women." He tells us the greater part of his story in one of the most unusual voice-over constructions in all of film noir: an extended confession which, drawing on overlapping flashbacks, is delivered to a real priest. The latter is a "jumping padre," a military chaplain who accompanied paratroopers—like Murdock and his buddy Johnny—on their missions during the war. Murdock addresses him as "Father" throughout the voice-over, so that as the facts of his story become more tawdry and depraved, the air in which they are delivered—the confessional framing—becomes increasingly solemn. Until finally it sounds as if Murdock is speaking to God himself from the depths of Hell, trying to unravel the bewildering series of events he has just endured.

It doesn't take Murdock long to solve the problem of Johnny's disappearance: with a simple inquiry on his first night in town, he learns that there has been a terrible automobile accident on the state highway in which Johnny may have been involved. Rushing to the morgue, Murdock identifies Johnny's body, pulled from a refrigerated drawer, "burned to a crisp." Solving the murder is something else altogether. Murdock's quest takes him first to a nightclub, where he has discovered in a newspaper clipping that Johnny's fiancée, Coral Chandler, is a torch singer. The nightclub is a place to which he would inevitably have gone on that first desolate night in a strange, hot city, under any circumstances. As he himself muses while sitting alone in his hotel room in the semidarkness, smoking a cigarette and sipping bourbon straight up: "What to do on a hot night, wind smelling of night-blooming jasmine, and nothing to do but sweat and wait and prime the body to sweat some more."

For a guy who especially doesn't trust women, Murdock wastes no time in getting Coral onto the dancefloor and into his arms. The night is steamy, but she's cool as snow. "Cinderella with the husky voice," Murdock calls her. (The same husky voice of the actress Lizabeth Scott that we will hear in *Pitfall* the following year when she plays the seductive model.) And to us, upon taking her in his arms for the first time, Murdock remarks, "Maybe she was all right, and maybe Christmas comes in July, but I don't believe it." He makes a point of telling her that he doesn't trust women. He tries to keep his hard edge intact. But Coral, whom Johnny nicknamed "Dusty," and whom Murdock nicknames "Mike"(!), remains unfazed. As a spider woman/femme fatale, she's right up there with Kathie Moffet in *Out of the Past*. Murdock ought to have stuck to his first impression, as Oscar Wilde advises, for Coral turns out to be cold, unflappable, triply duplicitous, and utterly treacherous. Christmas indeed does not come in July—even in the morally upside-down hothouse of Gulf City.

"Where have we met?" Coral purrs to Murdock as they glide along the dance floor.

His response is memorable. "In another guy's dreams," he replies.

From that exchange on, despite his outward mistrust, grumbling, denial, and wariness, Coral has snared Murdock.

The nightclub is owned by an urbane man named Martinelli—

that devotée of Nietzsche—who is a former gangster. He could be a poster boy, embodying the underside of the postwar boom, for all those noir nightclub owners who are simultaneously "legitimate" and criminal. He bears remarkable similarities to Janoth in *The Big Clock:* he is secretive, greedy, with a mania for control; he keeps an office hideaway upstairs from the nightclub; and not least of all, he employs a trusty and sadistic henchman/bodyguard, named Krause (interesting that he has a German name), who serves as his proxy in the infliction of physical punishment. Martinelli goes so far at one point as to dress down Krause for describing the bloody beating the latter has just inflicted on some enemy of Martinelli's—on the latter's orders! "You know I don't like to hear those things," Martinelli chides him. "Don't bring those things *here*," he goes on, meaning his office. Janoth, who committed a violent murder and plotted endlessly, in his office, how he would frame others for the crime, had no such effete compunctions. Janoth, the tycoon on the boards of museums and charities, had no problem stepping into the muck and mire of homicide; Martinelli, the ex-hoodlum in the tuxedo, is downright phobic on the subject, even while despatching paid killers. While Janoth is almost universally loathed by employees and colleagues alike—and could care less about it—Martinelli is obsessive about his "image" in the community. When Murdock, entangled in Martinelli's affairs, begins to threaten that image, Martinelli reprimands him too: "In a few days you'll manage to tear down what it's taken me years to build up." A familiar enough reproach, but in this case Martinelli is not worried so much about his material possessions as the false edifice of his fabricated identity in Gulf City.

In addition to his admirable reading habits, Martinelli speaks in measured tones with a British accent—never raising his voice—boasts a keen knowledge of the local flora, of European history, and of oenology and all matters culinary. Not formally educated like the criminal Dr. Soberin in *Kiss Me Deadly,* Martinelli has the same proclivity for lecturing others—including the obviously uneducated like Krause, and Murdock himself, for that matter, who for all his surface polish and coolness aspires to "running a fleet of cabs back in Kansas City." Just as Soberin employed Greek mythology, Martinelli packs his punches not with blackjacks but lightning epigrams from

Beyond Good and Evil. "Under peaceful conditions a warlike man sets upon himself." Quite a reproach to toss at a man like Murdock, who has just returned, highly decorated, from the battlefield. Especially when Martinelli has not only avoided action in the war, but also profited from it and grown soft with the good life in the process.

In fact, as in many noir films, the war provides an active subtext throughout *Dead Reckoning.* And Martinelli's nightclub is integral to it. Counterpointing the sacrifice and heroism of Murdock and Johnny is the obvious self-indulgence of Coral, Martinelli, and the regular patrons of the club, who have spent plenty of time there throughout the war years. But in this film the contrast really goes beyond those who took their licks in the trenches and those who stayed home living high off the hog. Martinelli's crowd is not just soft, but rotten. Not only do they not exhibit a modicum of shame, but they actively disdain—and are repelled by—those who, through enlistment or conscription, were drawn into the maelstrom of the war. Martinelli, in fact, makes a point of telling Murdock that he prefers, and prefers to serve his customers, food and liquor "unsoiled" by the war—wines of pre-1939 vintage, for example, and "prewar paté." This is another remarkably crass statement to make to a man obviously "soiled" and scarred in combat.

For Martinelli, who does not like to hear the details of the beatings he orders, it is as if the war had never occurred. And within the hermetic and hedonistic sanctuary of his nightclub, it really never did. Men like Murdock and Johnny, with mud and blood on their feet, bring back the war's commotion and disrupt the social order (as Martinelli defines it) that has evolved in certain quarters during the years of their absence. This is one of the classic noir themes: that the returning vet arrives in the city not just disoriented, and often destined for victimhood, but with his veins and nervous system electrified by the the war's violence. Beneath all the charm and quasi-erudition, Martinelli corrupts and rules through brute force, but Murdock, with his self-sufficient capacity to inflict terrible destruction (he needs no henchman and no gun) poses a far greater threat to Martinelli than the latter's rivals in the world of "legitimate criminals." As Murdock sees it, these rivals are as soft at their cores, after all, as Martinelli.

Murdock has been through the inferno already and was hardened by fire. In the war he lived through ferocious gunfire and conflagrations. With no pretensions to being any tougher—or more hardened—than he actually is, he barely flinches at the likes of Martinelli. Threats, beatings, double-dealing have little effect on Murdock when they're doled out by Martinelli. But Coral's treachery eats at him from within. For despite his frequent asides about the untrustworthiness of women and the folly of romance, Murdock falls for her. And just as he's coming to grips with this, he learns that she's really married to Martinelli!

Dead Reckoning has one of the most tangled plots in all of film noir, but the gist of it, the common denominator to its shifting equations, is that Coral has been "bad medicine" for everyone from day one. She has been Martinelli's wife all along—even when she got mixed up with Johnny before the war. Even when she married, and then murdered, a millionaire named Chandler and with Martinelli's assistance pinned the crime on Johnny. It's Martinelli himself who tells Murdock this when Murdock corners him in his office. Martinelli tells him that, even by his standards, Coral is no good. In this world of warfare and crime and vice, run by and for men, we are to understand that it is *the woman* (and she is practically the only woman in the entire film) who is truly the most sinister, malevolent, and dangerous figure. And certainly the most incendiary.

She is a "torch" singer, remember. And throughout the film, fire is the overriding symbol. Johnny is incinerated behind the wheel of a car. When Murdock learns that Johnny is wanted for Chandler's murder (Coral, of course, feeds him this misinformation), he remarks, apparently without irony, "Why would he have come back here where he was even hotter than the weather?" And finally it is Murdock who employs fire to kill Martinelli when Martinelli pulls a gun on him in that final scene in his office. It is, fittingly enough, a weapon of war that Murdock turns upon Martinelli. No ordinary weapon, but a napalm grenade which he has acquired, along with small arms, from a fellow vet who served in the Pacific campaign and now keeps a modest stockpile (the illegality of it is benignly glossed because this vet, too, was highly decorated for valor) of weapons in his home. So napalm intended for the Japanese a year earlier, and used upon them in the large-scale firebombings that preceded Hiroshima, instead transforms Martinelli's plush office into a charnel house. Martinelli and Krause burn alive—the latter, in a cocoon of flames, diving spectacularly through the picture window—as Murdock ducks out the rear door. He hurries to a waiting car in which Coral is coiled up in the passenger seat—but not before she has taken a shot at him in the darkness, claiming that she was expecting Martinelli to come out that door, not Murdock.

It's too late, though, for her lies because now Murdock knows everything. He tells her so as they speed along the same highway where Johnny went up in flames. "You're going to fry, Dusty," Murdock tells her, employing one last fire image, and—more significantly—dropping his own nickname for her, "Mike," and using Johnny's. It is because of Coral that the three men with whom she has been intimate—Chandler, Johnny, and Martinelli—meet violent deaths, and now Murdock barely escapes becoming the fourth casualty. Realizing that Murdock has her number, Coral shoots him point-blank in the ribs, he floors the accelerator, and they crash into a utility pole. Murdock survives, but Coral, her head swathed in bandages, dies in a hospital bed—with Murdock looking on—in a closing scene unlike any other in film noir, or in any other film genre, for that matter. As Borde and Chaumeton write: "The final image, done in documentary fashion, is that of a parachute which opens and then diminishes in size as it falls. For the first time in the cinema, we have seen death in the first person. The film achieves it by means of a fall into nothingness."

It is a fall for Murdock, as well. What little faith in his fellows he may have retained during the war has been blown to bits by his tortuous dealings with Coral/Dusty/Mike/Mrs. Martinelli. His insistent misogynism—so off-putting and repellant when we first meet him—seems to have been justified. The nasty asides about women become prophetic. What would have happened to him, we may venture to ask, had he *not* held a little of himself—a bitter, but self-preserving nugget—back from Coral? The answer is that he would have "fried," like the others. Unlike, say, Jeff Bailey in *Out of the Past,* Murdock is not just cynical, he's cynical enough to survive—which in the noir world is a crucial distinction. As for Coral, had Murdock, like Martinelli, read Part Four of *Beyond Good and Evil,* he might have served up the following typically misogynistic Nietzschean epigram as her epitaph at film's end before proceeding to Kansas City to pursue his dream of running that fleet of taxis: "In revenge and in love woman is more barbarous than man."

Criss Cross, too, has a blue-collar protagonist mixed up with affluent nightclub types. But Steve Thompson is no former paratrooper with fire in his veins; though fast with his fists, and nimble-witted enough, when it comes to his survival these skills are neutralized by forces beyond his control. From the film's opening scene, a stunning, aerial, panoramic pan of nocturnal Los Angeles that concludes in a nightclub parking lot where Steve Thompson (played by Burt Lancaster) is embracing Anna Dundee (played by Yvonne DeCarlo), we know that Steve is already, irrevocably, under her spell. Anna is the wife of Slim Dundee, the nightclub's owner. Her voice, her eyes, have Steve mesmerized. Whatever else happens to him, his passion for Anna, which will reign supreme, is the force in his life most completely out of his control. He will be consumed, night and day, with Anna in a way Murdock never seemed to be consumed with Coral, even when he fell in love with her. And whatever Steve does, we sense from the first that he will be destroyed by this passion. Dundee is also obsessed with Anna—his obsession fueled not by love, but by toxically pure wells of jealousy—and he, too, will destroy himself on Anna's account. This despite his worldly savvy, his harsher, more penetrating understanding of her, and his criminal's cynicism that far outstrips Murdock's.

In *Dead Reckoning,* we never see Martinelli outside of his nightclub. He is at once self-sufficient and imprisoned. In his private office, among hothouse flowers, he is like a spider at the center of a vast web—his holdings and interests—that radiates out into the city proper. Slim Dundee, on the other hand, is all over town. Expensively dressed, extravagent with money, he cruises Los Angeles in a flashy convertible with an entourage of bodyguards. He travels to Las Vegas on business, with much fanfare. He goes to the track. And he torments Anna, who accompanies him almost everywhere and always appears desperately unhappy while in his presence. At other times, her unhappiness is not so severe, but it never leaves her. Like many femmes fatales, she has a powerful sense of irony, and a sharp analytical faculty, able to anticipate other people's moves well ahead of time like a good chessplayer; but she never displays a sense of humor. Even in her most passionate moments with Steve, she seems joyless, soulless.

It is interesting that both of these nightclub owners, Martinelli and Dundee, for all their power, money, and acquired tastes for fine things, have marriages that are little more than charades. In fact, Martinelli's is a secret marriage—a phantom relationship—during which his wife marries another man and, after being widowed, is prepared to marry yet again. (It's odd that the word "bigamy" is never mentioned in *Dead Reckoning,* as if the other crimes committed diminish it completely.) As for Dundee and Anna, they fight, exchange jibes, taunt one another—usually in his nightclub, to the strains of dance music and the buzz of diners—but we never see them share a meal, a bed, a confidence, or a tender moment of any sort. In fact, we never see Anna in the home that we know she must share with Dundee somewhere in greater Los Angeles. We never hear about such a home. For all ostensible purposes, the nightclub is their family residence—the only place we see them together. Anna crops up in various bars, drugstores, train terminals, and even a pied-à-terre studio in the inner city where she trysts with Steve, but we never glimpse the fancy duplex apartment or sprawling mansion that would be commensurate with Dundee's wealth.

Is there a moral on display in these two films with regard to matrimony? For example, that the noir nightclub owner, shrewd in business (and a pioneer of white-collar crime), is incapable of something so elementary as maintaining a workable marriage—something even the least empowered 1940s petit bourgeois manages to pull off. Martinelli and Dundee, for all their machismo and sureness of touch in manipulating others, are shown to be somewhat less than complete men. Ruled at heart by volatile, out-of-control women, brought to ruin by greed and jealousy, in the end they are both reduced to committing capital crimes with their own hands. After working so long and hard to put insulating layers—hit men, patsies, lackeys, fall guys—between themselves and the crimes by which they have prospered, each finds himself directly implicated as a first-degree murderer.

When *Criss Cross* ends, Dundee is literally standing with a smoking gun over the entwined, bullet-ridden bodies of Anna and Steve while wailing police sirens close in on him in the night. They are in a remote beach house. Through a large window, framing the entire scene, the sea is shimmering a short distance from the house. The water is rippling and very much in flux, in contrast to the triangle comprised of these two men and this woman which has been rendered absolutely static. The three of them are at their terminus. Anna was about to ditch Steve, and he had finally—belatedly—seen through her; but when Dundee corners them, Anna, terrified, literally runs back into Steve's arms. And Dundee, all his jealous fantasies solidified before his eyes at that moment, leers at the two lovers while perversely egging them on. "That's it. Hold her, Steve. Hold her tight." As we have not once seen Dundee hold Anna. And then he sprays them with gunfire. His wife—hair thrown back, face darkly carved by shadows, eyes flashing, never more beautiful—dies in the arms of another man. A man she no longer loves, but with whom, at the moment of death—when all their wrong choices have collapsed in on them—she shares an intimacy that she never experienced with Dundee.

The noir nightclub as an amazingly elaborate, diversely populated, world-unto-itself establishment, with its own social codes and mores, has its cinematic roots in the fantastically baroque casino in the proto–film noir, *The Shanghai Gesture.* Directed by Josef von Sternberg in 1941, *The Shanghai Gesture* was in its way as innovative—if not as brilliant—a film as *Citizen Kane,* released just months earlier. Its impact on film noir was immense.

Born to a middle-class Jewish family in Vienna and raised in Jamaica, Queens, after they emigrated to the United States, von Sternberg had the "von" added to his name by a Hollywood producer who thought it would "look aristocratic" on a movie marquee. Considered one of the most exotic of "European" directors, von Sternberg actually received his essential film training at a small film production company in Fort Lee, New Jersey—advancing from patcher to editor to assistant director—and then in the Army Signal Corps, for which he directed training films in the First World War. After drifting around the Continent and the American hinterlands, he took up his career in Hollywood in 1924 after catching the eye of the film studios with a pioneering and aesthetically stunning documentary, *The Salvation Hunters,* about the lives of the waterfront derelicts on San Pedro Bay, south of Los Angeles. In Hollywood, after several misfires, he directed his breakthrough film, *Underworld,* in 1928. It was the first grittily realistic film depiction of American gangland, and was also unique in that it featured the criminals as heroes—now a commonplace, but back then a revolutionary concept.

Von Sternberg went to Germany in 1930 to direct the first talkie at UFA, then in its heyday as an Expressionist studio, where directors with backgrounds as diverse as Wilder and Hitchcock served apprencticeships. Like Fritz Lang, von Sternberg was one of those directors of Austrian or German descent who made films in Europe that would be seminal to the development of film noir, and later would direct films noirs in Hollywood. The film von Sternberg made in Berlin in 1930 was *The Blue Angel,* a fable of the nightclub if there ever was one, and it forever changed his career. He put Marlene Dietrich into the lead role after discovering her on the Berlin stage, and was responsible not just for launching her career (some characterized him as a Svengali to her Trilby) but for molding her image as a nightclub chanteuse and irresistible seductress, which she refined in subsequent films. Among these are six films (notably, *Blonde Venus, Shanghai Express,* and *The Devil Is a Woman*) that von Sternberg directed when he brought her—the two of them international sensations now—back to Hollywood with him in 1932. What he also brought back were the stylistic influences of his UFA experience, and an almost tactile apprehension, conveyed in his later films, of prewar Berlin and its violent streets and decadent nightlife—the clubs and dancehalls, singers, prostitutes, and criminals, the corrupt politicians and wealthy pleasure-seekers which were all to be staples of film noir.

Throughout his career, von Sternberg marched to his own drummer, professionally and otherwise, and was known to wear knee-high boots, a turban, and a lizard smoking jacket on the set when he worked. Often, in directing, he punctuated his instructions to actors and crew with a whip or a sword, as others might use a baton. He relished pushing the envelope when it came to what the studios would and would not allow on the big screen. He was literate in his tastes and contemptuous of the middlebrow pandering that is the bread and butter of the film industry. Once his association with Dietrich ended, and he began making film adaptations of material like Dostoevsky's *Crime and Punishment,* his honeymoon with the Hollywood studios came to an abrupt halt. Interestingly—but not surprisingly—von Sternberg's career followed an arc similar to that of his fellow pioneer, Orson Welles: after a meteoric rise and then a considerably bumpy long career, von Sternberg later in his life was forced to go abroad again (this time to England, and later even Japan) to raise cash and make films. He ended up embittered and nearly insolvent, though like Welles, he usually managed to live extravagantly, regardless of the state of his bank account. Four years before his death in 1969, he composed his autobiography, a serious book with an absurd title, *Fun in a Chinese Laundry,* which certainly ranks among the most acerbic and insightful books ever written about the film business. But in 1941, having already risen and fallen several times, familiar with vicissitude and with a keen eye for folly and hubris, he was the perfect man to direct *The Shanghai Gesture.*

The film was based on the 1925 Broadway play that went through more than three dozen film treatments, all rejected by the Hays Office, Hollywood's censorship enforcer of the so-called "Production Code" which went into effect in 1934. In their study of censorship and the Code, *The Dame in the Kimono,* Leonard J. Leff and Jerold L. Simmons describe the play as "a controversial amalgam of illegitimacy, miscegenation, white slavery, and murder." Von Sternberg's version, scripted by Jules Furthman, was only approved after undergoing numerous alterations based on Hays Office complaints. For starters, in the play the gigantic casino—a miniature city-within-the-city, a Vanity Fair rife with corruption and depravity—is a brothel whose proprietress is named Mother Goddamn. This was strong stuff at that time, though today the play reads like a tamer, Baroque precursor to Jean Genet's *The Balcony.* In Furthman's screenplay, the brothel is transformed into a gambling casino and Mother Goddamn is rechristened as Mother Gin Sling. But, as Alain Silver has written: "The true nature of Gin Sling's establishment is, in effect, revealed in such early scenes as her 'purchase' of Dixie, a blond playgirl, from the police and culminates in a New Year's auction of women suspended in cages outside the casino. Despite such exotic embellishments or the title disclaimer that 'Our story has nothing to do with the present,' *The Shanghai Gesture* obviously anticipates and has everything to do with the the postwar noir vision. . . ."

The casino is a spectacular, infernal, carnival construction, replete with mezzanines, balconies, floating platforms, secret rooms,
hidden nooks, and triple-tiered stages on which simultaneous entertainments are presented, often at glaring cross-purposes, engender-
ing visual chaos and an unceasing cacophony of voices and music.
Its initial blueprint might have been lifted from Piranesi's *Le Carceri.*
Scenes are shot with characteristic visual élan and with what
Ephraim Katz correctly identifies as von Sternberg's signature devices of "scrims, veils, nets, fog, or smoke between subject and camera." By way of a variety of overhead camera shots (he seems to have
had cameras all over the ceiling), von Sternberg places us at vertiginous, and dangerous, angles from which we feel we are gazing down
into Hell. It is a Hell into which we ourselves might at any second
plummet, a glittery Hell, clearly identified only when one looks beyond the swirl of lights, jewelry, expensive silks, and all the richly
textured commotion at one of the naked faces the camera might mo-
mentarily freeze. They are variously vicious, vengeful, bewildered,
lustful faces, contorted with anguish or electrified by greed, that
seem to have leaped right out of Hogarth or Bosch. Or Dante.

The crowds in *The Shanghai Gesture,* ever pushing, shoving, and
elbowing one another, most resemble the damned in the Fourth Circle of the *Inferno,* the "avaricious and the prodigal," who are condemned for all eternity to claw and butt while shouting and howling
into one another's faces. "Ill-giving and ill-keeping has deprived
them of the bright world . . . For all the gold that is beneath the
moon/or ever was, could not give rest to a single one/of these weary
souls." (Canto VII, 58 & 64–66). At the hub of the casino, the hub of
all transactions financial, social, and sexual in this hermetic world, is
an enormous roulette wheel which spins and spins. Through the entire film it never stops spinning. It is a wheel of fortune (and it is for
reviling and attempting to bypass Lady Fortune, herself in Paradise,
that the damned have earned their admission into the Fourth Circle)
and at the same time a grimly deterministic wheel of fate. In evening
dress, cramped and crowded on the surrounding tiers that spiral upward in the smoky darkness, the lost souls of the casino have fixed
their gazes upon the wheel as fervidly as ancient men gazed upon
the sun and the moon.

Whether the denizens of the casino are glitterati or decadents, merchants of flesh or of munitions, debauchers or debauchees, the casino is their temple, and the casino is the World. Overseen by a pimp named Goddamn. Where souls are bartered. And the games of chance include suicide and murder. And the house *always* wins. Stripped of pretensions, possessions, and dignity, these habitués of the first (and most all-encompassing) noir nightclub discover that when their resources—of body and spirit, as well as all money, jewels, and other collateral they may have held upon entering the casino—are exhausted, they are despatched into the night, into the other city, the *real* city in which the casino is nestled, that we have all but forgotten about during the course of the film. The real city which is also the fallen city of film noir, where all the casino's dynamics apply with a vengeance.

Which brings us to the most perfectly realized noir nightclub of all: the casino in *Gilda* (1946). Not a gargantuan construction, this casino is on the contrary a sleek, mysterious space in which the city-within-the-city and the "real" city have meshed; the casino is emblematic of the city in which it is located, but we do not lose sight—as we are meant to do in *The Shanghai Gesture*—of the fact that there is a city on the outside. While von Sternberg tried to achieve this balance in *Macao* (a film built around a gambling house owned by a drug smuggler), produced in 1952 twelve years after *The Shanghai Gesture,* it is *Gilda,* directed by Charles Vidor early in the classic film noir cycle, that is by far the more successful and evocative film.

Vidor, a Hungarian expatriate and First World War veteran, was yet another director who came to Hollywood by way of UFA, where he cut his teeth as an assistant director in the "street films" of the early 1920s after taking his degree at the University of Berlin. That he should have directed *Gilda,* in which he created a masterpiece, is an oddity for two reasons: one, Vidor never before, and never afterward, directed another film noir, or even a film that raised peripherally the issues with which noir films dealt; two, *Gilda* is one of the most erotic, psychologically probing, and eccentric films to come out of Hollywood in the 1940s, and though Vidor was a polished director, nothing else in his career would have led us to expect him to deal with such material with panache and subtlety.

Except for a handful of scenes, all the action in *Gilda* transpires in the casino owned by a man named Ballen Mundson. In his late fifties, Mundson is suave and urbane, and extremely formal in his manners and gestures. Like Martinelli in *Dead Reckoning,* he dresses impeccably and speaks with erudition. Like Martinelli and Slim Dundee, he is crooked—but on a far grander scale. His criminal interests involve not a single city, but an entire world market. The nature of his real business, the cash cow behind the casino, is at first murky, but eventually we learn that with the war over for barely a year he is fronting for an international tungsten cartel controlled by former Nazi officials who have escaped Europe. These Nazis see this cartel as the first step, politically and financially, in a wide-ranging plan to rise to power again from the ashes of the war.

There are numerous examples of this theme in film noir, fueled by public paranoia, as well as justifiable political concerns in the postwar years. For one thing, wartime propaganda in the United States—not least of all in films—had been all too effective, painting the Axis powers as awesome, nearly invulnerable, foes. People just couldn't believe at first that the war was really over, that the fascist empires of Japan and, especially, Germany, had been eradicated to their roots and their leaders brought to justice and taken out of circulation. And they were right. For every war criminal tried at Nuremberg, dozens of others escaped Germany and assumed new identities in other European countries, in South America or, as we continue to learn today, in the United States, where many (their true identities no secret to the authorities) were recruited by the C.I.A. for espionage or scientific work in the nascent Cold War.

Gilda is one of a troika of films noirs released in late 1945 and early 1946 set in Rio de Janeiro and that most labyrinthine of cities ("very large, sprawling, and almost endless," as Borges described it), Buenos Aires. With its long identical streets, crisscrossing alleys, ornate stone buildings with cage elevators, whitewashed walls that can run for miles, and enormous vacant lots, Buenos Aires serves as a highly effective and often surreal stand-in, atmospherically and thematically, for the American noir city. The other two films are *Cornered,* directed by Edward Dmytryk, and *Notorious,* directed by Alfred Hitchcock. In the former, the cabal of former Nazis is plotting resurrection around political subversion and disinformation campaigns in the war-weary Western democracies (referred to as "rotten fruit" by their new "führer"); in the latter, a group of wealthy Nazi officials and businessmen are also involved in a cartel, this time involving enriched uranium (the film was shot in the months after Hiroshima) which they are hoarding on the world market.

In *Gilda,* Mundson projects an icy persona. Always rigidly in control of himself—and of others—he is humorless, dictatorial, and ruthlessly efficient. His sexuality is perverse and cruel. Among his personal quirks is his ebony walking stick, which he calls his "little friend"; when he releases a catch in the stick's knob, a stiletto blade slides out the end of the stick, and the "little friend" has turned into a rapier. (And do we need Freud here to tell us, as he does in *The Interpretation of Dreams,* that "men . . . are in the habit of fondly referring to their genital organs as 'little man'"?) If one were going to set out to create a persona that would conjure a sophisticated and lethal Nazi to the postwar film audience, Mundson would be the model. And even before his politics are revealed, we see him as perhaps the coldest fish in all of film noir. And that's pretty cold, indeed.

Here's Mundson: hair slicked back, lips tightly compressed, spine stiff, and the skin drawn so tautly over his face that the underlying bones would seem to be sculptured of ice. On one side, his face is slashed from ear to mouth with a sword scar. His head is skull-like—a medieval death's head atop a body in formal dress (always)—and his manner is reptilian, swift and precise. While framing him in the darkest of shadows, Vidor illuminates him in an arctic light in nearly all his scenes—so white as to be sepulchral. Indeed, Mundson's casino, which appears to have no windows onto the outside world, is like a tomb. That world, like a hothouse city enwrapping the casino, seems to be one of torrid appetites, decadence, sexual ferocity, and barely repressed violence. And into the casino it sends daily, hourly, round-the-clock, a milling, ever-changing stream of humanity. Yet despite this frantic, exotic, carnival (indeed, at one crucial point in the film, it *is* Carnival) crowd, gathered around the gambling tables, congregating on the dancefloor, at the bar, and on plush sofas in the anterooms, the casino remains a tomb, its operations closely supervised by Mundson, with patrons and employees alike forever under his cold eye.

Literally so, as some of them know. For the casino does have internal windows—rows of them along the walls of Mundson's mezzanine office that seem to be suspended at the very center of things—with louvred steel shutters (rather than venetian blinds) that are both bullet- and soundproof. By opening the slats of these shutters, sometimes no more than an inch, he commands a panoramic view of the casino's interior. And he can manipulate, with an elaborate control panel, the lights and sound in the casino's various salons and chambers, as well as their whirling wheels, fountains, and dazzling chandeliers.

At the core of *Gilda* is an adulterous triangle; the casino serves as the Cartesian grid upon which that triangle shifts, contracts, expands, and ultimately spins out of control. The points of the triangle are Mundson, his stunning young wife Gilda, and her (unknown to Mundson) former lover, Johnny Farrell, an itinerant young gambler whom Mundson has hired as his major domo after rescuing him—with assistance from the "little friend"—from a street tough whom Johnny has just cheated at craps with a pair of loaded dice. "Three of us with no pasts," Mundson asserts the first time the three of them sit down together at the casino. Yet at some unspecified juncture in the recent past, Johnny and Gilda were apparently lovers who parted bitterly in some other (American) city. Shortly after Johnny's arrival in Buenos Aires, Mundson goes off on a "business trip," and returns with Gilda—from their honeymoon. From the first, Gilda begins taunting Johnny, which mystifies Mundson and arouses his jealousy. She spends much of her time at the casino. Mundson is there nearly all the time. And Johnny literally lives at the casino, in an elaborate bedroom (formerly Mundson's) with a private bath adjoining Mundson's crow's nest of an office suite!

So claustrophobic and complete is the world of the casino in the characters' lives that there are only a few scenes in the film which occur outside of it. Johnny makes a few brief visits to Mundson's house; once we see him in a hotel room; otherwise, we can count on the fingers of one hand the number of (even briefer) exterior scenes he has in greater Buenos Aires: a small airstrip; a courthouse's entrance; a hotel's; Mundson's garden courtyard; and a street corner (the floating crap game that opens the film).

Rita Hayworth's two greatest roles were the leads in *The Lady from Shanghai* and *Gilda*. As Andrew Britton notes in his essay on the former, "If *The Lady from Shanghai* is a misogynistic film, *Gilda* is a film *about* misogyny. Both Johnny and Ballen desire Gilda and wish to possess her, but her sexuality appalls as much as it attracts them because they experience it as an irresistibly powerful, independent force which generates intensities of feeling that they cannot master . . . one of *Gilda*'s most fascinating themes the perverse bonding of male sexual rivals united by their common hatred of the woman they both want. . . ."

Mundson is played by George Macready, interestingly enough, for in *The Big Clock* Macready also played Earl Janoth's urbane right-hand man, a kind of silken henchman who actually becomes an accessory to the murder of Janoth's mistress. In *Gilda,* Mundson oversees his casino with the same mixture of paranoia and vindictiveness we saw in Janoth, the tyrant of his own office building, with its enormous world clock, its army of security guards, and an array of technological controls with which he could manipulate employees and visitors alike. And Johnny has now become the silken henchman to Mundson. Whereas Janoth as a neurotic tyrant conjured up images of Hitler, Mundson is in reality a Nazi sympathizer. Again, it is as if the war, and the looming shadows of dictators both fascist and communist, had utterly recast Americans' notions of villainy, gangsterism, and corruption. What was the big-city crime boss of Prohibition and the gangland 1930s in the eyes of an American of the postwar era compared to what he had seen of Hitler, Mussolini, and Tojo, and to what he was still seeing of Stalin and Mao? It is not simply that Janoth and Mundson share dictatorial natures (as in the context of conventional character flaws), but that they embody an ethos of raw power, megalomania, and cold-blooded vengefulness which would seem to indicate that *control,* iron-fisted and absolute, has become their sole raison d'être. Control over their businesses, their associates, wives and lovers, competitors public and private—everyone around them, in other words, from intimates to underlings. Only to someone who had been a Rip van Winkle over the previous decade would they not conjure up the still palpable ghosts of the Axis dictators and the ascendent Cold War bosses of Eastern Europe.

So we have a totalitarian casino. A casino which, in the broadest sense, doubles as an office building, representing a hybrid of our two prime locales in the noir city. A casino at the beginning (1946) of the film noir cycle that prefigures all subsequent noir nightclubs. Suspended by a slender thread at its dark heart there is a toxic love triangle. Two expatriate Americans, a man and a woman, are being manipulated and are in turn manipulating—and torturing—one another. In their conversation, the word "hate" crops up more than "love." In this regard, Mundson sets the tone early on for all that is to come: "Hate can be a very exciting emotion," he says to Gilda. "Haven't you noticed that? Hate is the only thing that has ever warmed me." Then Johnny, in a voice-over, tell us: "I hated her so I couldn't get her out of my mind for a minute. She was in the air I breathed and the food I ate." And to Gilda he says: "Statistics show that there are more women in the world than anything else—except insects." And Gilda taunts Johnny: "I hate you so much that I would even destroy myself to take you down with me." Later, in her best bedroom voice, *in* her bedroom, she whispers to Johnny, echoing Mundson, "Hate is a very exciting emotion. Haven't you noticed? Very exciting. I hate you, too, Johnny. I hate you so much that I think I'm going to die from it. Yes, I think I'm going to die from it." All of this while they are locked in a hellish, extended minuet—pulling and pushing at one another, teasing, reviling, but never giving an inch.

Between the two of them, the young couple, there is an asexual man. White-haired, a father figure, a man without scruples. The casino is hermetic. Suffocating. It is an extension—and an emblem—of Mundson himself. As Gilda dresses the first night she is to go to the casino, he tells her solemnly, "Look your best, my beautiful. This will be the casino's first look at you." A man completely sealed off. A totalitarian state unto himself, with closed borders. Whose greatest excitement—if we are to believe him—comes in drawing others in and then sealing them off as well. In a scene in their bedroom, a husband-and-wife scene, Gilda is wearing a negligée and they are backdropped by their bed, piled high with pillows; it is apparently a bed prepared, not for lovemaking, but for suffocation. And Mundson says to her: "You're very excited about something tonight, my beautiful. Perhaps it's in the air. Perhaps you shouldn't have opened the window. Close it. There. See how quiet it is now? See how easily one can shut away excitement? Just by closing a window. Remember that, Gilda." Curiously, he makes a similar reference when speaking of his "little friend," the walking stick with the concealed blade: "It is silent when I wish it to be silent; it speaks when I want it to speak."

Entrapped, Gilda tries to use the casino to exact her revenge. She makes it her stage. First she flirts with other men, then dances with them, and finally begins picking them up in order to torment her tormentors, Johnny and Mundson. She manages to slip away briefly and returns with her hair wet—from "a midnight swim." Unknown to Mundson, but not to Johnny, who has to go fetch her, she has rendezvous with other men at hotels. Later, in a culmination of sorts, she takes over the floor show at the casino and, in a low-cut black dress and elbow-length black gloves (an outfit the art director appropriated from the painting of "Madame X" by John Singer Sargent), she dances and sings a song called "Put the Blame on Mame"—full of double-entendres with regard to her plight. This is another curiosity: as Richard Dyer points out, Gilda is the only femme fatale in film noir to dance onstage. However, when Gilda begins to do a striptease, Johnny has her dragged off the stage. Then he hauls her into a private office and slaps her. In fact, from the first, at each stage of her attempted rebellion, Mundson dispatches Johnny, this film's silken henchman, to reel her in. In this topsy-turvy world, it somehow makes sense that the jilted lover becomes the accessory of the cuckolded husband. Until, finally, he steps into the husband's shoes.

When Mundson spies Johnny embracing Gilda (in fact, it is the one and only time in the film that Johnny has dropped his mask of hatred and kissed her after bringing her home from one of her trysts), Mundson fakes his own death and disappears. And then Johnny replaces him, in all respects: following the dictates of Mundson's will, he takes over management of the casino and the tungsten cartel. And—something *not* in the will—he marries Gilda after sweet-talking her and professing his love. Then he rents her a plush apartment in which he has hung an icy portrait of Mundson. Imprisoning her as Mundson did, but with far greater effectiveness. Johnny never visits her, and though she is free to go out, he arranges things so that Buenos Aires itself becomes "her own private prison." She is literally a prisoner now. She can flirt, and dance, but every tryst, every dinner date, is broken up by one of Johnny's own henchmen. Bewildered, she pleads with him for an explanation—and she gets it, straight to the jaw. This is her punishment, he tells her bitingly, for deceiving Mundson. The dead father. "She wasn't faithful to him when he was alive," Johnny intones in the voice-over, "but she was going to be faithful to him now that he was dead."

When she does run away, to Montevideo, securing work as a singer and dancer in another nightclub, Johnny hires a man, a deceptively kind man with a milk-and-honey voice who poses as an affluent lawyer, to pick her up. The man promises that he will help her secure an annulment of her marriage and then will marry her himself. She returns to Buenos Aires with this man and checks into a hotel; as they enter their room, the hired man backs away and, bewildered once more, Gilda finds Johnny sitting calmly in an armchair. He tells her that she'll never get away from him and that he'll never allow her to get involved with another man. Her punishment will be interminable. And, breaking down finally, dissolving in tears, she pounds his chest with her fists and then sinks to the floor, to her knees, crumpling in on herself. This is the real end of the long danse macabre that was their romance. "You wouldn't think one woman could marry two insane men in one lifetime, now would you?" she cries to him.

Trapped in their tight private hell, Gilda and Johnny are oblivious to the fact that events around them have spun out of control. The complex web of Mundson's affairs, in which the two Americans were so caught up, has evaporated under police scrutiny. Detectives have unraveled his criminal activities and closed down the casino. The tungsten cartel has been shattered. The casino's income, and the cartel's, which of course was supporting Gilda and Johnny, has been cut off. In the end, after the tumult of the police investigation, the two of them find themselves alone at the casino bar. At first, they are still estranged, changed out of their formal casino attire of tuxedo and gown to which we have grown accustomed: he is wearing a plain business suit, she a simple traveling dress. They are pale, weary. Everything about them has been toned down. She is about to leave Buenos Aires for the United States. In the casino, it is after hours for the last time. For good. The roulette wheels have stopped spinning. Sheets have been thrown over the long crap tables and the round, felt-covered tables where the ladies in white gloves and the men with slicked-back hair played chemin de fer. The crowds of revellers have all left. The bandleader and his musicians, the croupiers and dealers, the waiters, cigarette girls, and shoeshine boys, the bouncers and attendants, the gamblers and the jigolos, the seducers and the lovesick, the exhibitionists and the voyeurs, the barflies and the freeloaders—the whole gaudy, floating population of the casino—they're all gone. The denizens of this particular outpost of Vanity Fair have folded their wares in the dead of night and glided on to another casino or nightclub.

Behind the bar, the washroom attendant—Gilda's one friend among the casino's employees—offers her a drink, "ambrosia for a goddess," he says. But Gilda refuses with a weak smile; she doesn't feel like a goddess. On her barstool she is humming her song, the one that says we ought to put the blame on her—but in a sad, subdued cadence now, without the bite, but not without irony. Johnny hesitates awkwardly at the end of the bar, fumbling with a matchbook. All the rancorous exchanges, the charged, passionate innuendo, the talk of hate are gone. She stops humming and gazes vacantly into the mirror behind the bar. He stares at his hands. The darkness seems to be closing in on them from all sides. The mirror before them, too, is darkening.

What happens next is a post-mortem effect. A tacked-on thing. Mundson returns suddenly, furious at losing the casino, his control of the cartel, his wife. He has been biding his time as a man who is legally dead, preparing to reappear on his own terms. And now there are no terms at all, much less terms of his own. He has nothing to return to. No casino. No Gilda. No power. So he surprises Gilda and Johnny, who only realize he is back when they see the steel shutters on his mezzanine office open and close quickly, as if the casino itself—those windows its eyes—has come to life again temporarily. Of course Mundson is bent on revenge. More blanched than ever, clothed to the chin in black, like the Grim Reaper, he emerges from his office, brandishing, sickle-like, his "little friend." He lays it on the bar and pulls out a pistol, with which, he says, he is going to kill Gilda and Johnny. His wife and son. His son and daughter. Considering all the raw animal energy they have exhibited, Gilda and Johnny remain strangely vacant, drained, backing away from him slowly. On the inside, resigned to death. And then, from offstage, unseen to us, the washroom attendant steps out of his role as a bit player and impales Mundson from behind with the lethal walking stick. And suddenly Gilda and Johnny, stepping away from death's door, are free to go. Back to America. Together.

An ending that is like a detour.

Mundson might have killed Gilda—the logical, and tragic, denouément for this woman whom these two men, in concert and independently, had seemed so hellbent on destroying. Or Mundson might have shot Gilda and Johnny, and then shot himself. Exploding the triangle. And the three of them would have sprawled out dead in the ashes of the closed-down casino, at the farthest reach of a dead end down which they had been plunging from the moment their lives converged.

The latter variation is how Orson Welles might have ended the film, much as he ended *The Lady from Shanghai,* which he directed in 1948. The wife in that film, also played by Rita Hayworth (Welles' own wife at the time!) dies violently with her husband, an older man, a cripple, in an amusement park after hours: the two of them in the Funhouse, in a room composed of mirrors, shoot one another to death—shattering mirror after mirror, false image after false image, man and wife indistinguishable from the countless images each projects and reflects, until they both collapse bloodied, bullet-torn. It is one of the greatest scenes in all of film. An archetypal scene in the mythology of film noir. (Camille Paglia refers to Rita Hayworth in this scene as "the siren of the labyrinth" in a "hall of mirrors.") The younger man, the wife's lover (played by Welles himself), a witness to this double murder, escapes and flees the Funhouse (falling through trapdoors, sliding down ramps, tripping over himself) and runs into the dawn. *The Lady from Shanghai* is itself—with all its twists and turns and its perverse, revolving sexual/marital triangle—a mirror-image (from a funhouse mirror) of *Gilda.*

I would posit a different ending altogether for *Gilda.* Truer. Faithful to the world of the casino. We have to go back a few steps. To Johnny and Gilda, still sitting vacantly, apart, at the bar. In limbo. Lit, separately, as Hopper might have painted them. The world of the casino—the world-within-a-world—has closed down, and the two star-crossed lovers have closed down with it. All their vitality, and negative energy, spent. Their true—and fullest—passion unconsummated. Fully resigned to death.

They would remain there, the prototypical noir couple in the deserted nightclub who will reappear, undergoing subtle metamorphoses, in countless subsequent films. The darkness closing in on them from all sides. The mirror before them darkening, too, and swallowing their images. Leaving only the darkness.

5. Grafters, Grifters, and Tycoons

Money.

In the noir city, the essential triangle—the building blocks beneath every foundation—is corruption, power, and politics. And at the triangle's center is always money.

Oswald Spengler writes: "The city means not only intellect, but money." And as Marshall McLuhan explains, "Not only do crowds of people and piles of money strive toward increase, but they also breed uneasiness about the possibility of disintegration and deflation. This two-way movement of expansion and deflation seems to be the cause of the restlessness of crowds and the uneasiness that goes with wealth. [Elias] Canetti spends a good deal of analysis on the psychic effects of the German inflation after the First World War. The depreciation of the citizen went along with that of the German mark." The lifeblood of the postwar American city, which rapidly loses its manufacturing base, is money. Paper money and its myriad offshoots—securities, bonds, contracts, IOUs—that create the endlessly crisscrossing paper trails of banking, finance, and law that might fill an atlas full of maps. Paper with which to construct speculative houses of cards. To entrap the powerless with interest. To pervert the political process, which determines who will be powerless and who won't.

Norman O. Brown in *Life Against Death* states that "the connection between money thinking and rational thinking is so deeply ingrained in our practical lives that it seems impossible to question it. . . . The money complex is the demonic . . . the heir to and substitute for the religious complex, an attempt to find God in things." He

151

goes on to set forth the relationship between money and the city: "Money is the heart of the new accumulation complex; the capacity of money to bear interest is its energy; its body is that fundamental institution of civilized man, the city. The archeologists note the complete rupture with the previous style of life which marks the foundations of the first cities. Heichelheim showed that the institution of interest-bearing capital is the key to this abrupt reorganization. . . . What then is a city? A city reflects the new masculine aggressive psychology of revolt against the female principles of dependence and nature. . . . The Iron Age, at the end of which we live, democratized the achievements of the Bronze Age (cities, metals, money, writing) and opened up the pursuit of kings (money and immortality) to the average citizen." A pursuit that Brown equates with the pursuit of death, in which "the real actuality of life" passes into "dead things." Money, which doubles for "the immortality of an estate or a corporation" or a city. Spengler says outright that the twentieth-century city *"denies* all Nature," and sees in it "a metaphysical turn towards death." To which Mumford adds that "the metropolis is rank with forms of *negative vitality.* Nature and human nature, violated in this environment, come back in destructive forms. . . . In this mangled state, the impulse to live departs from apparently healthy personalities. The impulse to die supplants it."

The first city is a "cathedral city," which, as the economist W. Sombart said, "is a settlement of men who for their sustenance depend on agricultural labor which is not their own." Hence, the temple buildings that dominate those (and all) cities are what Brown calls "monuments of guilt." A city is itself, "like money, crystallized guilt," he says. And quotes Frank Lloyd Wright: "To look at the plan of a great City is to look at something like the cross-section of a fibrous tumor."

The city, historically and mythically, has always been centered around an axis of gold and silver, of precious metals and gems (which in ancient Rome were the inherent property of Pluto, god of the dead—and of riches), and then that paper currency underwritten by a national treasury, which is the ultimate (metaphorical) temple building. Mammon has always been a city-dweller. As President Jefferson knew. Fearing the urbanization of America, he foresaw the noir city and stated unequivocally that if Americans were to build up cities as centers of wealth on the European scale, the cities "would be infinitely larger and infinitely more infernal."

But let's hear what some of the citizens of the noir city have to say for themselves about money, for which they have a slew of epithets, from dough, lettuce, and cabbage to moolah, juice, and scratch:

"Money. You know what that is. The stuff you never have enough of. Little green things with George Washington's picture that men slave for, commit crimes for, die for. It's the stuff that has caused more trouble in the world than anything else ever invented. Simply because there's too little of it." *(Detour)*

"To me a dollar was a dollar in any language." *(Gilda)*

"Every extra buck has a meaning all its own." *(Pickup on South Street)*

"You'll never make money, you're a two-bit guy." *(Gun Crazy)*

"Love rather than money is the root of all evil." *(Conflict)*

"He left me with two things: debts and beautiful memories." *(The Sleeping City)*

"Is that you . . . that nice expensive smell?" *(Murder, My Sweet)*

"What was it I asked myself—a piece of paper crawling with germs." *(Detour)*

"Money isn't dirty, just people." *(Pushover)*

Yes, and maybe money can clean them up.

Kenneth Rexroth, the poet and critic, made the astounding observation that in Daniel Defoe's *Moll Flanders,* published in 1720, there is not a single page on which some reference to money, in one form or another, large or small—sums, transactions, negotiations, reckonings—is not made. In a novel usually categorized as "lusty" or "bawdy," its heroine's name a synonym for licentiousness, the narrative—her story—is truly driven, not by sex, but hard cash. As Rexroth asserts, Defoe presents us with the "most authentic portrait of a prostitute" in English literature superimposed upon a scathingly detailed critique of capitalist morality—"the morality of the complete whore and that of the new middle class, which was rising around him." The world of Defoe's novel is mercantile London, a city about which the author possessed a unique understanding, for in his own life he was both a wildly successful businessman and an abject debtor. Defoe's London, according to Rexroth, is a place in which "all values are reduced to price and all morality to the profitable. Love is replaced by mutually profitable contractual relationships, which are worked out in actuarial detail even when they are illegal. Money is not something with which to buy sex and other sensual gratifications; on the contrary, sex is something to be bartered with shrewdness for as much money as it will bring."

While it is only one aspect of the noir city, where passion, lust, and love certainly thrive on their own terms and with their own dark permutations, the monetary ethos of Defoe's London—and its manifestations in human affairs: greed, covetousness, duplicity, self-delusion, and so on—certainly finds a home in film noir. Power equals Money equals Power is one bit of urban algebra that the noir city's population seems to know by rote. Money, the lifeblood of the city, is necessarily a central issue in all noir films, whether they be preoccupied with crimes of the streets or of the heart. The themes around money vary, from the hardscrabble plight of the urban poor, to the ascendent (or, increasingly, descendent) material preoccupations of the middle class, to the moral and financial imbroglios of the rich, but, as in *Moll Flanders,* the emphasis remains constant.

In post-Depression America, the noir city mirrors both the corrosive and the liberating influences of money on the society at large. In the city, in circular fashion, "currency" indeed means both the money supply and "the quality or state of being current" (Webster's), as in "being prevalent at the moment," that is, "dominant"—as in how much clout does one credibly wield. Backed up by what assets, how much cash, and—not to be diminished—what status symbols. When you go up or down the scale—*do, re, mi* or *do, ti, la*—you always end up back at *do.* This notion is reinforced daily in the city by the rough and tumble exigencies of making a living, perchance even *thriving,* and by the daily onslaught of advertising, public relations, and all the other effluvia of the entertainment industry which, with their thousands of direct or subliminal inducements to mass consumerism and a mass (anesthetized) sensibility, serve as satellites to the fixed constellation of power, status, and wealth.

Advertising, especially, has a volatile and dislocating influence in the postwar years when it leaps from billboards and radiowaves onto the far more powerful, and insidious, television screen. Using pseudo-art and other tools of deception, like sports personalities and other celebrities who clearly have no use for the product they are hawking (the aerobically taut model puffing a cigarette, the million-aire boxer shilling for a roach-killer company), advertising in its postwar boom becomes a scrambler of daily life: selling what is useless, harmful, or unaffordable, glamorizing the mundane, making *itself* a staple of modern life while diminishing the real staples of human sustenance, material as well as spiritual. As McLuhan notes: "The advertising industry is a crude attempt to extend the principles of automation to every aspect of society," so that, "instead of presenting a private argument or vista, it offers a way of life that is for everybody or nobody." It is a truism that advertising incites you to acquire what you don't need—to fill your life, literally, with everything money can buy, even if it is on credit, with back-breaking interest.

For long stretches in film noir it is not difficult to imagine the city as a sea of money, with currents, crosscurrents, and undercurrents, amazing depths and the barest shallows, safe harbors for the affluent, treacherous reefs to decimate the poor, and a whole range of ebbs and flows, tempests and tidal waves, predictable and otherwise, for everyone in between.

In the noir city, art works are frequently used to indicate the privileged financial lives of their owners. Objets d'art are often backdropped by a window that showcases the twinkling, diamond lights of the cityscape, which is meant to highlight the fact that the art works are emblems of the treasures the city has to offer. These treasures can take many forms: precious coins *(The Brasher Doubloon);* priceless jade *(Murder, My Sweet);* rare books *(The Big Sleep);* and exotic Native American artifacts *(The Leopard Man)*. Often, prized collections of gems, coins, stamps, or rare bric-a-brac are caressed and manipulated by their owners in the same way he or she caresses and manipulates people. For example, in *Sweet Smell of Success* the paintings, tapestries, and statuary strewn around a lavish penthouse mean no more to their owner, a ruthless public relations maven, than the gaudier emblems of his wealth—cars, personal jewelry, expensive liquor—and maybe even less; "I don't even like the stuff," he assures a visitor, nodding toward the Cezanne that adorns the wall over his fireplace.

The noir city is full of high art and its imitations—the real thing, that is, and the flotsam and jetsam of kitsch which wash up on our shores. Kitsch, in fact—not just imitations, but blatantly exploitative, low quality art and the ever-evolving art of forgery—is a high-growth industry in the postwar city. Fine art as a status symbol for the nouveau riche is still an emergent phenomenon in the postwar years, and a suspect one at that, in light of the United States' long-standing (still evident) anti-intellectualism, nativist tendencies, and general distrust of the artist and his productions. Artistic influences from abroad are often treated with hostility in film noir—as malignant influences. During the McCarthy era, the McCarran Act, which could block practically any foreign visitor from entering the United States on "political grounds," was invoked in alarming frequency to deny visas to writers, painters, and musicians. Artists in film noir are routinely presented as dangerous subversives or disgruntled radicals—though they rarely seem to be driven by coherent political philosophies. Notions of "radicalism" or "foreign influences" aside, in the films the presentation of art boils down to the following: the viability of art for the masses; the democratization of art appreciation (after liberating the Europeans from the forces of their own barbarism in the war, some of the films imply, why should Americans, especially those Americans who fought the war, feel less worthy than a Frenchman, much less a German or Italian, to enjoy the highbrow arts of those countries?); art as a sophisticated means of social climbing (through the knowledge, or acquisition, of art works); and art as an educational tool or recreational device.

More intimately fascinating than the implications of private acquistion and public appreciation of art works is the series of women's portraits, painted by highly skilled professional artists—sometimes even inspired ones—that runs through film noir. Often these paintings take on lives of their own, as important as the characters they depict. In *Laura,* for example, the heroine's portrait dominates her apartment; when she is believed to be dead, the portrait haunts the other characters, infuses their dreams, gazes down on them reproachfully, and even determines the course of the plot. Then, when Laura reappears alive, she somehow pales beside the portrait, which remains a more dominant image than the woman herself. The film's principal male characters are her two lovers; the first, whom she spurns, is her would-be murderer; the second, whom she embraces, is the investigating detective. Both men invest the portrait with fantasties and visions to which Laura refuses to conform upon her return. And it is at that point that the film's greatest turmoil begins; even after the climax, in the final shot of the film, the camera comes to rest, not on Laura herself, but on her portrait. In *Night and the City*, Helen Nosseross is coldly ambitious, destructive, and scornful of her husband, but he keeps an idealized portrait of her over his desk which he gazes at longingly, and lovingly, especially at the times of greatest stress in their marriage. In *The Blue Dahlia*, the glowing, smiling portrait of the hero's unfaithful, dissipated wife is central to the plot; folded into the back of its frame is a posthumous message which, after her murder, changes the course of the hero's life. And in *The Big Heat*, Mike Lagana, the immensely wealthy racketeer who has an entire city under his thumb, keeps a huge, idealized portrait of his mother in his home library, behind the desk from which he directs his crime empire.

Lagana's library is also filled with statuary and objets d'art, just as Laura's apartment is. In fact, in *Laura*, Otto Preminger spends a good deal of time panning across a series of immaculate glass shelves (the film opens with such a pan) filled with objets d'art in an elegant, coolly lit alcove of a very expensive New York apartment. Similarly, when we are introduced to her spurned lover, the radio personality, renowned columnist, and wealthy raconteur Waldo Lydecker (who writes, he informs us, "with a pen dipped in poison"), Lydecker takes us—remaining off-camera while the camera pans his opulent digs—on a tour of his apartment, past paintings under glass, ivory statuettes, and "rare Chinese porcelains of the Sung Dynasty," which concludes in his Roman-sized bathroom where we find him (on-camera finally) reclining in a huge marble tub with a marble shelf across the middle where he is rattling off his daily column on a typewriter. There is a cup of oolong tea in a delicate cup (antique, of course) beside the typewriter, and from the corner his voice suddenly pipes up on the radio, declaiming the column he wrote (in that very tub) the previous day. Lydecker and Laura lead privileged lives, financially and socially, and the art works they possess are constantly in view, and handled throughout the film, to remind us of this fact.

Crack-Up is a key film in the noir cycle with regard to the themes of art and money. The film itself—visually—is highly stylized. Much of it is shot at the Metropolitan Museum in Manhattan. The hero, George Steele, is a vocal proponent of art for the masses—he wants to open up the museum to the people. (His heart may be in the right place, but he is also one of those film noir characters who feels he must go out of his way to denigrate any and all examples of abstract expressionism; if it isn't representational, it's open to ridicule, he tiredly insists.) Pitted against Steele and his egalitarian efforts is a group of powerful collectors who are replacing masterpieces with forgeries and hoarding the originals or "renting them out" for profit. (During the war, Steele used his skills as an art detective to turn up Nazi forgeries—also created, by the Nazi brass, for hoarding or profit.) The process by which these forgeries are created, called "narcosynthesis," is also a byproduct of atomic research during the war—an abuse of the very same technology used to create the atomic bomb. And the means by which Steele exposes the forgeries is the X ray—a technique he developed and patented during the war. Both techniques, then—the one used to produce forgeries and the other to expose them—are radioactive, and both are linked to the war. And there is the obvious parallel between the forgery gang's methods (they're willing to kidnap, torture, and kill adversaries) and the Nazis', whose methods and ethos, it is implied once again, survive the war. Even in this film, shot between December 1945 and February 1946, within six months of Hiroshima—a film ostensibly about art and corruption among a sophisticated urban elite whose ringleader is a crooked psychiatrist (like Dr. Soberin in *Kiss Me Deadly*)—the themes of the war's cataclysmic end and the moral bankruptcy underlying the Atomic Age are lurking just beneath the surface.

Of course, one unshakable axiom in film noir, as in so-called real life, is that crime pays. Not all the time, but enough of the time so that it continues to be a worthwhile pursuit, with its own highly specialized professional class. Confidence men, embezzlers, and extortionists, thieves and fences, hijackers and safecrackers are all staples of the noir city. As are crooked lawyers, bribed inspectors, cops on the take, corrupt union bosses, and amoral tycoons.

But first and foremost there are the racketeers. They comprise the core of the criminal population, which is a highly liquid one; in film noir, despite the apparently black-and-white issues of guilt and innocence that abound, the line between criminals and honest citizens can remain considerably blurred. Racketeering (the word enters the language in 1928) in all its forms is a flourishing urban industry in the postwar years. And the ties between criminal racketeering and political corruption become inextricable; the rackets are a pervasive force, eventually a kind of shadow government. Crime is the iron skeleton camouflaged beneath the outer tissue (which grows ever thinner) of the city's body politic, and its major components are loansharking, protection, gambling, prostitution, counterfeiting, narcotics, and—the spine itself—murder, for hire and/or intimidation. All of these criminal pursuits after 1945 are organized around corporate business concepts; notably, the corporate pyramid, at the peak of which are white-collar managers with their legal mouthpieces and accountants and at the base street soldiers, enforcers, and runners. Money-laundering, instituting "legitimate" business covers, the absorption of political parties from the district clubhouse upward, and methods of creative bookkeeping are all practiced with increasing sophistication.

Like the casino and nightclub owners, but usually on a grander scale, the big-city crime bosses invariably live behind screens of respectability (the word becomes a mantra for such characters in film noir), their personal lawyers subcontracting to corporate law firms, their businesses endowing philanthropies, and their political influence inevitably edging them farther into the city's social mainstream. And also like the nightclub owners, they often have wives who do charity work and kids who attend private schools, and they acquire country houses and blue-chip investment portfolios which can make them appear indistinguishable from the businessmen who are their financial peers. But these men do not prowl the mezzanines of nightclubs: they remain out of the public eye, well behind the scenes, pressing other men's buttons from afar. The fear they have instilled is institutionalized, and their authority is unquestioned. A few of their exemplars are Lagana in *The Big Heat,* Sid Kubik in *The Brothers Rico* (1957), and Conners (no first name) in *Underworld U.S.A.* (1961). Lagana is presented, in smoking jacket and ascot, prowling the library of a mansion out of *Town and Country* and overseeing a black-tie prom party his daughter is throwing; we first meet Kubik, wearing a blue blazer and white ducks, on his way to his yacht that sleeps twenty plus crew for a day of deep-sea fishing off the Florida coast; and Conners is shown in his enormous natatorium perusing *The Wall Street Journal,* sipping fresh orange juice, and puffing on a corona at poolside with his butler poised nearby in the shadows.

In the descending tiers beneath these top dogs, however, the lieutenants and soldiers of crime organizations project an entirely different image. No prom parties, no swimming, and their activities around deep water do not include casting for marlin. Murder Inc., the Prohibition- and war-enriched Mafia, and the up-and-coming Tong triads in American Chinatowns which are celebrated in the tabloids, like Dillinger and Capone before them, feed into the film noir. In the films, a patina of glamour and cultish sensationalism is overlaid upon the raw brutality of these groups, producing an exotica of gangland violence which becomes part of the mythology of the noir city. We quickly find an incestuous relationship developing between films and the "real life" of the underworld. So that in the 1940s and 1950s, urban gangsters like the Anastasio brothers, who run Murder Inc., admit with pride that they picked up personal eccentricities of dress—white gloves, sunglasses, diamond tie pins—from film racketeers; and many actors portraying the latter (George Raft, Lawrence Tierney, Franchot Tone), in turn admit that they built their screen personas around real-life racketeers they knew personally.

Colin McArthur writes: "The gangster film which forms the watershed between the Forties and Fifties is *Murder Inc.* (1951). It bears many of the marks of the semidocumentary film—based on actual events, location photography, emphasis on the mechanics of investigation, large numbers of unknown players—but it also sounds for the first time the dominant note of the Fifties gangster film, the existence of a nationwide criminal organization." Nationwide, city by city. For it is always a city, often an entire city, money-corrupted from top to bottom, which is set forth in film noir as an island of amorality adrift somewhere in the greater U.S.A. (Never mind that the neighboring city, one hundred miles down the turnpike, may be equally corrupted.)

In addition to *The Big Heat,* films such as *The Big Combo* (1955), *Kansas City Confidential* (1952), *The Phenix City Story* (1955), and

The Captive City (1952) offer up such cities, utterly in thrall to corrupt, parasitical political machines which are limp appendages to organized crime. The two latter films take this formula to almost fantastical lengths: their respective cities seem to have been infiltrated, invaded, and annexed by a hostile external force. If this sounds like war, it's because both cities look and feel very much like war zones. And both films go well beyond standard docudrama fare into the realm of outright exposé.

In 1955, Phenix City, Alabama—it's a real place, and the entire film was made on location—is a city completely controlled by a gambling syndicate. The downtown has gone honky-tonk, with gambling houses, bars, and girlie parlors—there's not a luncheonette or drugstore in sight. The townspeople are presented in a state of debasement and fear, either working for the syndicate or cowed by it into silence. In fact, the film opens with a basso profundo narrator directing a tour of the town's "factories," where "workers" who look like they could blend in with the citizenry of any small city in the United States, are marking decks of cards, rigging slot machines, and loading dice. It is strongly implied that the powers that be in state government are the true overseers of the gambling syndicate, and the film ends on a note of hopelessness and despair, despite a small-scale victory by the single honest man in town, a crusading attorney.

Kennington, the "nice town" which could be "anywhere in America" in *The Captive City,* has none of the garish veneer of Phenix City: all of that has been pushed neatly underground, and on the surface—streets and parks immaculate to the point of sterility in bright light—it resembles a kind of moral ghost town, with phantom citizens going through the motions, equivocating, lying to themselves, or fixing themselves in a state of happy oblivion in order to get by. In this film, there is also a Diogenes—the editor of the local newspaper—stumbling about in the dangerous night, trying to shake things up. We first see him driving at breakneck speed along a highway with his wife grimly beside him, fleeing for his life, and then holing up in a small town in order to dictate the details of Kennington's corruption (a pathology report that seems endless) into a reel-to-reel tape recorder. This scene is preceded by a stiff-necked speech on organized crime in America by none other than Senator Estes Kefauver of Tennessee, a hero of the time for chairing a commission that bore his name and that first brought the names "Mafia" and "Cosa Nostra" into the American consciousness. Kefauver also delivered an upbeat polemical postscript at the end of the film, which in retrospect feels hopelessly inadequate; if the iron-fisted, nearly totalitarian control that the mob so easily imposed upon Kennington is a barometer, the political infrastructures of American cities after the war were in far more dire straits than Kefauver let on. *The Captive City* is the most claustrophobic of films noirs about "occupied" cities—that is, a nameless, ostensibly upright American city which beneath its placid, orderly surface is found to a be a chaotic, venomous, criminalized environment, from the Chamber of Commerce to City Hall. And how ironic it is in the postwar years to think of American cities, never occupied during the war, as occupied afterward, the occupier a criminal class that prospered—as illustrated by Martinelli and his associates in *Dead Reckoning*—while most of its later victims, the occupied, were engaged in the struggle against the Axis powers.

In film noir, we see over and over again that political corruption in the city invariably goes hand-in-hand with criminal power. From the Depression onward, graft becomes increasingly embedded, with increasing complexity, in urban culture. Earlier on, in 1870, at the zenith of Tammany Hall's power in New York City, Boss Tweed's urban plundering was remarkably simple: everyone who worked for the city padded his bill—first by ten percent, then sixty-six percent, and finally eighty-five percent. Tweed then skimmed the padding. Prefiguring later municipal and Pentagon scandals, in Tweed's New York forty chairs and three tables, purchased from political cronies, cost the city $179,000, and a single thermometer went for $7,500—in 1870 dollars. In the noir city, the enmeshment of politics and crime— shady contracts, rigged bidding, under-the-table payola, doctored books—is more surreptitiously executed. The corrupt political machine, unlike an outright criminal gang, has evolved: now it runs the city through the latter's institutionalized organs of government. It controls the entire civic nervous system, including—especially—the police. It is, by definition, systemic—a large-scale reflection of the cancers of angst and fear afflicting the postwar urban populace.

Even the well-worn, too-often-screened Christmas classic, *It's a Wonderful Life* (1946), directed by that celebrant of Norman Rockwell's America, Frank Capra, contains powerful noir elements. It is essentially an upbeat drama-fantasy that happened to be produced in the midst of the film noir era. Capra, like John Ford, was a native-born American director who, as McArthur points out, had a "more buoyant vision" than the German and Austrian immigrants like Lang, Wilder, and Siodmak who, after witnessing the disintegration of Europe after the First World War, were much more "sour and pessimistic" behind the camera. Yet at the center of *It's a Wonderful Life,* like a black hole, is the very image of the noir city: in a long, dream-like sequence, the hero glimpses a place called "Pottersville" (named after the film's villain, an avaricious banker who delights in foreclosures, it sounds like "potter's field"), which underlies the bucolic, wholesome, supposedly "actual" generic American city, Bedford Falls. The latter would have devolved into Pottersville had certain hypothetical events occurred—namely, the hero's suicide, whose aftereffects would have rippled into dozens of lives. And as the hero envisions this hypothetical Pottersville, it has become a thoroughly corrupt, depraved city: the noir vision carried to its limits.

A hyperbolic noir metropolis, Pottersville bears a passing resemblance to Phenix City, but would stand out for its grotesqueness in even the grittiest films noirs. Flashing neon is lighting up the night, and the blare of honky-tonk music fills the air. Violence, gambling, and public drunkenness dominate the streets, literally at every turn. Traffic laws are ignored. A hit-and-run victim is left to bleed in the street. An angry rabble crowds the street corners. Anxiety, cruelty, and fear strain the faces we glimpse in harsh light. Main Street is a strip of garish, seedy nightspots where prostitution is conducted openly and sexual assault is tolerated. Crooked cops, pimps, and criminals strut about with easy authority. The few "respectable" citizens left are objects of derision, fearful for their lives. This entire concoction is fantastical, but it feels real to us because, like much hyperbole of the aesthetic variety, it is not that far removed from our true, our worldly, knowledge of what is the norm. And therein lies its revelatory tension. For even in a holiday fantasy film, we see reinforced the noir theme that every city is really a tale of two cities, always, one underlying the other.

Charles Baudelaire and the other French Symbolists, inventing a language of hyperreality, are imaginative pioneers in defining the modern city as it was shaped by the Industrial Revolution. In speaking of Baudelaire's great sequence of urban poems, McLuhan writes: "Baudelaire originally intended to call his *Fleurs du Mal, Les Limbes*, having in mind the city as corporate extensions of our physical organs. Our letting go of ourselves, self-alienations, as it were, in order to amplify or increase the power of various functions, Baudelaire considered to be flowers of the growths of evil. The city as amplification of human lusts and sensual striving had for him an entire organic and psychic unity." And this is exactly the sort of unity we find in the film noir's depiction of the corrupt and unhealthy city: it is an extension and reflection of the corruption and sickness of its inhabitants. Again in these films, the city itself can be seen as a character, in the way of a metaphorical human giant—as with Joyce's Dublin in *Ulysses* and *Finnegan's Wake* or Italo Calvino's Venice in *Invisible Cities*.

With regard to wholesale political corruption, graft, and racketeering—with cities so sick as to be on the verge of moral implosion—two particularly notable films are *The Racket* (1951) and *The Street With No Name* (1948).

The Racket was directed by John Cromwell from a much-doctored screenplay, originally written by Sam Fuller. Howard Hughes produced it, with an obsessiveness bordering on mania, and vast, ill-advised, infusions of cash. The film's principal characters are a precocious police captain and a high-ranking mobster. Played by two noir icons, Robert Mitchum and Robert Ryan, the police captain, McQuigg (he is never addressed by his first name in the film), and the mobster, Nick Scanlon, are at odds from the first. Though Scanlon is more superficially coarse and brutal, the two men could be mirror-images of one another. In their methods and attitudes, they are often indistinguishable. Set in a corrupt midwestern city in the final days before a municipal election, the film makes no moralistic good-bad distinctions. McQuigg, the nominal hero, is a sharp-elbowed, aggressive, but ultimately ineffectual force; by default, and because of his less lethal faults (for example, endowing "a chair in civics" in order to facilitate his ne'er-do-well younger brother's college admission), Scanlon becomes the film's most sympathetic character. Certainly he is the most independent and single-minded character. As in *Force of Evil,* a national syndicate is absorbing a local syndicate, and Scanlon is the one racketeer bucking the takeover. The one who has the goods on "the big boys and the big graft," as he puts it. Both he and McQuigg operate outside the law, reflexively. In fact, the law has become, at best, an abstraction in this city—no longer merely broken down, but obsolete. A vacuum with no atmosphere to fuel activity, lawful or criminal. To operate within its perimeters would be an act, not of naiveté, but outright stupidity.

Slowly, inexorably, *The Racket* develops into a poisonously nihilistic film noir. Suffocating in its intensity of violence and claustrophobia, and cynical from every angle. Aside from a single honest, by-the-book cop under McQuigg's command (whom Scanlon shoots to death during a scuffle), and his wife and McQuigg's, who in walkon roles are like cardboard cutout emblems of virtue and passivity, not a single character with redeeming qualities surfaces. From Scanlon's oddly barren luxury apartment to McQuigg's icily bare precinct house, every space with four walls in this city seems to be closing in on itself. The moral implosion of the city, and of the main characters, is at all times occurring in tandem, the one informing and amplifying the other. Every scene—especially the most violent—occurs in a small, tight frame of reference, visually and psychologically. McQuigg lies, cuts corners, frames suspects, tears up writs of habeas corpus, and in the end helps to stage-manage the cold-blooded murder of Scanlon (while trying to flee the precinct through an open window, he is shot in the back). Scanlon's replacement, at film's end, is an even more vicious and destructive racketeer than Scanlon. And it is hinted strongly that the city's paramount crime lord, whose real identity is veiled throughout the narrative (he's always referred to as "the old man"), and who is glimpsed only once, early on, portentously initiating a bogus "investigation" into political corruption, is the state's governor! This is indeed a city of Hell, far removed from any possibility of redemption—quite off the map, in fact. But with coordinates that are very secure on the film noir map.

In *The Street With No Name,* directed by William Keighley, we enter another fictional, composite city, called Center City, with an utterly corroded body politic. The city is a garish, corrupt, and utterly nocturnal place (again, similar to Pottersville, except that this isn't the flip side, it's the whole story). The racketeer who runs Center City, Alex Stiles, makes constant use of society's supposed tools— City Hall, the FBI, the local police—to effect his rule. He frames ex-cons who want to join him, then through a crooked cop on his payroll has the FBI in Washington screen the ex-cons and send back their police records so he can see if they're bona fide criminals. Even the police ballistics lab is at his disposal.

Interestingly, most of the film's exterior scenes were shot at night on Main Street in Los Angeles' Skid Row. And because all the other, interior, scenes are set exclusively in a gang hideout, Stiles' apartment, a crooked detective's house, police headquarters, and a factory, this seedy honky-tonk district is all we see of the city proper. Stiles' formal occupation is boxing promoter, but his racketeering activities run the gamut, from gambling to armed robbery. As played by Richard Widmark, he is a strangely twisted, mannered character. A hypochondriac. A crude misogynist who beats and shames his wife before his underlings. He's asthmatic, and absolutely paranoid about drafts from open windows and doors, about underheated rooms, and germs that might be transmitted through handshakes. Bosley Crowther, reviewing the film in the *New York Times,* suggested that Stiles' voice possessed "the timbre of filthy water going down a sewer." Stiles always, superstitiously, wears a scarf imprinted with a certain print that is of private, though undisclosed, significance to him. Though a bully, who terrorizes through enforcers, he himself is frail, even foppish, a kind of inverted variation on that omnipresent noir character, the hard-bitten, returning G.I., crippled by the war but with an underlying masculinity. In his physical vulnerability, and his obsessiveness about his bodily welfare, Stiles also seems to be an overt reaction to (and rejection of) the invincible tough guy of the prewar gangster pictures; the characters played by Cagney and Bogart in those films had their tics and suffered their demons, but they certainly did not bundle up indoors fearful of drafts, much less fuss about the weather report with their underlings.

Sent up against Stiles by the F.B.I. is a young undercover cop named Gene Cordell. When we see Cordell with other cops, in character as a policeman, he is bland to the point of disappearing before our eyes. Self-effacing, laconic, a company man. Only when he goes undercover, posing as a prizefighter, gaudily dressed, affecting back-alley lingo and spicing up his body language, does he come alive for us—as if this criminal persona is his real self. Or, at the very least, another facet of his real self, for like Stiles and his men, Cordell grew up in the slums; like so many cops in film noir, he arrived early in his life at that fork in the well-traveled highway that cuts through the heart of the noir city: the one fork plunging into the underworld, the other meandering, with a thousand pitfalls, to the police force. (This is a point driven home in dozens of prewar gangster films and, more subtly, in many films noirs, which employ establishment figures—priests, policemen, lawyers—as the childhood intimates, and adult counterpoints, of the criminal protagonists.) But even so, it is not Cordell who most powerfully captures our attention. As with Scanlon in *The Racket,* it is the rackets czar Stiles who is the more textured and subtle character. Scanlon and Stiles are each a terrifying mix of the sadistic and the ridiculous that brings to mind the secondary tier of characters in Dostoevsky's *The Devils* or Gogol's *Dead Souls,* in whose company they seem far more at home than among the typical heavies of the police thriller.

In a wicked twist on the postwar celebration of military efficiency that had just subdued the Axis and was now revitalizing the operations of corporate America, Stiles continually boasts of the efficiency of his rackets organization. "I'm building an organization along scientific lines," he tells Cordell one night, with the pride of a company executive. "That's why I screened you . . . like in the army. Only I pick my own recruits." Indeed, the checks and double-checks, electronic and paper, that Stiles runs on the résumé created for Cordell's alias, bring to mind the machinery, not of gangland, but of an especially suspicious variety of corporate personnel department. Throughout the film, always in tones of deep pride, Stiles keeps using the word "scientific" to describe his operations and methods. And, certainly, there is a good chance that, as would be true with any "scientifically" constructed corporation, the foundation its founder has laid will outlive him. That is why, as with *The Racket,* the resolution of *The Street With No Name* is considerably downbeat, despite the overall (though messy) success of the authorities' undercover operation: Stiles is killed in a gunfight, and many of his associates are arrested, but it is implicit (to the point that it need not be spoken aloud) that the police have scant hope of dislodging the forces of corruption—of which Stiles was merely a transitory custodian—which have permeated their city.

In another instance of films noirs that are produced at the same time, by different studios, exploring similiar themes and utilizing similar motifs, *T-Men* bears an uncanny resemblance to *The Street With No Name*. Also filmed in late 1947, *T-Men* was directed by Anthony Mann and released less than six months before *The Street With No Name*. It features undercover agents (two men who work in tandem this time), criminals employing the latest "scientific" methods (as counterfeiters), and advanced police technology, from communications devices to elaborate laboratories. Again, the undercover men come most alive when they step out of their bland personas (a T-Man is a Treasury Department agent) and into their criminal aliases. In flashy suits and garish ties, with rakish fedoras, the agents seem right at home among the well-heeled hoodlums whose counterfeiting ring they infiltrate. Their own personalities, and their personal histories, are utterly subsumed—between themselves, and in their relationship to the audience—to their impersonations of ruthless criminal operatives.

Like *The Captive City* with its cameo appearance by Senator Kefauver, *T-Men* opens with a real-life former government official from the Roosevelt Administration, a man named Elmer Lincoln Iren who coordinated six Treasury Department enforcement divisions— "shock troops," he calls them. In an impressive aside, he adds that sixty-four percent of the inmates in federal penitentiaries were sent there by these six divisions of the Treasury Department. Iren extolls the virtues of the department in breaking up rings of counterfeiters. The film we are about to see, he informs us, is based on a real case known as the "Shanghai Paper Case." Then the same stentorian narrator (he seemed to have a lock on the job when a semidocumentary noir was made) who was used in *The House on 92nd Street* and *Call Northside 777* takes over. "The case started in L.A. just off Santa Monica Boulevard," he begins.

The counterfeiting ring, like the Nazi spy ring in *The House on 92nd Street,* turns out to have an attractive woman as its ringleader— the front-man for a murky, behind-the-scenes mastermind. Not only is the business of her organization the production of currency, but like Stiles she boasts to one of the undercover agents that she runs all her activities exactly as the operating officer of a large corporation would. In a dark take-off on that classic capitalist adage by a former General Motors chief executive that "the business of America is business," when she has a bad apple in her organization liquidated rather than showing him clemency, she explains, "The point of the business is business." The bad apple was a low-level operative nicknamed "The Schemer," a fallen mastermind who was once a big shot in counterfeiting circles. Now (again shades of Stiles) he's a hypochondriac who chews incessantly on medicinal Chinese herbs and takes a daily steambath. It is in a steambath that he is murdered by a hit man, in one of the most grotesquely balletic and stylized scenes in all of film noir; the bullets are "seen" as comet-like streaks, splintering into light, against the steamy blackness. (Here John Alton, undoubtedly film noir's greatest cinematographer, first used an effect that he was to perfect seven years later, working with a different director, in *The Big Combo;* in that film, similar flashes, against a steamy blackness, fill the screen when another character in failing health has his hearing aid pulled out by his assassins moments before they shoot him, so that we see gunfire he can no longer hear.) The Schemer's posthumous revenge comes about through a meticulous diary ("I got it written down in code," he boasts. "*My* code.") which the undercover agents use, once the code has been broken in Washington, to unravel the hierarchy of the gang and, eventually, to bring about its downfall. Though, once again, at the film's conclusion, we are reminded of the fact that this is just one counterfeiting ring out of many and, by implication, that the war against them, just beginning, might reasonably seem to be an interminable one.

Two notable points about *T-Men* that make it unique among "undercover" films noirs: it chronicles the swiftness with which criminal organizations slid over into the white-collar sphere in the years immediately after the war; and it lays emphasis upon the federal government's massive efforts to combat organized crime. A case can certainly be made that the second point is a direct result of the first. But there is more to it than that. With the end of the Second World War, and the Cold War just getting underway, the activist, mobilized federal government of the Depression era and the war years certainly was happy to help foster the public perception—via Hollywood in this case—that it was funneling its considerable power and energy into a domestic war against an increasingly sophisticated criminal community. If criminals were going to brag about their "scientific" methods and their open emulation of the operational efficiency of big business and the U.S. military, then the government—if for no higher purpose than raw public relations—had to turn up the heat themselves, or be made to look foolish.

Sound familiar? Certainly the polemical, quasi-documentary gangster films of the thirties—*Racket Busters* (1938), *Bullets or Ballots* (1936), *G-Men* (1935)—make much of the nascent F.B.I.'s heroic contributions to gang-busting. *G-Men* opens with a solemn and self-serving invocation—vintage P.R. material—not from some former Treasury official, but from the big cheese himself, J. Edgar Hoover, though we know now, in retrospect, how ineffectual most of his racket-busting operations were, and how, under his benign eye, the American Mafia was allowed to expand exponentially in the post-Prohibition era. And the so-called war on drugs initiated in the Reagan Administration, involving Coast Guard interdiction of smugglers on the high seas, high-profile spraying of marijuana crops in Mexico, and sporadic commando raids on various South American cocaine operations, seems to have been ninety percent public relations and ten percent action. It is significant that the most noteworthy, and highly televised, "battle" of this short-lived war was staged during the Bush administration, immediately after the Cold War ended and the Berlin Wall came down, when the United States invaded Panama, allegedly for its state-sponsored drug trafficking, and arrested, tried, and imprisoned its dictator, a man who for many years, beginning during Bush's tenure as C.I.A. director, had been on that agency's payroll.

In 1947, it was the Axis powers from whom we had just turned our attention, leaving a gap, apparently, in the mosaic of our national sense of purpose; in 1989, it was the crumbling Soviet Union and its satellites. Little surprise, then, that *T-Men* not only opens with a Treasury Department spokesman, but closes with a montage fashioned around a magazine-style layout, with that same stentorian narrator informing us of what happens to each of the film's principals—Treasury agents and criminals alike—and concluding with a paean to the virtues and vigilance of "the people of this country" (sound familiar again?) who made such a terrific law-enforcement operation possible in the first place. We also find out, in an aside, that the true boss of the "real" case, the Shanghai Paper Case, turns out to be someone who is not even portrayed in the film, a real-life "philanthropist and dealer in rare antiquities" named Oscar Gaffney! Gaffney must have appreciated, from his federal prison cell, that in a fictionalized docudrama, not only was he—the mastermind—relegated to an offstage role, but his was the only name left unchanged for the movie audience. It is also interesting, from a journalistic/public relations angle, that despite the film's gritty and hard-boiled milieu, its notoriously low-budget studio, Eagle-Lion, provided it with a massive publicity campaign; it is even more interesting and surprising that *Life* magazine, which usually lent its support only to the glossier efforts of the big-name studios, in its issue of February 23, 1948, featured a pictorial spread on the film.

Kansas City Confidential, directed by Phil Karlson, is one of several noir caper films that are literally obsessed with money. The smell, feel, and almost otherworldly magnetism of the stuff. Other such films, built around racetrack or jewelry store heists, are *The Asphalt Jungle* (1950), directed by John Huston, *Private Hell 36* (1954), directed by Don Siegel, and Stanley Kubrick's early tour-de-force, *The Killing* (1956). But, for sheer tightness of plotting and internal tension, and the fact that it is such a wonderfully concocted morality play whose twin poles are concealment and betrayal, *Kansas City Confidential* occupies a niche all its own. A low-budget, critically undervalued film, it takes as a given the proposition that money is filthy lucre, a corrupting element to all who touch it—which means just about everyone in the city in which the film is set. It is a film that examines the minutiae of money laundering, the marking of paper money, and the monetary obsessions of its major characters, from the physical characteristics of the stuff to its metaphysical potential. But, most importantly, it fixes on the actual money which is at the core of the plot: bags of unmarked bills snatched from an armored car, bills which we frequently see and even—via the characters' senses—touch and smell, in various locales, from a Kansas City bank to a fishing boat off Mexico called *The Mañana* where it is stashed in the hold as "bait."

In this film, the corruption of the city is presented in miniature, in the shifting roles that the two major characters play in one another's lives. Timothy Foster is an ex-cop turned criminal; Joe Rolfe, an ex-con gone straight. Foster engineers a complex heist by blackmailing three felons; not one of them knows the identity of another, and none of them knows Foster's identity. He remains anonymous throughout the film. On the day of the crime, he brings them all together wearing masks. Rolfe, whose delivery truck they hijack for their getaway, becomes the fall guy for the robbery. The police brutalize him, but eventually must release him for lack of evidence. He then sets out on a quest—blindfolded, for all intents and purposes, in the murkiest of labyrinths—to track down the real robbers. Money, like spoor, provides the only trail, and it is a meager one. He has to find four men, and because three of them are completely in the dark as to the identities and locations of the others, his quest rapidly devolves into the surreal, employing logic more apt for nightmare than ratiocination. In the *Film Noir Encyclopedia,* Alain Silver sums it up quite neatly: "The narrative scheme, which brings [Foster and Rolfe] into direct conflict, not only reverses their previous roles as criminal and policeman but ironically keeps them unaware of the other's true identity and purpose until the film's conclusion. . . . Like Galt in *The Dark Corner,* Rolfe is assailed and nearly destroyed by unknown forces, forces that he will discover bore him no personal malice. His unrelenting and brutal search is both a moral vindication and a simple assertion of existential outrage."

In this film, the moral corrosion of the noir city is presented in an extended shadow play between, and in the minds of, two angry, embittered men who become emblems of the general population. Foster clearly defines his own motives for turning criminal: he has been retired on a paltry pension after twenty years of wearily and thanklessly fighting crime, especially during the Depression, and seeing the "hoodlums always come out on top." Now he wants compensation, in the form of the stolen loot, and vengeance; to achieve the latter, he manipulates the investigation in such a way as to embarrass the Kansas City Police Department. Rolfe, for his part, has been shaped by the same mold as the disgruntled and disillusioned veterans who populate films like *Crossfire, The Blue Dahlia,* and *Somewhere in the Night:* the war.

The theme of money and vets is a recurring one. Soldiers and sailors returning home to straitened circumstances while the rest of the country is entering a boom period was social dynamite, and in film noir we often see the explosion up close. Quick-tempered and quick with his fists, Rolfe speaks for all of these vets in one of the classic, paradigmatic bits of dialogue in all of film noir. Framed for the armored car robbery, getting the third-degree under hot lights in a cement cell from the cops who are all but brandishing their rubber hoses, he hears the district attorney remark about him to one of the cops, "He won a Bronze Star and a Purple Heart." To which Rolfe snaps, "Try buying a cup of coffee with them." How revealing it is that his reflexive indignation is not directed at their callousness toward his distinguished military service or his heroism, but to his precarious financial plight.

The most popular sport in film noir is also the most violent, existentially intense, ritualistic, and money-driven athletic exhibition that the city has to offer, and invariably it is controlled by organized crime. That boxing and the subculture it populates loom large in these films should not surprise us, for the world of boxing is truly the noir world in miniature. Boxing offers film noir a rich cast of characters: the fighters, their trainers and managers, promoters, mobsters and gamblers, wives and girlfriends, hangers-on and confidants, society swells and low-lifes. Official corruption and street-level violence find their common ground in boxing arenas and gymnasiums. Never far from the sweet science is the art of the fast buck.

Isolated and isolating for spectators and boxers alike, the sport is both a potent metapor and social symbol in film noir. A kind of diorama—like the ring itself, seen from above—of the noir ethos.

Noir has this to tell us about boxing:

At the heart of the professional prizefight is cash, and at the heart of the fighter is a man attempting to claw his way, with fists and guile, from the city's slums to its glittery heights. If he has the physical talents—speed, agility, raw strength—if his hubris is large enough, his conditioning relentless enough, his chin solid enough, *and* if he catches some luck, he might become a contender—one of the nine men in the top ten trying to topple number one, the champion. The latter possesses the hubris, the guile, and the punch, like the others, and then something powerful on top of all that. Devotees of the fight game try to put a word on it: guts, class, magic. It is not an over-abundance of luck which gives him that something extra, though he has to be lucky too. If other fighters have a flame burning inside them, he has a bonfire, stoked by some fury he could never define. Maybe not even acknowledge. Back in the 1940s and 1950s, during the classic noir era, boxing titles still meant something; there were, respectively, a single flyweight, bantamweight, lightweight, welter-weight, middleweight, light-heavyweight, and heavyweight cham-pion. (Today, amid an alphabet soup of sanctioning bodies and multiple-menu weight categories, dozens of fighters hold devalued title belts.) The spotlight on the champions of the postwar years was intense, as were the rewards they reaped. So when, after waiting for his shot and pounding his way to the front of the line, a fighter did win a championship, he might indeed climb very high very fast out-side of the ring—and then plummet even faster.

Thus the boxer lends himself naturally to tragedy. In film noir, the arc of his parabola is rapid and steep; and though there may be a pot of gold at one end of it, the arc is no rainbow.

That arc of his professional life is also the arc of his youth, and along it the boxer spans many economic strata; he often tangles with every obstacle, hardship, and vice, followed by every temptation and luxury, that the city can throw at him in a compressed period. The business entrepreneur may go from rags to riches in a short period, early in his life, but, just as often, his career climb may stretch over decades; the successful boxer, by definition, leaps from rags to riches practically overnight. It is axiomatic that he is a child of immi-grants; skimming through the listings of champions in a boxing en-cyclopedia is as revealing of the immigration patterns of the United States as any government document on the subject. Irish fighters predominate at the turn of the century, then we see a sudden mix-ture of Italian, Polish, German, and Swedish fighters, a host of Jewish champions in the 1930s, and beginning in the 1940s the large wave of African-American fighters, followed in the 1960s by Mexican, Caribbean, and Latin American fighters, all of whom dominate the sport to the present day. The farther up the economic ladder these immigrants climb, the fewer boxers they produce. In film noir, these boxers are the products of distinct ethnic neighborhoods, usually

Irish, Italian, Jewish, and African-American. So the champion, in so-
cietal terms, is always a creature of economic extremes. As for the
vast majority of his brethren—pugs, palookas, sparring partners,
also-rans, and tankers—they start off at the bottom, stay at the bottom, and nine times out of ten end up on Queer Street, bodies battered, senses scrambled, even worse off than when they started,
when they were poor but at least able-bodied.

The boxer, alone in the ring with his opponent, bathed in harsh
white light in a sea of blackness from which voices shout, jeer, hoot,
and whistle, is a prototypical, existential noir hero, deep in his
labyrinth: that is, the labyrinth of his mind, where the chess match of
the fight unfolds milliseconds before the action of the physical fight,
which lies within the labyrinth of the ring; the ring's lethal, phantom
corridors and chambers—negotiated with jabs, hooks, and feints—
invisible to all but the boxers, in turn center the carefully evoked
mini-labyrinth of the boxing arena, which lies within the greater
labyrinth of the city itself. The tight rectangular ring both entraps
the two fighters and gives them license to do what they would be arrested for doing just twenty feet away, among the spectators.

Watching footage of old championship fights—Dempsey and
Tunney, Louis and Schmelling, Marciano and Walcott—is like looking through a window to a place where time has stopped. A black and
white limbo, one man in dark trunks, the other in light, circling one
another, inflicting punishment and absorbing it, fighting off pain, exhaustion, and death—both literally and metaphorically. All the great
noir films whose subject is boxing were powerfully influenced by
such footage; like the early documenatry films noirs that took their
cue from the wartime newsreels, *Body and Soul* (1947), *Champion*
(1949), and *The Set-Up* (1949) offer us viscerally authentic boxing
footage that propels the dramatic action throughout each film and,
inevitably, constitutes its climax.

In these three films we run the gamut, in compressed form, of
noir boxers: from corrupt *(Champion),* to corrupt and then re-
deemed *(Body and Soul),* to upright and punished for his upright-
ness *(The Set-Up).* The boxers in *Champion* and *Body and Soul* are
truly emblematic of the postwar era: both in the ring and in their
complex private lives, they suffer enormous stresses and strains,

seesaw between disciplined power and slothful greed, and graphically evince both the abysmal depth of their failures and the dizzying height of their triumphs. Everything about them is writ large.

In *Champion,* directed by Mark Robson and based on a wonderfully acidic short story by Ring Lardner, the hero, played by Kirk Douglas, is an unrepentant heel who has used and abused every person—wife, brother, manager—in his life during his climb as a fighter. At his triumphal moment, signing a contract that will make him rich, he looks out at Manhattan from the fortieth-floor window of an office building, turning his gaze finally, with great self-satisfaction, upon the tiny black dots (shades of Harry Lime contemptuously surveying the crowds from the ferris wheel in Vienna) that are pedestrians—"suckers," the fighter calls them—pounding the pavement of the workaday world over which he now feels he towers. The hero of *Body and Soul,* starring John Garfield and directed by Robert Rossen from a script by Abraham Polonsky, at a similar moment, having just signed on with the corrupt promoter who absolutely controls the fight game in New York City, shouts at his mother, his girlfriend, and his former manager (whom he has just double-crossed), all of whom disapprove of his selling out in order to get a title fight, "It's money. It doesn't think. It doesn't care who spends it. Take it while you can."

It was Polonsky and Garfield who worked together the following year on *Force of Evil.* Like that film, *Body and Soul,* as Robert Ottoson writes, "not only attacks the free-enterprise system, but also the American success ethic. Judging from the fate that awaited the creative forces behind *Body and Soul,* it seems that the film's 'message' did not go unnoticed by HUAC, and other professional patriots." Rossen, Polonsky, and three of the film's major actors would all be blacklisted out of the movies, and John Garfield and Canada Lee, who plays the black champion dethroned by Garfield in a tainted fight, were, as Ottoson observes, "hounded by HUAC into early deaths."

Ottoson lays down a simple and terrible "equation" for *Body and Soul:* "greed = money = corruption = death." It certainly holds when the promoter who is the story's puppeteer at one point delivers his credo, that life is just "addition and subtraction—everything else is conversation." And our hero, without blinking an eye, and thinking he will somehow escape the hard truth that, like all the boxers in the promoter's grip, he is no more than an economic investment to be unloaded when he no longer pays dividends, proclaims, "I just want to be a success. You know, every man for himself." But no sooner is he clutching in each of his fists a wad of that money that "doesn't think" than he begins his terrible descent, money through the entire film dangled before his eyes and pouring from his pockets as he dissipates his talents in the ring and wrecks his personal life careering down the fast lane.

The Set-Up, directed by Robert Wise, is the only film noir I know of in which the screenplay is adapted from a narrative poem (by James Moncure March). A surprising winner of the Critic's Prize at the Cannes Film Festival in 1949, the film is a curiosity for a number of reasons. For one thing, like Hitchcock's *Rope,* it is set in real time. Seventy-two minutes long, *The Set-Up* chronicles seventy-two minutes in the life of an aging journeyman fighter, played brilliantly by Robert Ryan. Like other noir icons, including Robert Mitchum, Jack Palance, John Huston, and Tom Neal, Ryan in his youth had boxed professionally. The film is set about as far from the fast lane as one could get, in a hellish town called Paradise City, which is depicted solely through its shabby rooming houses, greasy spoons, dark filthy streets, and most important, through the warrens of a rundown, sweltering arena. *The Set-Up* is entirely nocturnal, much of the composition black on black and brilliantly cut (Wise was Orson Welles' editor on *Citizen Kane*). The film is hands down the bleakest boxing film ever made—certainly the harshest ever to come out of Hollywood. Even the criminals are seedy, small-bore types who play viciously for penny-ante stakes—no big-time promoters here, with diamond rings, cashmere coats, and limousines. And the crowds in every way exceed the coarse, vulgar stock players we find in other boxing films; here they are outright sadistic, with a blood-lust verging on hysteria. When the hero's left eye is swollen shut by punches in the climactic fight, a blind man in the crowd shouts to the other boxer, "The other eye, Nelson, close the other eye!"

Ryan plays a fighter who wants only to make enough money in his last fight to open a beer hall or cigar stand: that's about as far as his dreams carry. Very soon it becomes clear that that is much too far.

His manager has sold him out, accepting a bribe and promising that his fighter will take a dive; furthermore, the manager has so little faith in his fighter that he doesn't even inform him of the arrangement! And it happens that the latter, having promised his wife this will be his last fight—and thus his last shot at that cigar stand—takes a terrible beating in the early rounds, but fights his heart out, rallies, and emerges victorious. He's very pleased with himself, a terrible weight lifted from his shoulders—but, cruelly, in this universe only for few minutes—until he realizes that the double-crossed crooks are waiting on him. They've sealed off every exit in the arena. Trapped, he's taken refuge in the ring, of all places, and there is a memorable shot of him from on high in which we see enforcers sauntering down every aisle, converging on him. Aerially, the arena appears in the form of an infernal mandala that has come alive, spinning in black space. The thugs give him a terrible beating, breaking both his hands in the end and tossing him into the gutter in front of a dance hall called "Dreamland," where his wife finds him. He can never box again, and it's doubtful he'll ever put together enough money for that cigar stand. Maybe he ought to feel lucky that he's not dead; maybe not.

And that's it. There's no saga of a rise and fall here—no parabola of any kind—as in *Champion* and *Body and Soul*. For this boxer, we see only the tail end of a downward spiral that began a dozen years earlier, when he set out as a club fighter and never broke into the ranks of the contenders, much less the challengers, for a championship. *The Set-Up* is less a morality tale than a nihilistic sprint that skirts the abyss. It is worth noting that in this film the fighter is in no way a kid from the slums who craves sharp clothes and a snazzy pad, but rather a low-key working-class stiff—he has the demeanor of a weary plumber or handyman—faithful to his wife in her drab dresses, uncomplaining, a clock-puncher who happens to labor, and be exploited, in a sweaty arena rather than a sweatshop.

The low-key stiff is an anomaly in film noir; invariably, like the insurance agent in *Pitfall,* he is someone eager to bust out, whatever the costs. Broken families, soiled reputations, and criminal records lie in the wake of such flights into the whirlwind of upward mobility, one of the bywords of the postwar era. Luxury living, sexual emancipation, and the leisure toys which are the spin-off of the country's latest technological marvels are among the lures that beckon—and tempt—the forty-hour-a-week man. Whereas at Delphi the inscription in marble of "Know Thyself" was the distillation of centuries of oracular wisdom, in film noir, distilled in the time it takes to ponder a fast buck—and without apology—the most universal adage could be "Money Talks." (With the addendum, perhaps, that "Everybody Dies.") The critic Michael Wood makes a crucial point when he says that the film noir world is "a state of mind made visible in furniture and sidewalks, and that it presents us with a picture of "what life would look like if crime *did* pay." Like the city itself, with its polarities of rich and poor, and the yawning chasms in between, films noirs (more than ever today, for they were certainly prophetic in this respect) owe much of their tautness and bite to the tightropes that are strung between those poles for the characters climbing, the ones descending, and the great majority who are suspended, and buffeted, between the worlds of the haves and the have-nots.

From the highest, most opulent penthouse, the slums are visible in the distance; and from the slums, the lights of that penthouse twinkle brightly as the stars, and remain equally out of reach. (Or not so out of reach, the films would suggest, for those willing to ditch scruples and other inconvenient baggage and enter the noir labyrinth in search of a shortcut to those stars.) In film noir, Spengler's city of high culture, fueled and regulated by wealth, coexists symbiotically with the city of "refined, socially accepted crime"—a development that he saw as an inevitable urban condition in the late stages of empire in the mid-twentieth century. The American Empire, that is, and the American city. So, increasingly, as we ourselves plunge deeper into the noir labyrinth, we find it assuming the properties, not of a stark dingy maze, but a teeming Amazon rife with intoxicating perfumes, its black rivers branching into countless tributaries, clotted with human beings both predatory and exotic, protean and faceless—a place ruled by the dizzying calculus of the jungle, whose prime functions emanate from sex, violence, and death. This is where the greatest urban novelists—Smollett, Balzac, Dickens, Dreiser—found their material and where even today's tabloid readers take it as a truism that the boundary between crime and legitimate enterprise increasingly blurs. As Hillman points out, "In the underworld all is stripped away, and life is upside down." The cop

and the criminal, the gangster and the tycoon, become interchangeable, and the crime that is socially acceptable, behind its succession
of veils, may be responsible for more deaths in real numbers than
the violent street crime.

The tycoon is a seminal figure in film noir who often bridges the
deceptive terrain of respectability and culture and the treacherous
provinces of crime. Enamored of luxury and power, seemingly invulnerable, equipped with jungle instincts, the tycoon comfortably becomes a repeat offender of the socially acceptable crime (and gets
away with it), only to teeter, in a moment of hubris, along the razor's
edge of committing the unsanctioned (or too-glaring-to-ignore)
crime—like Janoth or Mundson—for which he pays with his life.
Whereas in gangster films of the 1930s ultimate power resided in a
mayor or a city's political boss, after the war, with the rise of big business and its octopus reach into both the functions of government
and of the individual citizen, this same power has clearly begun slipping into the private sector. The tycoon's city mansion and country
getaway, his skyscraper business lair and the pied-à-terre he keeps
to rendezvous with his mistress, his fleets of cars and other accoutrements of wealth, the army of people from aides-de-camp to nameless blue-collar workers whom he controls, are all important noir
fixtures. Characters running magazine empires or tungsten cartels
become increasingly common, with many variations: the blackmailing, bullying movie-studio chief in *The Big Knife;* the reclusive
Boston shipping magnate in *Mystery Street;* the ruthless electronics
and aerospace czar in *Brainstorm.*

Caught, directed by Max Ophuls in 1949, is in a class by itself in
this respect. Ophuls was another German expatriate who appren-
ticed at the UFA studios in Berlin. He was famous for his virtuoso direction and the painterly approach he brought to the camera. His
rendering of objects—like so many still-lifes frozen together in the
fore- and backgrounds of his frames—was textured in a baroque,
minutely detailed manner. In *Caught,* the most baroque of all his
films, he is stylized without being flashy. Much of the film is shot in
a millionaire's mansion that rivals (and was reputedly modeled after)
the pleasure palace Xanadu that Orson Welles created in *Citizen
Kane.* The house, like Kane's, is filled with cavernous rooms and
walk-in fireplaces, gigantic doorways and dizzying stairwells, and

corridors wide enough to drive a truck through. Within those rooms are enough jewels, minks, hats, gloves, and shoes for a hundred people. But the principal residents, with their squad of servants, are the millionaire himself, Smith Ohlrig, and his new, young wife, Leonora Eames.

Leonora is played by Barbara Bel Geddes, an actress with a shy, studious, and somewhat dazed persona. Ohlrig is played by Robert Ryan at his most hard-bitten. It's interesting to note that he made *Caught* and *The Set-Up* simultaneously in late 1948; the former was released in theaters by Metro-Goldwyn-Mayer on February 19, 1949, and the latter by RKO on March 29, 1949. So the films ran at the same time, and one could literally go from theater to theater and see Ryan playing men stationed at the opposite ends of the socio-economic scale who possessed wildly contrasting dispositions, the one a user, the other among the most squeezed-out of the used. To-day, with video rentals and VCR machines, this is not at all a novel proposition—I reviewed the two films, along with two others by Ryan, in a single weekend—but in 1949, when films shown on television were themselves a rarity, it was a different story altogether.

Also, it must have been a delicious irony for Howard Hughes' many detractors in Hollywood to learn that Max Ophuls had secured the services of both Bel Geddes and Ryan for *Caught*—especially Ryan, who, along with Robert Mitchum and Robert Young, was one of the most important contract players at RKO, Hughes' studio. Ophuls and Hughes had had a terrible falling-out in 1946 when Hughes hired and fired him as the director of a turgid melodrama, *Vendetta,* a vehicle for Hughes' most recent "protégé," Faith Do-mergue, which eventually required the services of five other direc-tors and turned out an utter flop. So the fact that Ryan was playing Smith Ohlrig, who, rumor had it, was based as much on Hughes (Ophuls settling his own vendetta)—tyrannical, workaholic, misogy-nistic—as on the fictional Charles Foster Kane of *Citizen Kane,* must have galled Hughes. Uncharacteristically, he did not retaliate against Ryan, but he never forgave Ophuls.

The focus of *Caught* is the terrifying, ultimately obliterating, emo-tional void that the Ohlrigs inhabit in lieu of a marriage, all the while drowning in their material possessions. Even the most modest of the latter turn out to be anything but modest. When Ohlrig makes

Leonora a present of a handbag, for example, he tells her with his characteristic gruffness (his emotional range runs from harsh to caustic) that the bag is constructed of the rarest skin. "Lizard from the Amazon," he boasts, "ten days upriver to find it." Not that he has done the finding. But he always knows, and revels in, the respective histories of his luxury acquisitions.

And "luxury" is the operative word in *Caught,* both as a catch-all for the physical pleasures it describes and as a state of mind—and existential condition. Ohlrig enforces an idleness upon Leonora that devolves into imprisonment; then, even while chastising her for accepting this condition, he continually reminds her that it is "a luxury." The title of the film, too, works on a multiplicity of levels, from describing the innocent, and annoyingly passive, young woman caught in a malevolent relationship, to a whole class of people thrashing in the web of their materialism, to the tycoon himself caught in a net of rage and self-loathing. It is a film in which the ordure smeared in the wake of money is always apparent, tainting everyone from Ohlrig and Leonora to the yes-men and hangers-on whom he keeps around (primarily, it seems, to absorb his abuse at all hours) and who evince little shame in their roles as parasites.

Once again, in *Caught,* we have a film that is remarkably similar in plot, theme, and characterization to another film noir released within a year of it, *Where Danger Lives,* directed by John Farrow and starring, ironically enough, Faith Domergue, whom Howard Hughes was still trying to make into a star at RKO. Both films have idealistic (and not very interesting) young doctors at their centers, trying to rescue the young wives of dangerous, wealthy men from their husbands. Both wives become the doctors' lovers. But in Farrow's film, the wife is a murderess herself, and a psychopath; Domergue dies on an electrified fence at the Mexican border, wearing sunglasses and a white trenchcoat, while the doctor (played by Robert Mitchum) watches helplessly, in a drugged stupor. In *Caught,* the young wife is a hopeless dreamer seduced by opulence into a tormenting, crushing, and finally murderous marriage. But in the end, she survives in the care of her doctor, while Ohlrig dies of a massive heart attack.

When we first meet her, Leonora is a poor working girl, holding down a secretarial job, living in a tenement walkup apartment, fantasizing about a life of glamour and leisure that seems permanently out of reach. She has been to charm school. She is pretty in a conventional way, and introverted—bookish, judging from outward appearances. But it is not books that she reads. In the opening scene, on a stifling summer night in New York, she and her roommate, in their pajamas, are curled up on the sofa in their tiny living room flipping through the pages of fashion magazines, mesmerized by the glossy advertisements. They are chattering excitedly about the furs, jewels, and designer outfits on each successive page. The magazines are a veritable catalogue of the city's booty, a Roman inventory, that seduces Leonora long before she meets Ohlrig.

The labyrinth into which she is drawn, in the end filled with ever-darkening turns and sheer drops, is at first a hall of mirrors where Leonora is blinded by diamonds, sapphires, and emeralds (like the hapless peasant girl in the Andersen fairy tale who loses her way, dazzled by gems, in an underground cave). She is a kind of Proserpine to Ohlrig's Pluto, and his house, darkly lit and surrounded by black gardens and unswaying trees, is like a palace of death, the Hades in which Leonora is imprisoned, broken, and nearly murdered. Like Proserpine, she is a wife with an absentee husband; he may not be reaping souls with a sickle, but Ohlrig, who literally works day and night (à la Hughes, sadistically keeping a battery of subordinates awake with him) and who apparently never sleeps (does Pluto?)—and *never* with his wife—is certainly mowing people down left and right through the ruthless manipulation of his wealth and industrial holdings.

Ohlrig is an amazingly modern prototype of the junk bond dealers and leveraged-buyout sharks who thrived in the 1980s, gutting entire companies and communities for a fast profit. Pride and avariciousness are the least of his character flaws, however, and we soon discover that he is capable not only of erratic and abusive behavior but of physical violence. In fact, it is all but spelled out for us that, by any measure, he is clinically insane. Ohlrig is the only film noir villain I know of who is actively undergoing psychoanalysis (usually only a war- or crime-battered hero gets to be an analysand). In fact, we are allowed to observe him in sessions with his psychiatrist. In 1949, this was a very new film experience. It is during one of these sessions, which he breaks off in a fury at his doctor, that Ohlrig decides—in order to spite the doctor—to marry Leonora, a young woman he met casually the previous day and in whom he showed absolutely no interest. And he goes through with it, though he has only contempt for her; then, from the moment they leave the altar, he begins his mental torture of her.

Ohlrig is one of those tycoons, like Ballen Mundson in *Gilda* and the copper mining magnate in another, later film noir, *A Kiss Before Dying,* who is at the center of a story woven around the themes of marriage, money, hatred, and class. And, like Mundson, his cold demeanor and utter ruthlessness, his iron grip on everyone around him, would recall to the popular consciousness the Nazi *uberman* who had been rightly demonized in the newsreels just four years earlier. It was no coincidence right after the war that Scandinavian (as in Nordic—as close to "German" as one could get in the negative, wartime sense) tycoons would be used as Nazi surrogates, embodying all that had come to be seen as sadistic, depraved, and dictatorial during the war. Within months of their wedding, Leonora, who barely ever sees Ohlrig, has still not had sex with him (this is his neurotic "revenge" on his psychiatrist, whom he now blames for his marriage!), and never hears a kind word from his lips, is lamenting (at poolside) to a friend that "I've been taking pills ever since I came East . . . instead of the honeymoon we never took, instead of seeing my family in Denver." And she's not going to see them: Ohlrig may not be around, and he may despise and ridicule her openly, but he keeps Leonora on the tightest leash you can imagine. She's spied upon, followed, and practically confined to quarters in their death palace with the priceless furniture, the paintings, and the ubiquitous, tight-lipped, blank-faced servants in white, who might just as well be orderlies seeing to her needs, while keeping the doors and windows secured, in an asylum.

I would be surprised to find a crueller American film ever made about marriage—a problematic subject to begin with in film noir, where the nuclear family is distinctly absent, or actively attacked as an institution. *Caught* begins as an exploration of money and its ramifications in human affairs and turns out to be about insanity. That is an appropriate segue from this chapter to the next, but first note this gem from Leonora Eames, in that poolside conversation with her friend after a few months under Pluto's roof: "The moment you get rich, you get neurotic." Money can surely corrupt one's morals, but more profoundly, as we see in film noir, it can tear apart the psyche, leaving not a clean divide but a livid, irreparable zigzag. And, though it may have offered Smith Ohlrig's wife little consolation, it's too bad her friend didn't know enough to tell her that often enough you can get plenty neurotic without a dime in your pocket. As we shall see.

6. The Dark Mirror: Sex, Dreams, and Psychoanalysis

In late 1924, as his fame was rapidly spreading from Europe to the United States, Sigmund Freud received two interesting offers from two unlikely sources on this side of the Atlantic. The first was from the powerful publisher of the *Chicago Tribune,* Colonel Robert Mc-Cormick, with regard to the sensational murder trial of Nathan Leopold and Richard Loeb, two wealthy young men who had killed a friend, apparently in an attempt to commit the perfect crime (a plot Hitchcock would appropriate in *Rope* two decades later). Mc-Cormick sent Freud a telegram offering him $25,000 "or anything he name" to come to Chicago and psychoanalyze the two defendants and then publish his findings in the *Tribune.* Knowing that Freud was in ill health, the publisher added that he would be happy to charter the doctor a transatlantic steamer. Freud declined the offer.

Several months later, the Hollywood producer Samuel Goldwyn, another man accustomed to having people jump when he called, offered Freud, whom he called "the greatest love specialist in the world," $100,000—an enormous sum in those days—to "commercialize his study [of psychoanalysis] and write a story for the screen, or come to America and help in a 'drive' on the hearts of the nation." En route to Europe at the time, Goldwyn requested an interview with Freud. And as recounted by Freud's biographer, Peter Gay, Goldwyn then remarked that "'there is nothing really so entertaining as a really great love story' and who better equipped to write, or advise on, such a story than Freud? 'Scenario writers, directors and actors,' Goldwyn thought, 'can learn much by a really deep study of everyday life. How much more forceful will be their creations if they know how to express genuine emotional motivation and suppressed desires?'" Freud declined the interview with a one-sentence letter: "I do not intend to see Mr. Goldwyn." Or as the *New York Times* headline of January 24, 1925, reported it: FREUD REBUFFS GOLDWYN./VIENNESE PSYCHOANALYST IS NOT INTERESTED IN MOTION PICTURE OFFER.

A pity. Love stories aside, Freud might have singlehandedly hastened the film noir era by a generation. In fact, it was just after his death in 1938, at the outset of the war, that many of Freud's major concepts were beginning to wash up into the American consciousness, especially, as one would expect, in metropolitan centers. The popularity of Freudianism and the onset of the film noir era correspond exactly. The intense European interest in his writings—the seminal theories of the unconscious, of dreams, sexuality and humor, dark and otherwise—was part of the intellectual baggage the Austrian and German expatriate directors brought to this country when, like Freud, they fled the Nazis on the eve of the war. After the war, and its dislocations and traumas, it is not surprising that film noir should turn out to be the most psychologically oriented of all film genres, with enormous appeal for that very reason. As James Greenberg wrote in the *New York Times* in May 1994, "Film noirs were movies about adults, made for adults who had just been through a war." It is axiomatic that in film noir the city of dreams and the city of reality merge, with an effect that is not harmonious but disjunctive.

"Almost from its earliest emergence," Mumford writes, "the city brought with it the expectation of intensified struggle within: a thousand little wars fought in the marketplace, the law courts, the ball games, or the arenas. To exert power in every form was the essence of civilization: the city found a score of ways of expressing struggle, aggression, domination, conquest—and servitude." And it is no wonder that psychoanalysis, dreams, and sexual interplay in all its varieties take on such a prominent role in the noir city. The labyrinths of dreams and sexual fantasy overlap, interconnect, and merge in each individual within the greater labyrinth of the physical city—which itself is a catalyst of dreams and fantasies.

Sexual mores changed dramatically in the United States after the war. From a purely social perspective, we see that huge numbers of women had entered the urban workplace during the war, and even late in the Depression, to labor side by side with men. With the return of G.I.s to fractured marriages and romances gone sour, and the influx of single men and women from rural areas, the familiar grid of interpersonal relationships—and notions of romance and sexuality themselves—were turned upside down. The faster, more freewheeling social scene, and a less restrictive, lurid nightlife—radiating around those tremendously popular nightclubs and casinos—rapidly took root. Many returning servicemen, after living for years in combat zones, exclusively in the company of other men, continued to seek a sexual outlet in the only place it had been available to them during the war: among prostitutes. Along with a postwar reaction to the straight-laced, Depression-dampened sexual habits of the 1930s, among vets and non-vets, this helped account for the vast increase in the population of prostitutes nationwide, and for the explosion of so-called illicit sex in every large American city.

Thus in film noir, just as the numerous female executives, journalists, and doctors reflect changes in the legitimate workplace, so does the large number of prostitutes—streetwalkers, call girls, and party girls—reflect the fast-evolving sexual underworld after 1945. Often these women are depicted as exploited victims *(Pickup on South Street, Party Girl, The Big Heat)*, other times as predatory *(The Glass Web, Scarlet Street, Pushover)*, but their constant presence lifts them from the marginal roles, heavily sanitized or camouflaged, which they played in prewar films to a position of some prominence in the urban social fabric as depicted in film noir. Here as elsewhere, in chronicling the subterranean reality, film noir subverts the surface reality. For the first time in American film, Americans' sexual preoccupations, obsessions, and perversions are explicitly dealt with. Film noir is filled with sexual exotica and issues of deviation and fetishism. Love triangles on a highly charged erotic and psychological level, sexual obsession (even—often—to the point of violence), and deep sexual conflicts, confusions, and rifts comprise the most dominant constellations in the noir universe. Promiscuity, priapism, impotence, bisexuality, and homosexuality appear on the big screen with varying degrees of camouflage at first, and then later with broader, more realistic strokes. The now routine (and tiresome) inside stories or "exposés" in contemporary films and television dealing with escort services, wife-swapping, incest, high school prositution rings, and so on, are direct offshoots of those first unvarnished, and far more eclectic, glimpses of the sexual underworld in the noir city.

Today, more than half of all American marriages end in divorce. In cities, the percentage is even higher. Adultery, multiple marriages, out-of-wedlock births (among not just the poor but the middle- and upper-middle classes), and the number of couples, both straight and gay, cohabiting (socially, in many circles, this was still a no-no in 1960, much less 1945) have all increased astronomically since the war, as has teenage—and now pre-teenage—sexual activity. With this greater license, the accompanying cultural changes have at times been seismic. And again, in film, these postwar shifts were first depicted not in the arid domestic dramas and repressed comedies (Doris Day et al.) of the times, but in film noir.

The Marxist critic Sylvia Harvey writes, "In the world of film noir both men and women seek sexual satisfaction *outside* of marriage." Seldom permitted the more socially comfortable, and far safer, pursuit of a discreet affair, noir lovers are required—by inexorable fate, moral law (film noir is unequivocally the most morally driven of all American film genres), lack of hypocrisy, and sheer destructiveness—to carry out, as Harvey says, "the violent destruction of the marriage bonds." "Paradoxically," she goes on, "the destruction of the sanctity of marriage, most notable in *Double Indemnity,* results in placing the relationship of the lovers under such strain, so beyond the boundaries of conventional moral law, that the relationship becomes an impossibility, and transforms itself into the locus of mutual destruction. In *Double Indemnity* the act of killing the husband serves as the supreme act of violence against family life. . . . It is perhaps most clear in this movie that the expression of sexuality and the institution of marriage are at odds with one another, and that both pleasure and death lie outside the safe circle of family relations."

The issues of sexual deviation and fetishism, seldom dealt with in American cinema before 1944, are presented with startling frankness in film noir, often as outgrowths of overcrowded, overpressurized, ultimately decadent urban environments. Among the countless examples of formerly taboo subjects, treated head on in many films noirs, there is foot fetishism in *Where the Sidewalk Ends,* lipstick fetishism in *While the City Sleeps,* pedophilia (the miscreant is the city's foremost child philanthropist) in *The Naked Kiss,* and drugs, pornography, and ritualistic murder in *The Big Sleep.*

At the same time, the films display a ceaseless fascination with murder and betrayal, frequently in tandem with sexual obsession or inversion. If the depictions of psychosexual material are veiled, the veil is a transparent one that distorts the unreality of the censored elements back closer to reality. Because of the censorship imposed by the Hays Office, which stifled even indirect representation of physical love and sex to the point where the byplay around cigarettes between male and female characters (proffering, tapping, lighting, blowing, stroking, extinguishing) served as a stand-in for sexual activity, and the lingering kiss came to be emblematic of sexual intercourse (accomplished in the vast, timeless realm between the cutaway and the next scene), noir directors after the war found in the concepts and catch-phrases of psychoanalysis and psychiatry other essential reference points through which audiences could trace the necessary (and necessarily omitted) connections to emotional and sexual behavior.

In sexual and social matters, it cannot be emphasized enough, noir is first and foremost a subversive form, galaxies removed from the usual cinematic concerns of marriage, conventional romance, love as elixir, and even "acceptable," ultimately redemptive, depictions of infidelity and divorce. To rah-rah wartime films that glorified the gal back home in the kitchen and the guy overseas in the trenches ("family-values" films, the political hucksters would call them today), film noir responds with the desperately manipulated, and in turn manipulating, postwar woman and the scarred and twisted returning G.I. who become enmeshed in the incendiary emotional terrain of the big city. It is a city of increasingly shallow roots, a stopping ground for an ever-shifting, barely settling population of human tumbleweeds. A city the stolid, repressed, blue-collar families, entrenched for generations before the war in ethnically divided neighborhoods and enclaves, desert for the expansiveness, physical safety, and cultural sterility of the suburbs. (It is the more alienated members of these families who gravitate back to the noir universe of the inner city.)

So the city is no longer American society's melting pot, but its cauldron, where high art and low-brow entertainment, opulence and penury, sanctioned white-collar crime and the dirty knife-in-the-alley variety, and every other human contrast imaginable all simmer—and sometimes boil over—in the same black, phantasmagoric broth. The suburbs may be spiritually barren, but they are also reassuringly static to their denizens, a place apparently not subject to tremors from the tumultuous currents underlying the city. They are a kind of limbo in which nothing changes, unless the change is initiated in, or spills over from, the nearby city. This remains true today, of course, when the many varieties of violent urban crime have made their way to the suburbs, victimizing the very people who fled the city for fear of them.

The illicit noir couple, volatile and frankly sexual, operate far from the orbit of conventional morality. They begin as rebels and end up as outlaws. If and when, like the young gunslinging couple in *Gun Crazy,* they attempt to circle backward, toward home and family (in this case, it happens, in those very suburbs), they quickly discover that they are no longer welcome. Discover, too, that they have been seen first as an irritant, then an "infection," and finally as the manifestation of a terrible disruption in the fabric of family life. So they find themselves, not romantically alone together and footloose as they once longed to be—escaping the suffocation of that same family structure—but coldly isolated and trapped. And when it sinks in that it's for keeps, that they're truly doomed, unable to escape even one another, they explode even farther into limbo—not just outlaws, but outcasts. Inevitably they wander into a wilderness which we know they will never leave. Sometimes this is a remote and forsaken corner of the urban wasteland: an abandoned factory, a condemned building, a tenement basement, a boxcar, a piece of cold ground beneath a bridge; or it can be part of the natural wilderness outside the city: a desert *(Split-Second)*, mountains *(High Sierra)*, or the swamp at the end of *Gun Crazy.* At the dead center of a deadened emotional landscape they find themselves hunted, utterly depersonalized, and they die violent deaths. In these films—*They Live By Night, Raw Deal, Out of the Past, Detour, Double Indemnity, The Postman Always Rings Twice,* and dozens of others—sex is not just hot stuff, but literally dynamite. We know the moment the two lovers meet that they are the catalyst of their own destruction, lighting a long zigzag fuse which will chart their abbreviated, but seemingly interminable, journey into the night.

Gun Crazy is notable for its overt sexuality, its highly charged (and stylized) eroticism of violence. From its example spring an enormous number of films noirs with young couples in the fast lane on the short road to oblivion, a score of notable *hommages noirs* by French New Wave directors, such as *Breathless* and *Pierrot Le Fou* (Godard) and *Shoot the Piano Player* (Truffaut), in addition to the countless American films, *Badlands, Bonnie and Clyde, Vanishing Point, Wild at Heart,* that are bleak but straight-ahead road movies rather than films noirs. The inextricable relationship of sex and violence in his work—mirroring their dark nexus at the heart of American culture—and the finely calibrated, ever-ramifying effects of his characters' violence and sexuality on the world around them make the creator of *Gun Crazy,* Joseph H. Lewis, one of our most important postwar directors. For Lewis, America, and everything that big word encompasses, boils down to Sex and Violence. Imitated widely, warmly admired by the likes of Billy Wilder and Otto Preminger, Lewis was a free-wheeling, tough-talking, and meticulous director whose stature—as both a craftsman and psychological innovator—has grown with time. He cut his teeth churning out low-budget quickies for small studios: war movies, horror flicks, singing Westerns, serials, and several Bowery Boys pictures. His first critically acclaimed work was a tightly constructed film noir (centering around the classic noir themes of identity, amnesia, and madness) he made for Columbia Pictures, *My Name Is Julia Ross,* in 1945.

In *Gun Crazy,* a film which was to make him a cult figure, Lewis presents us with a pair of improbably and wildly memorable lovers. Bart, played by John Dall, is a reform school graduate (sent up for robbing a gun store) and army vet (a sharpshooter, of course) who is obsessed with guns. The only toys he wants as a kid are firearms; when he hits adolescence, it's not girlie magazines, but *Guns and Ammo* that he hides in his sock drawer. Laurie, played by Peggy Cummins, is the female sharpshooter in a carnival. She's as worldly and hard-edged as Bart is naive; in this film, it's the young man who plays the ingenue. Sex and guns are Laurie's weapons; when we meet her, she is trading the carnival owner sex for a higher salary and bigger billing. When Bart, adrift, unable to hold a job, joins the carnival with his suitcase full of rare firearms, he and Laurie instantly hit it off. From the first, she's the initiator, the aggressor; at first, in her short-skirted, high-booted, tight-waisted, bust-accentuating cowgirl outfit, she's every bit the female sexual object, fifties-style. But as soon as she is involved with Bart, as the critic Jack Shadoian has written, "she's dressed in pants, and of the two she makes most of the decisions. Bart is compelled by her. She assumes the male role while Bart fusses, hesitates, and hangs back. . . . She is a psychopath. . . ." In terms of gender switching, overt sexuality, and "masculine" assertiveness in her dealings with both men and other women, in 1950 Laurie was light-years ahead of her time. And even among femmes fatales, she is particularly potent.

"I want action," Laurie tells Bart, twirling her six-shooters. And she gets it, in spades. They run away from the carnival, get married in a quickie ceremony, and when they run out of money, spending without a care in the world, begin sticking up grocery and liquor stores. Then, in their carnival cowboy outfits, they move up a few rungs on the criminal ladder and hold up a bank. Guns blazing, this is the beginning of their serious robbery spree. But the surface similarities to the other young-couple-on-the-lam films end here. With Laurie and Bart, we zip right by the notion of criminal motivation per se and dive directly into the corridors of their sexual enmeshment. As Alain Silver points out, "The relationship of Laurie and Bart is one of the most purely sexual in film noir." Despite Bart's fascination with guns, he abhors murder, and it is Laurie who initiates their criminal activities just as she initiated their sexual relationship. "When they have run out of money," Silver continues, "she sexually blackmails him to prevent him from pawning his collection of sidearms." When he begins to balk at the notion of further bank robberies, she threatens to leave him. And she means it. Laurie is consistent from the start: ruthless, greedy, and self-sufficient. Murder for her is merely another option when the situation warrants it. She never veers and never flinches. In her manipulation of Bart, she uses violence as a sexual stimulus which in turn becomes a further stimulus to violence, round and round, a deadly circle.

That the sexual content of *Gun Crazy* should be so powerful is no surprise. Listen to Lewis himself on the subject of what he describes as "his favorite film." In a 1993 interview with the *Village Voice,* upon the occasion of a tribute to him at the Public Theater in New York, he said: "*Gun Crazy* was a great joy to make. I wanted to make an intense love story with the audience rooting for this couple of young killers. Before shooting the scene where they meet at the carnival during the shooting match, I got hold of John Dall and Peggy Cummins and said, listen, you're two dogs in heat, sniffing each other out. And you can tell from the way that scene is done that although she's looking at his eyes, she's really eyeing his pecker." (And that's one of the film's tamer scenes; it's too bad Lewis hasn't disclosed the instructions he gave them for some of the film's more explicitly charged moments.) In his essay on Lewis, "Joseph H. Lewis: Tourist in the Asylum," Myron Meisel has dug up another statement Lewis made with regard to Bart and Laurie's sexual relationship. Meisel writes that the lovers' "competition at marksmanship and their robberies become their means of expressing their feelings toward one another," and that Lewis "centers his narrative around sexual tensions; he has said that he wanted to show that 'their love for each other was more fatal than their love for guns.'"

Five years after *Gun Crazy,* Lewis would direct another masterpiece of the noir canon, *The Big Combo,* a film notable for the sexual obsessiveness of every one of its major, and most of the minor, characters. It is also unique for its time in a number of ways. First, it presents us with a pair of openly gay hit men. Fante (Lee Van Cleef) and Mingo (Earl Holliman) are literally inseparable: they work, relax, and eat together, and they even sleep in twin beds in the same bedroom in their apartment—surely a Hollywood first, previously reserved to the domain of farce, as in the Marx Brothers, Laurel and Hardy, or the Three Stooges. (Fante and Mingo die together, too, in domestic circumstances, when at the dinner table they open a gift box of cigars containing, not Havanas, but a high explosive.) The film also depicts, during a love scene, a thinly disguised portrayal of oral sex; we see the head of the urbane mobster Mr. Brown (Richard Conte), first nuzzling, then sliding down the body of his Junior League mistress, moving clear out of the frame while the camera remains on her face which, moments later, begins to register sexual arousal and then ecstasy. Then there is the detective, Diamond, in love with Brown's mistress, who has a sadistic, hot-and-cold relationship with a stripper ("I used her like a glove that I put on and took off when I felt like it," he says remorsefully after she is gunned down by Fante and Mingo).

Mr. Brown has literally driven his first wife mad during his years of climbing to power in the underworld. And though Brown's mistress, after Brown is shot by Diamond, takes up with the latter, theirs is clearly a relationship that is going nowhere; the road behind them is not so much rocky as cratered, and the road ahead (in the film's final frames they disappear together into a thick, nighttime fog) is inked out by darkness. As for Brown's ex-wife, we leave her at an isolated country cottage, looked after by a permanent housekeeper, where Brown has ensconced her for many years. She's like the woman in white, in Wilkie Collins' novel of that name, the woman of the Victorian era, who is put away by a powerful, criminal husband. And like those hapless, powerless Victorian women, she has lost her mind. When Brown makes reference to her at one point as "his family," it would be laughable if it weren't so terrifying.

Indeed, as noted earlier, in all film noir there is almost a complete absence of the American family. And once again, in their treatment of such a significant subject, the films are chillingly prophetic. The institution of the family is often portrayed with contempt and anger as a claustrophobic relic, a nuisance—something to be exposed, compromised, or fractured in the course of the individual's struggle for *self*-preservation. In short, the family is presented as something wholly unsuited to the stresses and strains of a disintegrating social structure, and then dismissed as just another, often feeble, tool of repression.

One of the most savage portrayals of a "family" in film noir is the household of Norma Desmond in *Sunset Boulevard* (1950). She is a faded silent film star (played by the faded silent film star Gloria Swanson) who has become a recluse in her moldering mansion in Hollywood. She hires Joe Gillis, a failed young screenwriter, as her gigolo. They are waited upon by a butler who turns out to be her ex-husband. Here is Oedipus turned upside down: the son and the mother operate in flagrante under the ministering eyes of the father, and in the end it is the mother who murders the son and the father who is her accomplice. Norma's other substitute child, who dies peacefully and is granted a solemn and macabre funeral, buried by candlelight in a white casket in the garden, is her pet chimpanzee. In this household, the failure of romance, marriage, and family is laid out in spectacularly ironic fashion, with razor-sharp touches of the absurd by Billy Wilder, in his script and direction.

But Norma Desmond is a rare bird among the central women in film noir, who tend to be as young, strong, and magnetic as they are manipulative and destructive. In fact, the role of women in film noir is considerably complex. In no way do we find the crude, sexist, madonna-or-doormat formulations of 1930s gangster films in which the women are usually cardboard cutouts. While the principal female figure in film noir is the femme fatale/spider woman/dark lady, she comes in many forms, wears many masks, and is never one-dimensional. She tends to be more enigmatic, more textured, and more powerful than the noir hero. And however evil she may be, her *real* power, it is made clear, derives not from some malignant core or deformity of character, as it does with the most negative male characters, but from her sexuality.

This is a great departure in American cinema, where so often women's sexuality has been depicted negatively—from a male viewpoint—as a source of weakness and uncertainty. In comparison to the housewife or other maternal figure traditionally found at the nucleus of family life, the femme fatale (usually as the other woman) is nearly always the more intriguing and energetic figure in the films, imbued with intelligence, guile, charm, and unambiguous sexual electricity. Not to mention the sort of street smarts that were previously evident solely among male characters. From the very first, in fact, and certainly today, the surge of interest in film noir among men and women alike has to do in large part with its compelling, complex representations of women and women's sexuality. The critic Janey Place insists that the classic noir era "stands as the only period in American film in which women are deadly but sexy, exciting, and strong," and in which they are "active, not static symbols . . . intelligent and powerful, if destructively so."

These women are the most memorable characters in film noir. Ava Gardner as Kitty in *The Killers,* Yvonne DeCarlo as Anna in *Criss Cross,* Barbara Stanwyck as Phyllis Dietrichson in *Double Indemnity,* Claire Trevor as Velma in *Murder, My Sweet,* Jane Greer as Kathie in *Out of the Past.* While the hero remains a constant—often a passive, self-destructive one—in these films, the femme fatale undergoes numerous metamorphoses, sometimes at a dizzying rate. As Christine Gledhill has written: "The femme fatale is noted for changeability and treachery . . . not only is the hero frequently not sure whether the woman is honest or a deceiver, but the heroine's characterization is itself fractured . . . for instance, in *The Postman Always Rings Twice,* Cora (played by Lana Turner) exhibits a remarkable series of unmotivated character switches and roles something as follows: 1. sex bomb; 2. hardworking, ambitious woman; 3. loving playmate in an adulterous relationship; 4. fearful girl in need of protection; 5. victim of male power; 6. hard, ruthless murderess; 7. mother-to-be; 8. sacrifice to the law." The male hero, Frank Chambers, played by John Garfield, all the while remains relatively linear, even to guiding us through the story in flashbacks through his voice-over; a shifty, weak-willed drifter, he stumbles into a whirlpool from which he spends the entire film (unsuccessfully) trying to extricate himself. Turner, incidentally, while playing the quintessential black widow in this film wears pure white in nearly every scene and has bleached her hair a blinding platinum. Also, though MGM bought the film rights to the James M. Cain novel in 1934, because its two basic themes were long-term, unrepentant adultery and a husband's cold-blooded murder by his wife, the Hays Office blocked production of the film for twelve years; only after the novel had been adapted to film twice in Europe, in France by Pierre Chenal in 1939 *(Le Dernier Tournant)* and in Italy by Luchino Visconti in 1942 *(Ossessione),* did it find its way onto the American movie screen.

As vivid and exciting as the femme fatale can be in film noir, her antithesis, the nurturing, supposedly redeeming woman is usually unrelievedly pallid and passive—to the point of repulsing us, as well as the hero. She is most often the girl back home, or the faithful, long-suffering wife, or the steady fellow worker at the office, or the platonic friend futilely in love with the hero. She is very much *not* a denizen of the night. In fact, she tends to be portrayed in the few daylit, pastoral scenes in film noir, usually with flat, high-key lighting, in the kind of wide open spaces to which the femme fatale would be a rare visitor, indeed. Ann, the small-town fiancée Jeff Bailey leaves behind for Kathie in *Out of the Past,* is the perfect example of this type. Antiseptic, static, sexually repressed, socially rather dull, she lives with her parents and works as a schoolteacher; she wants to marry and have kids and never leave her hometown. Should we be surprised that when reunited with Kathie, who is freewheeling, worldly, intellectually (if criminally) active, dangerous, and highly sexed, Jeff finds it so easy to fall back under her spell?

Our first glimpse of the femme fatale in a film noir often centers on her stockinged legs, resting on a desk, crossed on a bar stool, striding down a street or corridor, descending a set of stairs. Or on her long mane of hair, seen from above, catching the rays of a street-light or being combed out before a dressing-table mirror, or fanning out on white satin sheets. These "disastrous women" (as the French literally translates) are equally at home in shadowy dives or ritzy apartments, hugging the shadows down hazardous byways or sashaying into the leather-and-walnut-appointed boardrooms of large corporations. Their dress runs a tight gamut, always between the twin poles of sexuality and power. For example, in the boudoir, where their sexual wiles predominate, they may be dressed in the slinkiest of gowns or negligées, fluid and at ease within their bodies; in the world of business they often appear in aggressively male-style clothing: pinstripe suits with padded shoulders and boxy contours, such as Joan Crawford wears throughout *Mildred Pierce,* for example, playing a successful restaurateur, or Audrey Totter in *The Lady in the Lake,* as the president of a publishing company. The femme fatale may also indulge, around either of these two poles, in various eccentricities of dress that will serve to heighten, literally or metaphorically, her sexual allure or power lust: a wardrobe that is completely red, or white; a closetful of monogrammed silk robes; a sable coat and hat to match the sable upholstery on her automobile seats; jewelry custom-made around a single gem, such as sapphire or onyx; a perfume specially created for her that is like no other, and so on.

Approaching the femme fatale from a purely compositional point of view, Janey Place writes that "the strength of these women is expressed in the visual style by their dominance in composition, angle, camera movement, and lighting. They are overwhelmingly the compositional focus, generally center frame and/or in the foreground, or pulling focus to them in the background. They control camera movement, seeming to direct the camera (and the hero's gaze, with our own) irresistably with them as they move. In contrast, the 'good' women of film noir and many of the seduced, passive men are predominantly static, both within the frame and in their ability to motivate camera movement and composition." The femme fatale is portrayed as most comfortable moving through the nocturnal city alone—not on a man's arm, but *without* a man—which was also a new phenomenon in American films.

Depicted on the other end of the social and economic scale from the high-powered female business executives, advertising whizzes, doctors, and newspaper columnists are the numerous women, initially seen as femmes fatales, who barely survive on the fringes of show business, the arts, or the world of all-night restaurants and nightclubs. They can be waitresses looking for (and sometimes dating to get) their break out of obscurity *(Fallen Angel* and *I Wake Up Screaming),* bit actresses *(The Crimson Kimono),* artists' models *(Killer's Kiss* and *Nocturne),* carnival extras *(Nightmare Alley),* as well as prostitutes, criminals' molls, and other social outcasts. Sometimes these women—neither conventionally good nor bad regardless of their occupations, and inhabiting no archetypal extreme— surprise us and turn out not only to be the most multifaceted character in a film, but also the first (setting an example for the hero) to embrace, or stumble onto, her own brand of spiritual regeneration.

In other words, they are femmes fatales who undergo conversions, like Lily (she has no last name) in *Road House* (1948). Lily is a down-and-out jazz pianist. At first she appears in the guise of a classic femme fatale, opening the film with her legs propped suggestively on a desk. She has come to town to audition at a cocktail lounge. One of the bartenders refers to her as "the new equipment," and one of the patrons, listening to her play the piano, turns to another patron and says approvingly, "She reminds me of the first woman who ever slapped my face." Yet it is Lily, cynical and streethard, who deflects the hero's (after he's given her nothing but grief) otherwise certain plunge into the abyss. In the opening scene of *Party Girl* (1958), the title itself a euphemism for a call girl, Vicki Gaye is one of a dozen showgirls who parade onstage in a large garish nightclub; one by one, the most attractive of them are picked out of the lineup by men who pay them a hundred dollars to attend a party where they will be matched off for the night with other men.

Yet after her roommate's murder and her own ordeals at the hands of sadistic mobsters, Vicki evolves into the film's most regenerative character, helping the crooked hero to see the light. In *Pickup on South Street* (1953), Candy (she too has no last name) is an outright streetwalker, garishly dressed, poorly spoken, vulgar at every turn, who turns out to be the most moral character in the film (as well as the most patriotic!) long before the hero, a shameless and self-centered pickpocket, ever takes a single action beneficial to someone else.

These three women are exceptions in the pantheon of femme fatales, yet still they spend most of their working lives trading sex for favors or selling their sexual services outright. The fact is that whether the femme fatale is presented as a powerful "legitimate" citizen (however threatening) or an exploited fantasy object, never before the film noir era were women found in such roles, with carefully textured, unflinchingly delineated characters.

It should be noted, too, that there are several important films noirs in which the character who enters the labyrinth on a quest—the principal character, that is—is a woman. These heroines, decidedly *not* femme fatales, but equally powerful when it comes to intelligence, resourcefulness, sexual energy, and pure independence of action, have the added distinction—unlike many of their male counterparts—of surviving the labyrinth and resuming their previous lives, battle-hardened as only men could be in films before film noir.

The heroine of *The Reckless Moment* (1949), the film that Max Ophuls shot right after *Caught,* is a suburban housewife, Lucia Harper, who has plunged into the bowels of the Los Angeles underworld to disentangle her young daughter from a murder which she thinks—erroneously—the girl committed. In fact, the girl's lover, an aging roué, died accidentally. Lucia finds herself the victim of a blackmailer who has spotted her disposing of the roué's body. Thus begins her dizzying journey through the noir labyrinth, which ends "successfully"; that is, though scarred and not a little shaken when they return to their humdrum existence, Lucia and her daughter find themselves at film's end in the clear of both criminals and police. Lucia heightens the irony of her ordeal when she receives a Christmas Eve phone call from her husband, who has been away on business, and tells him (with no irony in her voice) that "everything is fine."

Raw Deal (1948), directed by Anthony Mann, is another such specialized film noir in that it not only revolves around a woman's descent into the labyrinth, but also is one of the very few films noirs (*Mildred Pierce* is another) in which the voice-over narrator is a woman. *Raw Deal,* like *T-Men* shot by the cinematographer John Alton, stunningly evokes postwar San Francisco, its mists, fogs, and deceptive shadows and its many-layered nocturnal tableaux, textured with Alton's customary black-on-black compositions. Pat (again, a woman with no surname), played by the redoubtable Claire Trevor, is the girlfriend of a jailbird named Joe Sullivan. It is Pat who addresses us in a complex and understated voice-over. Early on, she becomes the film's "other woman" when Joe falls in love with Ann Martin, a young woman leading an uneventful life with no criminal ties. This is where *Raw Deal* charts out new territory; here the familiar sequence of a femme fatale drawing an innocent man into her web is inverted. As critic Carl Macek writes, "Joe Sullivan exists as a *homme fatal,* seducing Ann Martin into a world filled with violent action and murder, enticing her with a promise of sexual fulfillment that goes beyond the realm of normal relationships. She surrenders completely to Joe, committing murder as the ultimate expression of her love." And Pat is left to become their chronicler. She remains with Joe to the end, but as an appendage and no longer an active partner in his sexual or criminal activities.

In fact, in chronicling the journey with Joe and Ann through the labyrinth, Pat turns further and further inward herself, lapsing into digressions from her own history (the labyrinth of her memory) as well as lengthy invocations of the city itself (the physical labyrinth). When her love affair with Joe is put on ice, it is San Francisco that absorbs her attention. She relates to it both geographically and spiritually, and invokes it most powerfully just before the film's climactic scene when she is holed up with Joe, hiding from his gangland enemies, in a harbor-front hotel. While the fog off the bay rolls past her window, Pat confides to us in her voice-over: "In less than an hour we'll be leaving San Francisco. Now that we're actually going, I have a kind of feeling for the city—even Corkscrew Alley, way over on the other side. It's where I grew up, jumped rope, cried, fell in love, and now. . . ." And at that moment she realizes she isn't going anywhere; Joe has taken his gun and slipped out into the night to find Ann. Within the hour, he will be gunned down, appropriately enough in Corkscrew Alley (the film was based on a story of that title), a name that is emblematic of the twisted moral world the characters inhabit. Ann will cradle him in her arms on the pavement, her life a shambles, and Pat, their chronicler, will fade back into the thick fog, swallowed up, literally, by the city.

In *Phantom Lady,* one of the most expressionistic of all films noirs, directed by Robert Siodmak, an engineer's secretary sets out to clear him of the charge of strangling his own wife. A Beatrice-figure named Kansas (ostensibly a model American girl from the heartland), this secretary enters the sweltering and harrowing nocturnal labyrinth of New York during a heat wave in pursuit of a mystery woman who is her boss' lone alibi. The mystery woman turns out to be mentally deranged, cocooned in a world of her fantasies and utterly incapable of providing an alibi. It is ironic that the night of the murder, when she crossed paths with our hero, was the one and only time in months she had put on street clothes and escaped her home confinement (in the far suburbs) in the care of private nurses in order to have a night on the town. The murderer turns out to be a sculptor who was the engineer's best friend—and the dead wife's spurned lover. His studio, where in the end he attempts to strangle Kansas, is full of gigantic busts that look as if they might have adorned one of those grotesquely oversized temples to fascism erected by Hitler and Mussolini during the war. He is an artist with a penchant for psychological patter. Throughout the film, and especially in his last hours when he entraps Kansas at his studio, he pontificates to her about art, the masses, and the workings of the psyche—a far cry from the nickel-plated street lingo of 1930s villains.

Many noir characters engage in such psychological banter; usually it is interspersed with other, thoroughly "realistic" dialogue. Two examples: in *This Gun for Hire* (1942), Raven, a contract killer, comments to a girl who has befriended him, "Every night I dream. I read somewhere about a . . . about a kind of doctor. A psychsomething. You tell your dream, you don't have to dream it anymore." And in *Gilda,* a film in which we have seen that the triangle of lovers never seem to leave off analyzing one another in psychosexual terms, Gilda at one point, standing by the casino's roulette table in the shadow of a potted palm, turns to Johnny with a twinkle in her eye. "Any psychiatrist," she purrs casually, "would tell you your thought associations are very revealing. . . ."

Our sculptor/strangler in *Phantom Lady* prattles on and on with such talk, analyzing himself and tossing out wildly involuted symbolic references; then he moves on to his hands, first rhapsodizing about them as the tools of his art and then lamenting them as the weapons with which he murders. In both instances, he speaks of them as if they operate independent of his mind and body; and here we see Siodmak's German roots, for the silent "street films" made in Munich and Berlin in the 1920s are full of such murderers. Again, modern art and mental deviance are linked in a film of the 1940s; some attribute this to Hollywood's bedrock anti-intellectualism, but the roots of this connection relate more to the country's anti-intellectualism and deep ambivalence about ideas foreign, especially European in origin—especially Germanic—immediately after the war. Kansas is rescued by the dogged detective who pursued the case with her even after her boss had been convicted and sent to death row. And the sculptor—off-camera, in the style of Greek tragedy—jumps through a large window high above the streets, leaving a fearsome jagged hole in the plate-glass. Black on black, like the hole in his psyche. His insanity.

Phantom Lady much resembles *The Dark Corner,* in which another faithful secretary enters the noir labyrinth to clear her ex-con boss of murder, and *Black Angel,* in which a chanteuse teams up with a drunken pianist (just as Kansas does with the sculptor, and like the sculptor, the pianist turns out to be the real murderer) to exonerate her jailed husband of a murder he did not commit. In *Black Angel,* as in *Phantom Lady,* the murder victim is the femme fatale, who in both cases is presented as a knockout blonde with a scalding temper and a vile disposition—the absolute antithesis of our two Girl Fridays. And neither of the men that these "good" women are trying to save are particularly appealing; certainly for the better part of each film they are presented as self-centered ingrates. In *The Dark Corner,* it is the femme fatale's crooked, gigolo boyfriend who is murdered. Interestingly enough, *Black Angel* and *The Dark Corner* are yet another pair of films with similar plots, identical themes, and overlapping symbolism that were made at different Hollywood studios (Universal and 20th Century-Fox) by different directors and producers at exactly the same time, the early spring of 1946.

There was another film noir released that spring, *Nocturne,* directed by Edwin L. Marin which is built around a fascinating conceit. A composer is murdered while working at his piano—by someone he knows, who has come right up beside him and shot him at point-blank range. He is a womanizer, and his living room walls are filled with photographic portraits of his many conquests. The only clue as to his murderer's identity is the piece of sheet music the victim was annotating at the moment of his death, called "Dolores." After having "Dolores" played for him over and over again, the detective on the case must first aesthetically, then concretely, link the music, its moods, colorations, and intonations, to one of the many female suspects—none of whom is actually named Dolores, but one of whom had it applied to her fictively. And until he finds her, he refers to her always as "Dolores"; thus the woman takes on the name on the sheet music.

Music plays a crucial role in *Phantom Lady,* as well. It is by far the most psychologically charged of all these films, and though *Black Angel* is entirely set in the world of popular music and nightclubs, and *The Dark Corner,* as we have seen, ingeniously incorporates music as a motif throughout, and *Nocturne* makes music its cornerstone, it is *Phantom Lady* that employs music with the greatest resonance as a purely psychosexual device. Midway through the film, sex and music become fused into a single entity in one of the most famous scenes in all of film noir.

Kansas, early in her quest, disguises herself as a prostitute in order to win the confidence of a jazz drummer whom she is certain knows the identity of the real murderer. For a girl from the heartland, with hayseed in her hair, she is immediately convincing in her role switching—both to him and to us. In no time at all, and with hardly any effort, she puts together an impressive ensemble: short clinging skirt, stiletto heels, mesh gloves, a see-through plastic raincoat, tons of makeup, a flashy hairdo, and a wad of gum in her molars which she chews with relish. Except for the heels, which hurt her feet, she seems very much at home within this persona, and we begin to wonder just how much of the seamy side of the city our Girl Friday is acquainted with. Pint-sized and zoot-suited, with an out-sized swagger to match his ego, the drummer is very much a ladies man. He is performing at a theater with a big band, and Kansas, flirting with him from the front row, catches his eye immediately. Then she accompanies him to a basement room down an alley where an intense jam session is in progress. There are a half dozen jazz musicians playing bebop, but the stool behind the drum set is vacant. The drummer sits and, literally without missing a beat, joins in with a vengeance. And what follows—yet another example of how an inventive director could bypass the Hays Office censors—is one of the steamiest simulations of sexual intercourse in film, with neither participant ever once touching the other. The drummer plays with increasing frenzy and Kansas reacts every inch of the way, dancing, gyrating, or just rocking on her heels with incredibly suggestive body language, until he launches into his solo—the sweat streaming down his face, her breath coming in short bursts through parted lips—which reaches a tremendous climax and then leaves them both looking exhausted, post-coital.

All of this is shot by Siodmak, with rhythmical visual cuts syncopated to the music, from various bizarre (up-from-the-floor, through clouds of smoke, or along the planes of long shadows) angles in an utterly claustrophobic space. A kind of dream space. For despite the music, the scene has the look of dream footage in a silent film: hallucinatory yet utterly realistic, compartmentalized but imaginatively spacious. Talk about wish-fulfillment and its ambiguities: here is an atmosphere of freewheeling sexuality in an impossibly confined area; clandestine and exquisitely private, but with other people present; simultaneously orgiastic and chaste; a ferocious climax with a complete lack of physical contact! Sex at once mental and subtly palpable, attainable and terribly elusive—as in a dream.

As should be obvious by now, Orson Welles was correct: a film, above all else, is certainly a dream, and within that dream dozens of other dreams open inward and outward, radiating powerfully. Film noir is filled with dreams within dreams, sometimes as pure dreams, other times in the form of flashbacks, fantasies, or episodes of psychic flight. Often in the films we may lose track exactly of where the putative (so-called real life) narrative leaves off and the dream narrative begins.

C.G. Jung states, "The dream is a spontaneous self-portrayal, in symbolic form, of the actual situation in the unconscious." And a film noir may be the distillation of such a situation, once frozen in time and now rendered cinematically fluid. The film, in short, like the dream in psychoanalysis, may be an explanation in itself, through its symbolism, its juxtapositions, and its story, however fractured. As with purely technical considerations such as lighting and camera-angling, the psychological aspects of film noir are often more concerned with *concealment* than *revealment,* constantly reinforcing the notion that the characters' motives are ambiguous, furtive, and frequently overridden—and distorted—by fear and anxiety.

The film noir hero is always on a quest, sometimes in the role of a detective or private investigator, sometimes investigating without that formal investiture. But even when playing a detective, he is not like the detectives we find in the 1930s (with their own series of films, each film the unraveling of a different case)—Philo Vance, Nick Charles, Perry Mason, Mr. Moto, Charlie Chan—who *employ* psychological stratagems from a highly detached, objective plateau, like a chessplayer who rarely soils his hands; rather, the noir detective operates from an intensely subjective psychological perspective within the murk of the labyrinth in which he himself is actively venturing (or trapped). In short, the life of the noir investigator, whether he is formally or figuratively in that role, may depend on how well he can read the psyches and deduce the motivations of other characters, especially his antagonists. Often, this ability, rather than his aptitude for physical violence—skill with his fists, marksmanship, pain threshold—is far more crucial to his survival.

The critic Deborah Thomas, putting the noir hero on the couch rather than behind it in discussing his investigative urges, compares him to the classic Freudian neurotic, first observing (and she quotes Peter Gay) that in both types "the desire to recall is countered by the desire to forget," and then concluding that "the frequency of flashback structures in the [film noir] genre is suggestive of the neurotic's compulsion to repeat, as the noir protagonist, too, reworks the past to try to master it through his narration." Whether as metaphorical doctor or patient, and however sly or bewildered he may be, the noir hero will find that the investigative onus—the equivalent of Odysseus' vaunted "wiliness"—is on him.

The characters in film noir often walk a shadowy borderline between repressed violence and outright vulnerability. The returning G.I.s who seem to be walking around in their own nightmares are a prime example. For example, there is Gerard (only once do we hear his first name, "Lawrence") in *Cornered* zigzagging through the perilous darkness of Buenos Aires; and Buzz, with a steel plate implanted in his skull and "monkey music" thundering in his ears, lurching through the rain in *The Blue Dahlia;* and George in *Somewhere in the Night,* a man with no memory and no identity, wandering a hostile maze full of dead ends; all three manifest their fears and vulnerabilities immediately, on the surface: it takes but a single scene with each for us to see how lost they are. The themes surrounding the shell-shocked G.I. as a character in film noir can be viewed as a comprehensive critique of urban society both before and after the war. The embodiment of such a critique would be the veteran's psychological traumas—from amnesia to homicidal compulsions—and his sense of displacement, rejection, and cynicism as he tries to reenter American society. The film noir can be seen as a reflector (some would say, deflector) of the society's responsibility for the war: that is, the hero may be murderous or violent because of his role in the war, a war which itself, in circular fashion, reflected the vast, murderous undercurrents of the society as a whole.

"You knew he was dynamite. He has to explode sometimes." This is how Dixon Steele's agent rationalizes (to Steele's new girlfriend) the fact that Steele, without provocation, has beaten a man mercilessly in a nightclub. And at this point we are only midway through *In a Lonely Place,* a 1950 film directed by Nicholas Ray. Steele is icily and jaggedly played against type by Humphrey Bogart, who anticipates his role as the paranoid Captain Queeg in *The Caine Mutiny.* Bogart's Steele is a literate man—too literate for his own good as a screenwriter in Hollywood—with a brutal temper. We witness many acts of violence on his part. He is a war vet. His career is in a shambles, his few friendships are dissolving, and he is suspected of a murder he did not commit. Trying to salvage a screenplay that won't be salvaged by driving himself to exhaustion, he has gotten involved in a love affair which also begins to come apart because of his paranoid fantasies. In the end, he cracks, and after an escalating quarrel with the girlfriend, begins strangling her. At that moment, he is interrupted by a call from the police and informed that he is no longer a murder suspect: the real killer has been apprehended. Shortly thereafter, without a word, Steele walks out of his girlfriend's life. As Nicholas Ray (it is his wife, Gloria Grahame, perhaps the most battered woman in film noir, who portrays the girlfriend) pointed out in an interview in 1963, we don't know if Steele "is going to get drunk, have an accident in his car, or whether he is going to a psychiatrist for help."

The latter course of action is not always the safest in a film noir. Many of the films revolve around sophisticated urban psychiatrists as central characters, often villains, who manipulate the hero's mental labyrinth in exactly the way more pedestrian villains like gangster overlords or corrupt politicians manipulate the workings of the greater urban labyrinth to achieve their ends. Their knowledge of the human mind empowers these doctors in the way the mobsters of the prewar gangster films were empowered by their street savvy and criminal know-how. The psychiatrist as a specialized variety of criminal mastermind makes his debut in film noir.

In *Nightmare Alley* (1947), directed by Edmund Goulding, a former carnival worker and nightclub mind-reader, Stan Carlisle, sets himself up as a spiritualist who bilks wealthy clients. Carlisle is played with chilling ferocity by Tyrone Power, who after years of playing handsome golden boys and swashbucklers had to beg his studio to cast him in such an unsavory role. Most of Carlisle's clients want him to bring back the spirit of a dead loved one, and through various technical tricks with sound and light, he manages to hoodwink a number of powerful and well-connected people. "The spook trade," he calls it, because of the apparitions he conjures. Soon enough Stan begins referring to himself as Stanton Carlisle—"The Great Stanton" is his billing—when he plies his trade. His two partners are his wife Molly, and a "consulting psychologist," Lilith Ritter (brilliantly portrayed by Helen Walker), who provides him with intimate information about various patients whom Stan engineers into becoming his clients. Armed with this information, which only the client himself (and the unsuspected and above-suspicion Ritter) possesses, Stan can dupe him with impunity and subtlety. And that's exactly what he does until Molly, seeing first-hand how one client, a rich industrialist, collapses with grief (Stan has convinced Molly to play the "spirit" of a long-deceased young woman the man loved), exposes Stan by taking flight midway through the staging of this elaborate scam in the man's garden.

Stan's fall is as quick and brutal as was his ascent, when he stepped on or destroyed every person with whom he came into contact professionally, including the strongman in a provincial carnival (from whom he seduced Molly), and Zeena the mind-reader, his first partner, from whom he stole an oral code used by mentalists, and before that, Zeena's drunken husband to whom Stan unwittingly, but lethally, gave a bottle of wood alcohol that killed him. Stan is the consummate conman, glib, smooth as oil, supremely self-confident, and ruthless to a fault. But with Lilith Ritter, he turns out to be quite out of his league. In fact, with the utmost ease, and certainly without a qualm, she pulls off what seems impossible after we've watched Stanton Carlisle outmaneuver everyone from nightclub owners to business tycoons: she outcons the conman.

Dr. Lilith Ritter is one of the greatest femmes fatales. She is icy, calculating, avaricious to a fault—and piercingly intelligent. Helen Walker specialized in such parts, though this was her zenith; only twenty-six, she was involved in a serious automobile accident before the filming of *Nightmare Alley* was completed, and her career was never again the same. She appeared, in smaller parts, in two subsequent films noirs, *Call Northside 777* and *The Big Combo;* in the latter, she portrays Mr. Brown's ravaged, deranged, locked-away wife. That was her last film, and soon afterward Walker died of cancer at forty-seven. She was one of those noir actors—like Tom Neal (imprisoned for murder), Gail Russell (a terminal alcoholic), Lana Turner (involved in sex scandals), and John Garfield (a victim of political persecution)—whose off-screen life, rife with accidents, illness, and mental instability, seemed to mirror her noir persona.

When Stan opens up to Lilith Ritter (as he never has to the two warm women in his life, Zeena and Molly), she delivers her credo to him, with no mincing of words: "I think you're a perfectly normal human being: selfish and ruthless when you want something; generous and kindly when you've got it." And in her very first two scenes in the film, Lilith appears, without contradiction, at either end of the femme fatale scale (persona-wise): in a nightclub wearing a strapless gown and diamond earrings, her hair provocatively styled and her makeup thick, every inch the vamp; and in her office wearing a box-shouldered, mannish suit, hair tightly bunned, and with only a trace of makeup on her face. Stan has met her at the nightclub while performing his mentalist act; she is the one member of the audience who tried to trip him up with a lie when he was performing. And he parried her—for the first and only time, it turns out.

But she has aroused his pique, and in the next scene he visits her office (at both her office and home she has powerful female attendants seeing to her needs) to find out more about her. He finds out plenty. But first she turns to him, hand on hip by her large desk, and says, "Have you ever been psychoanalyzed?" His reply is offhand and—from our point of view—delicious: "I saw it once in a movie," he says. Stan discovers that Lilith records all her patients' therapy sessions with an elaborate recording mechanism involving (in those pre–tape recorder days of 1947) a phonograph that records on vinyl. And so begins their unholy alliance.

But while Stan feels at all times that he's in the driver's seat, it turns out Lilith has been playing him for a sucker from that first meeting. Though his considerable worldly success has been achieved by publically performing every conceivable kind of clairvoyance, from mind-reading to mentalism, Lilith is a clinically trained psychologist: when it comes to the human mind—and to human foibles—she can run rings around him. So when Stan is exposed, and runs to her apartment for his share of their shakedown loot (hundreds of thousands of dollars in cash) which she has been safe-keeping for him, Lilith does to him, with frigid efficiency, what he has been doing to everyone else.

For starters, she feigns bewilderment and tells him she doesn't know what he's talking about. Partners? She was never his partner. Scam? What scam? She's a respected psychologist with a thriving practice, a solid citizen in her city, while he is a visiting nightclub entertainer whom the police are seeking for fraud. Then she pulls out a "confession" he made to her early on when, spooked by an unfavorable tarot reading by Zeena (and a whiff of rubbing alcohol recalling Zeena's husband's death), he ran to Lilith and talked his head off until dawn. It turns out she had switched on her hidden recording device that night.

"Please, Mr. Carlisle," she tells him sternly moments after he has barged distraught into her apartment, "try to understand that these delusions of yours in regard to me are a part of your mental condition." Throughout the scene, never wavering, Lilith acts as if he is just another of her patients. And she turns up the psychological jargon—still a novelty to movie audiences—full-throttle, spinning him all around, and upside down, with a kind of Freudian Esperanto. "When I first examined you," she continues, "you were being tortured by guilt reactions concerned with the death of that drunken mentalist during your carnival days."

Exasperated, Stan demands to know what she's trying to pull. "You can't prove anything," he says. "Besides, it was an accident—I told you that."

"I'm a psychologist, not a judge," she snaps. "What I want to explain to you is that all these things you think you have done lately—or think have been done to you—are merely the fantasies and guilt of your past life projected on the present. . . . You must regard it all as a nightmare. . . . And speaking of records: would you like to hear a playback of the recital you made that night?" When Stan, weakening visibly, in a cold sweat, insists that she was complicitous in his crimes, Lilith throws the final switch: "That's another thing, Mr. Carlisle, which clearly indicates the serious nature of your malady. You've made a strange transference onto me as a confederate of yours. You must have hospital care . . . these hallucinations of yours—we simply can't have you wandering about getting into trouble, can we . . . Please, Mr. Carlisle, put yourself in my hands. You can trust me absolutely."

And hearing police sirens approaching (on Lilith's orders, her maid has called the cops), Stan snaps and takes flight—without his money—clambering through the window onto the fire escape and disappearing into the night. When we next see him, he's sitting dazed in the waiting room of a train station—subdued as we've never seen him before: as if Lilith, in their mental combat, has scrambled his senses and intellect irreparably. She's also put him on the front page of all the newspapers, a large mug shot beneath the word FUGITIVE.

After hiding out in a succession of cheap hotels and flophouses, broke and desperate, Stan starts drinking, and soon enough finds himself riding the rails with other hobos, guzzling gin from the bottle and bewildering his companions with fractured versions of his old mentalist routines. Finally he wanders into a carnival in search of a job, and after much pleading he is offered one—as the Geek. The Geek is a man who is given a bottle and a place to sleep it off in return for putting in several hours a day in a cage biting the heads off of live chickens. It is the crudest and most bestial of sideshow attractions, a human being at the absolute nadir. When the carnival owner asks him if he can handle the job, Stan, throwing back a shot of rye, contorts his lips and says, "Brother, I was made for it." Instead, he breaks down completely after a single night in the Geek cage, and hits his bottom, alcoholically and emotionally. He runs amok and has to be restrained physically by a group of carnival hands. One of them recognizes him as a former big-time performer and remarks to the carnival owner: "The Great Stanton. How could he fall so low?" Without missing a beat, the owner, evoking the ethos of middlebrow businessmen everywhere (despite the oddness of *his* particular business), replies impassively, "Because he reached too high."

This is not a charge that could be leveled at the hero of Alfred Hitchcock's *Spellbound* (1945), a young psychiatrist who wanders around for nearly the entire film in a thick, amnesiac haze. *Spellbound* is a veritable viper's nest of psychiatrists and psychologists, among whom its hero is trying to clear himself of a murder he did not commit. Unfortunately, he has no memory, and scant mental reserves for clear thinking. Enter a female psychiatrist who throws herself wholeheartedly into assisting him, taking on the role of Beatrice not only to guide him through the hostile labyrinth of the physical world, but also through the pitch-dark maze of his unconscious. In short, she becomes his analyst, trying to unlock his memory. For a while, she maintains the veneer of her external professionalism during their floating therapy sessions (on the run from the police), but soon enough, and with less consternation than we might expect, she also becomes his lover. This psychiatrist couple, amorously and psychically entwined, and played without a gleam of irony by Ingrid Bergman and Gregory Peck, is the only one I know of in film noir.

But that's only the beginning. Much of the film is set at a sanitarium, filled with psychiatrists who work, dine communally (at a long table), engage in banter and debate, and otherwise live together day in day out in deluxe boarding house style. (This is one asylum where the keepers are more interesting, and possibly more tormented, than the inmates, whom at any rate we seldom see.) It turns out that the murderer is the elderly director of the sanitarium—the head psychiatrist; his victim was yet another psychiatrist, a much younger man, who had arrived to take his job. Rather than relinquish his position (talk about a Freudian plot!), the older man murders the younger one and then frames our amnesiac.

There are two other notable films noirs with female psychiatrists at their centers that were made within a year of *Nightmare Alley*: *The High Wall* (1947) and *The Accused* (1949). Both were directed by German expatriates of the expressionist school, Curtis Bernhardt and William Dieterle, respectively. In *The High Wall*, the psychiatrist (played by Audrey Totter) is a nurturing type who will go to any lengths to rescue her patient—both from the law and from his own demons. Again the patient is an amnesiac who is deeply incriminated for a crime he did not commit: he's actually found unconscious at the murder scene, in an automobile beside his dead wife. Institutionalized, he comes under the care of this psychiatrist who first helps him track down the real murderer, his wife's boss as it turns out, a stodgy older man who runs a conservative religious book publishing company; then, after our hero has knocked him out in a scuffle, the psychiatrist administers sodium pentothal to the murderer and extracts a confession from him.

In *The Accused,* the female psychiatrist is a more problematic case. For one thing, though she is also a professor of psychology at a university, she seems utterly adrift when it comes to reading the emotions of other people—or having even a minimal understanding of her own motivations. Played at her most cloying and spinsterish by Loretta Young, this psychiatrist holds an unusual and coveted position in the world for a woman of her time, but seems to be as unworldly as one could imagine. And so it is that she finds herself, in all innocence apparently, alone on a remote beach at night with one of her male students. He kisses her and she becomes highly agitated, clearly upset at having been aroused—as if this is her first schoolgirl kiss. Moments later, in a panic, she bludgeons her companion to death with a steel bar. From then on, utilizing all her professional knowledge, she does everything she can to cover up her crime. She manages to fill the dead student's lungs with water (a difficult trick, even for a doctor) and arranges both his body and the surrounding terrain so that it appears as if he has drowned in the sea. (We see all of this—murder, attempted cover-up, and eventual discovery of the crime—through a series of flashbacks presented in the form of her hallucinations and nightmares.)

And suddenly she's not so spinsterish anymore: as if committing murder (in lieu of having sex) has brought out the "real woman" inside her: powerful, calculating, resourceful, and sexy. In other words, discarding her wire-rimmed spectacles, flat shoes, and academic's cardigan sweater, she reveals herself as a true femme fatale— a siren on the beach where men wash up dead. Outgoing now and loquacious, even while concealing her crime, she starts to juggle (and she turns out to be a fast learner) the emotions of two grown men of considerable worldliness: the guardian of the murdered student and the police detective investigating the case.

The guardian is a successful trial lawyer; he falls in love with her and then defends her in court when she is tried for his ward's murder—and he gets her acquitted. She is convicted only of concealing the crime, not committing it, though it is absolutely clear that she and only she could have committed it. So in the end the student is dead and the psychiatrist will only be perfunctorily punished before moving on to marriage with the young man's surrogate father. That is, she kills a man who arouses her sexually, and after many twists and turns, ends up not on a jail cot but in a marriage bed—with the man's father. As Robert Ottoson points out, the female protagonist here displays one of the classic attributes of the femme fatale: she is simultaneously "the woman as both Destoyer and Victim." She is difficult to punish, but sometimes not so difficult to reward—even in Hollywood, where, because of the Hays Office, crime must be shown never to pay. A formulation which, as we've seen, doesn't always hold true in film noir.

Imagine what the outcome of *The Accused* might have been had the gender grid been reversed: if a male psychiatrist, aroused while kissing his female student, had clubbed her to death, concealed the crime, and after romancing the girl's adopted mother, a lawyer, gone on to be acquitted in court with the mother's expert help before marrying her. Spelling this out only heightens the absurdity of trying to picture it on the screen; for even in film noir—or, I should say, especially in film noir—the question of the femme fatale, the sexual woman, is forever a divided one. We are attracted even as we are repulsed, and vice versa. The femme fatale takes the extra, forbidden step that differentiates the transgressor from the aggressor. She violates codes. Personifies doom. Becomes the woman with a gun who is the woman with a penis. Yet she is more womanly—even to that pale corollary of her real self which might be called her "feminine" aspect—than other women. In a world of violent men, who are often afraid, she is unafraid. She shuns and abhors, not men, but passive women. She often disguises herself. She sometimes looks into mirrors and is surprised by what she sees. Which is what? A beautiful—the most beautiful—woman doing "what only a man would do," though it is forbidden to him, and getting away with it. Often finding that men, indeed, help her to get away with it. Want her to get away with it. And why? Kill my son and I will take you as my wife. Transgress and I will diminish you, but slyly. You will be domesticated and declawed. Is that not the final, crucial, feminist subtext of *The Accused*, that the woman's relegation to marriage after transgression is no more or less than a substitute for prison?

This brings us to the most interesting film noir psychiatrist of all, appearing in not one but two films: the dark, dapper, and urbane Dr. Judd, of Greenwich Village. His specialty would seem to be female pathology. His most notable patient is his final one: a woman who, after marriage, refuses to have sex with her husband for fear she will be transformed into a cat—a large black panther—at the moment of coitus and immediately kill him. (Once again, because of the Hays Office, a single kiss does its usual stand-in for sexual intercourse.) Judd is intrigued by this woman, named Irena and played by Simone Simon, who is so catlike even *before* any feline transformation occurs that canaries panic around her and house cats hiss and arch their backs. Though her tireless and much put-upon husband, a ship designer, finally throws in the towel and turns to a female colleague for platonic solace, Judd, supremely confident of his prowess, intellectual and sexual, is convinced that *he* can cure Irena.

As it turns out, he fails miserably and pays for it with his life. Yet despite the fact that he is killed at the conclusion of *Cat People* (1942), Dr. Judd reappears in *The Seventh Victim*, filmed the following year at the same studio by the same producer, Val Lewton, but with a different director and screenwriter. (*Cat People* is one of those rare films that deservedly achieved immediate—and enduring—cult status; it is, for example, the film that the character Molina synopsizes in loving detail for his cellmate Valentin in the opening forty pages of Manuel Puig's 1976 novel, *Kiss of the Spider Woman*.) Anyone who watches Lewton's tightly constructed noir thrillers chronologically—as film audiences in the forties obviously did—are startled at first by Judd's resurrection. He goes by the same name, is played by the same actor (Tom Conway), sports the same expensive clothes, haughty demeanor, and slick bedside manner, and dispenses his psychoanalytical services at the same brownstone office on the same tree-lined street just off Washington Square Park.

"All of us carry within us a desire for death," he tells us right off the bat in *Cat People*. In *The Seventh Victim,* a truly frightening film about the inner workings of a well-disciplined satanic cult in the Village, Judd numbers among his patients several of the more affluent cult members. One of these is a successful businesswoman (the founder and chief executive of a perfumery) who disappears, then resurfaces dazed and fearful, and is driven relentlessly to suicide by the other cult members. With his highbrow superiority, moral ambivalence, smarmy ladykiller instincts, and obvious lack of sexual boundaries with female patients, Judd reprises in this film his behavior in *Cat People,* though without stepping to center stage nearly so often.

In *Cat People,* Judd is a highy stylized character beside whom others seem drab; only Irena, the heroine, stands out as powerfully. And it is not his pinstripe suits, pencil moustache, or cocksure attitude that set him apart so much as the whiff of suppressed menace that he exudes—as sharp and memorable as the cologne that he is surely wearing. He and Irena seem equally dangerous at times; and this is a great paradox in the film, for while she seems to be a far gentler, and more tortured, soul, she is in reality infinitely more dangerous than he. She is also highly intelligent, and with an insufferable condescension that never lets up, Judd underestimates her badly on that count. Until, in the end, we hope he will get his comeuppance—which he does, quite horribly.

If one were to couch Irena's affliction in noir terms, from her own lips, it might sound like this: "Sleep with me and I will become a femme fatale such as you have never seen before—literally a wild cat, sleeker and more beautiful than you can imagine, who can blend into the night, walk cunningly on silent feet, and tear you apart in seconds." She is the dream girl who becomes your worst nightmare: another good working definition of the femme fatale. Irena's fate would seem to be the opposite of the female psychiatrist's in *The Accused,* for she refuses domestication preemptorily. She can't really cook (cats eat their food raw, after all), she is an indifferent housekeeper (nomadic as a cat, she prefers roaming the city parks, especially the zoo, to dusting furniture), and she unequivocally refuses the marriage bed (she will not submit to her husband physically, and seems never to be in heat, though—contradictory as a cat—she professes love for him). The only other creature in the film to whom Irena even remotely relates is the black panther prowling a cage at the zoo. She seems capable of watching this other cat for hours on end: the film begins with her drawing the panther on a sketchpad and ends with her dying beside his cage, coiled up catlike in her black plush coat which is so shiny as to be iridescent—like a cat's fur.

Dr. Judd first treats Irena formally after she and her husband come to his office for help. We see her lying on his analyst's couch, only her face bathed in bright white light, stony as a death mask. Judd has hypnotized her, and she is relating her background while in a trance. She is an immigrant; her native land is a mountainous country in Central Europe—"in the Carpathians"—whose recorded history began with an interminable civil war in which all the men fought. Among the women they left at home, a cult evolved around the panthers that populated the mountain forests. Ravenous in winter, these animals descended on the towns; and the women, making a deal "with the Devil himself" to secure their survival, produced with him a race of infernal panther women who allowed no mortal man to touch them. (Which did not make for a very happy community when the men returned from war.) Irena goes on to say that as a child she herself liked to play, to hide, in those same forests. Recently, she adds, she has dreamt of herself as a panther.

Judd doesn't believe a word of this story. In fact, he doesn't put stock in much of anything Irena says, in or out of hypnosis; he is certain she would fabricate and prevaricate in order to avoid sex at all costs. And we get the impression that he wants to learn why this is the case only because he is so attracted to her himself.

When Irena gets up off the couch and Judd switches on the lights, it is he who yawns. "Hypnosis sometimes exhausts me," he complains. When she asks him if he remembers all she related while hypnotized, he taps his notepad. "It's my duty to remember," he chides her. "I have it all here." When she asks him what conclusions he has drawn, he replies without hesitation, and with his customary self-assurance: "These things are very simple to psychoanalyze. You told me about your childhood. Perhaps we'll find this trouble starts in your childhood." Judd is a Freudian—no surprise there—and he'll be seeking the key to her sexual confusion, he soon makes clear, in her relationship to her father.

This course of treatment doesn't take them very far, and after this very first session Irena breaks off her therapy, lies to her husband about continuing, and starts going to the panther cage at the zoo at the hour she is supposedly being treated by Judd. That doesn't deter Judd, however, whose doctor-patient boundaries are allowed an elasticity that would have horrified Freud. He seeks her out at her favorite haunt (which he learned of in that one session), and stepping up close to her tells her in no uncertain terms that he can relieve her of this absurd fear she has of turning into a cat. Realizing that he is propositioning her, Irena recoils and runs off. But Judd doesn't let up. Soon enough he discovers from her husband (and at the same time informs the latter that Irena has stopped coming to his office) that things have come to a head in her marriage. Irena has learned of her husband's warming friendship with his female colleague and has begun terrorizing the woman: following her through Central Park, first in her human form, then as a cat (unseen) rustling through the high grass, and later growling from the deep shadows surrounding a basement swimming pool where the woman is swimming solitary laps.

Now even Irena's husband has begun to fear her, and to fear that she has been telling him the truth all along about her dual nature— that her other persona is, indeed, that of a cat. Judd is still in pursuit of her. After speaking to her husband, and learning that Irena is home alone, he phones her up and tells her he will be right over. He says he understands her predicament now, and that he will help extricate her once and for all. He finds her waiting for him, alone, smiling—for she knows what he wants and what he intends to do. Irena watches Judd approach her from the door, with his self-assured gait and suppressed ladykiller's smile. He is dressed to the nines, as always, and carries a black walking stick. Her smile broadens and her eyes twinkle, and for once her torment seems to have left her. She no longer looks afraid. She allows him to take her in his arms. She gazes up into his eyes and he is smirking now. And he kisses her, hard and full on the lips; that is, in 1940s censorship terms, she has opened herself up and allowed him to enter her.

All at once the camera pulls away from them and fixes on the wall where their shadows are cast by the one burning lamp. We hear a struggle erupt. Furniture is knocked over. A vase shatters. Other objects fly to the floor. Suddenly one of the shadows on the wall is transformed: Judd's silhouette is now locked in a struggle with the shadow of a large cat standing on its hind legs.

The camera cuts to Judd. The smug expression is gone, but still he doesn't look frightened. It's as if he was half-expecting this. Certainly he came prepared, for in the next instant he snatches up his walking stick, presses a button in its knob, and—presto—a sharp blade snaps out the other end. It is a lethal weapon now, identical to the walking stick Ballen Mundson would brandish in *Gilda* four years later. Judd is thrown across the room, badly clawed, but he jumps up quickly, and finally we see fear creeping into his face. Then the camera takes us back to the shadows on the wall: Judd and the cat are one now, wrestling upright. Suddenly Judd's shadow raises the stick high over his head and plunges the blade into the cat. The cat keeps coming on, however, and a moment later we see Judd's shadow slide to the floor. And all the commotion ceases.

Irena's husband arrives with his lady friend and they run up the stairs to the apartment. The camera remains on the stairwell, and a moment later we see Irena, in her plush coat, her hair tousled, slip unsteadily from the shadows of a large plant—catlike—clutching her left shoulder. She is bleeding badly. And as her husband discovers

Judd's mangled body in their apartment, his throat torn open, Irena limps from the house. It is a cold, windy night, and she hurries to the zoo, the panther cage, which she opens to free the black panther she has so frequently visited. The panther leaps over her head and knocks her down. Then he races out of the zoo, scales a stone wall, and runs into the street, where he is hit by a police car answering the call that has been put in from Irena's house. At that moment, Irena collapses and dies outside the panther's cage. Crumpled, coiled up there on the pavement, like a black iridescent shadow. Like a cat.

At the center of *Spellbound,* there is a famous dream sequence which Hitchcock commissioned Salvador Dali to choreograph. The psychic "setting" Dali came up with is a kind of funhouse without walls, elastic, multidimensional, and dense with symbols—bent wheels, forking paths, vertiginous balconies, spinning gears— among which our hero is tossed helter-skelter. In this regard, it is much like the final funhouse scene in *The Lady from Shanghai,* which Welles was to film two years later. The symbols, as Dali visualizes them and Hitchcock employs them, contain all the keys we need to unlock the film's complicated plot. Some we can recognize immediately; others come clear later. In film, as in life, symbols are the language of dreams.

The dream in *Spellbound* is among the more extreme, and sophisticated, sequences in film noir. There are other such dream progressions, fantastical and wildly inventive, as in *Murder, My Sweet* and *The Dark Past;* and all of them appear, interestingly enough, at the very beginning of the classic film noir cycle. Many other films noirs use dream motifs and dream logic, not as mere stylistic devices, but as vehicles for the essential purposes of advancing plot and revealing character. At the same time, films like *Nightmare Alley* and *Cat People* are themselves, in their entirety, little different textually and compositionally from the formal dream sequences contained within the fabric of other films noirs. Noir films as a group are the only films in which the presentation of dreams is consistently identical to the presentation of straight narrative action. One might miss the cutaway to a dream in film noir by blinking at the wrong moment; such moments are seldom bracketed, and there are few obvious or heavy-handed segues. At most, we'll get a quick dissolve—but rarely a complete one—in which the frame for an instant becomes gauzy or liquid.

All of this reinforces the fact that in film noir putative reality and the world of dreams are crucially interwoven, indivisible in light of the internal progressions—those darkly luminous spirals and zigzags—that underlie the external grid of a man's life. Since the noir quest is on its most elemental level a revelatory journey into the mind, memory, or imagination, the noir labyrinth owes its numerous (Borges would say infinite) blueprints to Psyche, who, in the end—as an architect of dreams rather than a guide through their mazes—must figure far more formidably in the noir pantheon than the various Ariadnes and Beatrices our heroes encounter.

7. Black and White in Color

As early as 1945, a film noir was shot in color. This may sound like a contradiction in terms. A film with a black-and-white aesthetic and a multicolored plumage. Technicolor, at that: luscious reds, oranges, and yellows. Much of it shot in daylight. In the desert.

Of this film, directed by John M. Stahl and with cinematography by Leon Shamroy, Lee Sanders and Meredith Brody write: "The predominant color in *Leave Her to Heaven* is an orange that suggests the same sickness and corruption as the high-contrast photography of black-and-white film noir and also dominates other noir films shot in color, such as John Alton's *Slightly Scarlet.*"

The same John Alton who is perhaps the finest black-and-white cinematographer in the history of American film. A master of shadows and light, and black-on-black compositions. Of Alton, who was born in Hungary, Paul Schrader writes that he was "an expressionist cinematographer who could relight Times Square at noon if necessary. No cinematographer better adapted the old expressionist techniques to the new desire for realism, and his black-and-white photography in such gritty film noir as *T-Men, Raw Deal, I, The Jury, The Big Combo* equals that of such German expressionist masters as Fritz Wagner and Karl Freund." And yet, by 1956, Alton is shooting some films in color, lush, exploding, tropical-fruit colors, in such a way that they still feel like black-and-white films. Bitter fruits.

This reliance on orange, apparent in color films noirs through the 1950s and 1960s and in the neo-noirs right up to the present day, functions in place of the chiaroscuro of the black-and-white films.

Orange provides the sort of deep-contrast, low-key photographic effects previously achieved with black-and-white contrasts.

Or as Sanders and Brody go on to say about *Leave Her to Heaven:* "In contrast with cold blue shadows and night exteriors, the warm amber glow of *Leave Her to Heaven* occurs in the films of many of the most prominent photographers of this pre-1954 Technicolor period, giving a distinctive tone that can be, in context, as ominous as the grays and blacks of standard film noir."

Robert Ottoson employs the following adjectives in writing about the Technicolor in *Leave Her to Heaven:* "glossy," "garish," "psychedelic," and "delirious." It is all of those things, and more. At times, the film lights up the screen like a Christmas tree.

John Alton, in turning to color, Blake Lucas observes, "continues to utilize extensive shadows and large black areas, while also accentuating a garish array of pinks, greens, and oranges, producing a startling effect in many scenes."

Slightly Scarlet is a study in scarlet. In fact, the title comes off as something of a joke, for the film—thematically and stylistically—could not be *more* scarlet. Eclectically directed by Allan Dwan, it focuses on the duality of two sisters, one the femme fatale, the other the Beatrice/good sister. The film opens with the bad sister being released from prison and being picked up in a red convertible by the good sister. Often, visually, we cannot tell them apart when they first enter a scene. In fact, the actresses playing the two sisters, Rhonda Fleming and Arlene Dahl, strongly resemble one another. These two sisters—at the dead center of the Eisenhower fifties—exude enormous sexual energy; quite predictably, they rapidly slip into a sexual rivalry, first for one man, then another. Both sisters are knockouts, zaftig, with hourglass figures. Both wear stunning outfits that highlight their busts, hips, and long legs. They are in a constant state of décolletage, with slinky robes slit up to the hips, lacy bustiers, tight slacks or even tighter pepper-red short-shorts, halter tops, gold pumps, and swishy silk pajamas. They have green eyes, almond-shaped. The high planes of their cheeks are rouged. Bright crimson lipstick glistens on their wide mouths. And of course both women have manes of flaming orange hair.

The femme fatale in *Leave Her to Heaven* is centered along a very different sexual axis—an extreme Electra complex for which the flamboyant, but ultimately chilling, color compositions serve as an accurate barometer. In this film, the femme fatale plays the role of an icily crazed manipulator sexually and emotionally obsessed with her father, before and after his death. Her character is easily delineated by a summary of her activities. First, she aborts her own child, neurotically certain that her husband will prefer the child to her, by purposely falling down a flight of stairs. Out of possessiveness, she murders her husband's younger brother, an invalid, by urging him to swim across a lake while she follows in a rowboat; then, when he founders, she rows away from him—just a short distance—and watches him go under. And, finally, she poisons herself in such a way that both her husband and her sister, with whom he has grown close, are incriminated and tried for murder.

At the crux of both *Slightly Scarlet* and *Leave Her to Heaven,* then, is the sexual rivalry, jealousy, and possessiveness that erupt between two sisters over the same man: a very scarlet subject.

These color films noirs present a rich assortment of impeccably designed sets, interior and exterior. The highly charged mix of colors produces a stream of surreal effects: colored telephones, deco or early–Space Age furniture, two-tone cars, wild and provocative clothing, and the Dayglo panoply of the honky-tonk night in which neon signs span a nocturnal rainbow.

There is a series of films noirs set in the desert—the topographical antithesis of the city. The wasteland which by definition is post-urban, post-atomic. Some of these films are shot in black-and-white: *The Big Carnival* (1951), whose credits roll over a background of sand rather than the customary cityscape; *Split-Second* (1950), in which the characters are trapped on an atomic testing ground; *Border Incident* (1949); *The Hitch-Hiker* (1953); *The Tattered Dress* (1957); and *The Prowler* (1951). Of the latter film, which begins in central Los Angeles and ends up in the desert, Foster Hirsch writes, "The Mojave Desert is a novel and expressive noir setting. The parched landscape reinforces the barrenness of the characters . . . and proves to be as suffocating as the city environment."

And then there are the desert films noirs shot in color, the most notable of which, aside from *Leave Her to Heaven,* is *A Kiss Before Dying* (1957), also set in New Mexico. Also about two sisters. Twins, this time, who are the daughters and sole heirs of a copper magnate.

To get at the old man's money, a handsome, psychotic schemer from the wrong side of the tracks romances, then murders, one sister, and goes on cold-bloodedly to romance and marry the other. When he tries, unsuccessfully, to murder her, he is instead killed himself. Like *Leave Her to Heaven* and *Slightly Scarlet, A Kiss Before Dying* is a film awash in oranges and reds; set as it is in baking desert heat, those colors appear even more infernal than they might in a metropolitan setting. In all of these films, the oranges and reds become the very colors of Hell, emanating from the fiery lake, the furnaces of lost souls, to which the respective protagonists are inexorably drawn, and consumed.

Red is also the central color in *Party Girl* (1958), the last color film noir made during the classic noir period. But it's a cold bloodred, the red of a bell being rung—or shattered—in subzero air. Its complementary colors are not desert oranges and yellows, but sleek wintry blacks and whites.

Party Girl is set in Chicago in dead of winter. The winds swirling off the lake are bone chilling. There is much snow and ice, and sleet like broken glass. Like those films noirs set in the desert, we find here an environment of extreme weather conditions, in which the city's inhabitants are blindly buffeted about the streets while predators, political and criminal, perch high above in the rock canyons of office buildings. Again the city is presented as a force larger than life (and inhumanly frigid), a place where human destinies are meager, disposable things. It is the antithesis of that gritty optimism and firm belief in the individual's paramount importance, every man the captain of his fate, equal under the law, and so on, which are ingrained American dicta. None of that adheres in this Chicago, which is mapped (truer to life) in strict accordance with the noir ethos.

The film is entirely nocturnal, with few primary colors outdoors; but its night colors, while not broad, are brilliant. Especially the blacks, which run from the flattest matte to a silvery ebony flecked with mica. The whites can be so deep we fall into them, like sheets upon sheets of snow, or so electric that they're piercing. At times we wonder why Nicholas Ray, the director, did not simply shoot the film in straight black-and-white, like all his other films noirs *(On Dangerous Ground, Knock on Any Door, In a Lonely Place)*, and then suddenly amid all that luminous black and white he'll show us why, planting something bright red in the frame that shoots to life, like a flare in the night: a glove, a handbag, the fender of a red coupe otherwise covered with snow.

When we move indoors, it's a different story: golds, silvers, metallic blues and greens hit us at once like a shower of confetti. The opening dance sequence, showgirls in scant glittery outfits with feathered boas, platinum stiletto heels, and shimmering capes and gloves, begins only after the camera slides slowly through successive waves of brightly colored curtains, tinsel, and a profusion of brilliantly red Christmas tree balls. The apartments we visit, owned by wealthy political bosses and lawyers, are filled with colorful bric-a-brac and gorgeous pastel furniture. Even scenes in restaurants and courthouses—places we expect, even in color, to be fixed in a sea of gray and tan—are garishly splashed with color.

Ray uses color in this film, we see from the start, not to distance it from the noir statement he has to make, but to intensify that statement. It is the noir elements of the film that demand color: the wild swings in the characters' emotional lives, their intense sexual energy, and the violence rippling all around them. We find these qualities presented with the intensity of the rawest and most visceral films noirs, like *Kiss Me Deadly* and *The Naked Kiss*. But in those films, Aldrich and Fuller, respectively, achieve that intensity employing high-definition black-and-white cinematography, not color. The paradox in *Party Girl* is that while standing out among the darkest films noirs, it utilizes color, and color techniques, with a hallucinating clarity we might expect in a film with radically different subject matter—like a Jerry Lewis comedy, a biblical spectacular, or a splashy musical.

In the cinematography of one of the earliest harbingers of film noir, the silent film *Manhattan Sunrise* (1927), heavily influenced by German Expressionism, character is for the first time revealed most powerfully through lighting changes. In fact, this would become a device without which one cannot really envision film noir as we know it. Add to the power of light the startling impact of color and the possibilities of expression grow exponentially with regard to character delineation and imagery development. Thus, in *Party Girl,* as in the other color films noirs, background colors are used to reveal and open out the characters' inner emotional states, to tint the fault lines of their shifting relationships, and to define the director's intentions rather than simply to ornament the scene of action.

Which brings us back to that red glove or handbag flaring in the black-and-white Chicago night. The color symbolism around clothing in *Party Girl* is crucial to an understanding of the film. The hero is a "a mouthpiece for the mob," a crooked lawyer—literally so, for he is a lame man who walks a crooked line through life physically and morally. Throughout the film, he wears only black and white: suits, shirts, ties, shoes, even his cane is black. His hair, too, is jet, slicked straight back, and he has pale skin and sharp black eyes. In other words, he could just have stepped from the frames of a black-and-white film. Characterwise he is certainly a throwback, almost all the way to the 1930s; he is a bit stuffy for his years, despite his high-risk profession, and he does not have the tastes or attitudes of a postwar man. On the other hand, the heroine, the party girl—a Beatrice in this particular labyrinth—always wears something red. Usually it is a bright scarlet dress like the one she is wearing at the beginning and end of the film, so that in scenes with powerful mobsters, lawyers, and policemen—with every single man in the film, that is— she always dominates the screen. When it is not her hat, dress, scarf, or nightgown that is bright red—when she is not dressed, in other words—it is her bathtub that is full of red (with blood) water. Or she stands behind a huge red lampshade, with only her face visible in the frame.

At the film's climax, when the vicious boss of the city's crime machine calmly pours a bottle of acid onto a red paper bell (a Christmas tree decoration) which is exactly the same shade as her dress, we understand that this bell is a thinly veiled metaphor for the heroine. When the bell dissolves down the middle with a hiss, and splays open, the suggestion is clear: this is what the acid would do to her face. She is wearing her red dress, which initially she wore when she was most vulnerable, and as Colin McArthur observes, ". . . the reappearance of her red dress in the final sequence causes the audience . . . to see Ray's colour symbolism as, in the clearest sense, red for danger, the danger to Vicki—in sexual terms early in the film, in terms of violence at the end—of her proximity to the gangsters."

In this orgy of red, her most incredible moment comes when the heroine, wearing a crimson evening dress, with red earrings and red bracelet to match, and fingernails gleaming with red polish, reclines on a scarlet sofa with scarlet pillows, and before pulling a red blanket over herself, sips from a glass of tomato juice and switches off a red lamp! In this freezing winter city, frozen by crime and corruption as well as Arctic winds, she is the one character with blood in her veins, rather than on her hands.

In *Party Girl,* at the tail end of the classic noir cycle, we literally have a black-and-white film in color. It is a pioneering film in its way that helps to close the cycle, for after 1958 almost all the neo-noirs will be shot in color. Textually they will be modeled, directly or indirectly, on *Party Girl:* dense compositions, shot through with bright primary colors while employing luminous black-and-white motifs. The best of them do not look like other color films. A minority—*Blast of Silence, Cape Fear, Experiment in Terror, Underworld U.S.A., Shock Corridor*—all released in 1961 and 1962, will be shot in pure black-and-white, but after *Party Girl* we will begin to wonder, with the rarest exceptions, why such a choice is made. I think the choice for black-and-white becomes a retro impulse, a self-conscious throwback, even for the above-mentioned films, which are integral to the noir cycle, when their directors—from Blake Edwards to Sam Fuller—were such highly skilled practitioners with color film. I would go so far as to say that there is no aesthetic purpose served, going into the late 1960s and beyond, which justifies leaving color *out* of film noir. The films noirs of today, conceived and shot in color, the best of them approaching the stylistic assurance of Nicholas Ray's masterpiece, retain their vitality and power as noir films precisely because they speak to us in the same visual language as their predecessors in the 1940s—updated and expanded by color, not diminished.

8. Paint It Black

In speaking of lighting in film noir, the French cinematographer Allen Daviau said, "Darkness is not a negative space. Darkness is the most important element in the scene. *The most important lights are the ones you don't turn on.*" Or the ones you begin by turning off.

In the first great wave of neo-noir films after 1960, those lights are not just turned off, but short-circuited and blown out. Just as *Kiss Me Deadly* is a very late entry in the classic noir cycle, *Brainstorm,* released in 1965, is a straggler to those black-and-white films noirs of the early part of the decade. While *Party Girl* marks the onset of the color film noir era, *Brainstorm* is undoubtedly the last of the truly great black-and-white films noirs. I have tried to imagine it, too, as a color film—on the hyperchromatic, mid-sixties psychedelic scale of *Point Blank*—but more than any other film of its own immediate period, *Brainstorm* feels metaphysically like its own negative. If *Kiss Me Deadly* is the definitive noir statement about the onset of the Atomic Age, *Brainstorm* is its post-mortem. It is unquestionably the most nihilistic film noir of either the classic or present-day cycle; it serves as a precursor to the neo-noirs of the present day, which both draws on the earliest films noirs and anticipates unerringly the obsessions that will inform all subsequent ones.

Brilliantly directed by William Conrad, who often played a heavy in early films noirs *(The Killers, The Racket)*, *Brainstorm* employs a number of other actors from that era, including Dana Andrews, the detective in *Laura,* and Viveca Lindfors, the expatriate Swedish actress. Its hero is played by Jeffrey Hunter, who had previously been cast in the role of Jesus Christ in *King of Kings*—improbably directed by Nicholas Ray—and, more typically, as the absolutely clean-hewn, blue-eyed young American hero of countless 1950s westerns, including *The Searchers*. Here he plays the role of a research scientist, a high-tech aerophysicist who first flirts with insanity and then veers across the line into deep psychosis. He complains unceasingly about his splitting headaches. (And, shades of Helen Walker, of *Nightmare Alley,* who met a noir-like demise in her own life, Hunter would die at forty-four, four years after *Brainstorm*'s release, of a cerebral hemorrhage.)

Like *The Naked Kiss* by Fuller, *Brainstorm* is a film conceived and shot in the year following the Kennedy assassination, and its insistent references to madness, murder, mayhem, and conspiracy reflect the tenor of those times. In plot and character, the film is constructed radially around a spinning center of rage and paranoia. Nearly every character betrays someone close to him or her. All of them lie fluently. Nothing is what it appears to be, which is not unusual in film noir; what is unusual is how clearly it's spelled out, as a moral axiom of this universe, that nothing *can* be what it appears to be. Here the noir world is not subversive, but anarchic. In this regard, *Brainstorm* is to other films noirs what Lobachevski's geometry—in which parallel lines eventually intersect—is to Euclid's.

Most of the film is set in three locations: an insane asylum; a scientific laboratory undertaking "dangerous atomic research" (to develop weaponry for deployment in outer space); and a tycoon's mansion, where the lady of the house, a wild, young, blonde party girl tyrannized by her sadistic husband, is constantly attempting suicide (by swallowing a drug overdose, slashing her wrists, and even parking her car on railroad tracks after washing down sleeping pills with vodka!) and constantly being thwarted in her attempts. In the locales alone, this film synthesizes numerous central noir elements: the asylum with its team of predatory psychiatrists; the secret atomic research with its devastating implications; the megalomaniacal tycoon who uses his wealth and power to manipulate and destroy others, especially those closest to him. The research scientist works for the tycoon, and it is the latter, in conjunction with the scientist's duplicitous female psychiatrist, who eventually breaks and ruins him.

Brainstorm is the terrifying cinematic portrait of a sophisticated, educated man's descent into madness; in the bleakest of urban wastelands we watch an integrated and (in the mid-1960s, with NASA at the height of its popularity) iconic social figure, the aerospace scientist, disintegrate before our eyes. The film takes the noir theme of the complex mental labyrinth to new heights—and depths. Set in a Los Angeles that has been rendered even more vacant— morally, emotionally, and aesthetically—in the ten years since the making of *Kiss Me Deadly,* it feels now like a wasteland beyond all possibility of redemption. Its ashes could no longer feed a fire: all that is left now for them is to freeze. The urban desert of the city has spilled over into the literal desert in which our hero finds himself whenever he ventures beyond the city limits. In *Kiss Me Deadly,* the only way out seemed to be through the nuclear apocalypse that concludes the story. *Brainstorm* is post-apocalyptic: you cannot reduce a desert any further; you can only stagger around it, trying to stave off the inevitable, inflicting, deflecting, and absorbing pain, running toward death even as you run away from it. In the end, circling yourself over and over again, until the trail you leave is a radial one, concentric circles that collapse in on themselves.

The hero, descending the circles of his own Hell, commits adultery with the tycoon's wife, who is his own age; murders the tycoon, who is old enough to be his father; falls in love with his psychiatrist, old enough to be his mother; sabotages the atomic project on which he has been working; first feigns insanity (to get off the hook for murder) and then finds himself after the fact declared clinically insane and incarcerated. All the while, he goes from being a buttoned-up whiz-kid with a slide rule in his shirt pocket to a wild-eyed loner who hurls prophet-in-the-desert sorts of tirades at anyone who crosses his path: the judge trying him for murder, the journalists at a press conference, the guests at a lavish banquet in the tycoon's home, and, finally, his fellow inmates at the asylum. There is also an amazing scene in the asylum in which the hero, through a two-way mirror, views another patient, a boy about twelve who bears a striking resemblance to him, going berserk and smashing to bits an architect's "model city" replica of Los Angeles that takes up an entire room; the boy literally destroys the city while the hero watches raptly. Soon afterwards, the hero reaches the juncture in his own madness where his feigned insanity has become self-fulfilling and propelled him into genuine derangement.

Thus we have a post-apocalyptic Oedipus: he kills his father, sleeps with his father's wife, and tries to seduce his own surrogate mother. And it is the latter, when he escapes the asylum, who has him pursued by armed security guards. As he screams into the blinding desert sunlight, his eyes rolled back in his head, they drag him back to confinement. To be confined for the rest of his life. Which is how the film ends.

It is fitting that *Brainstorm,* filmed in the twelve months between two defining national tragedies—a traumatic assassination and the massive escalation of a war that would be decisively lost—is the final, essential entry in that long line of films noirs that begins at the end of the Second World War. Its narrative unfolds like a dream, evincing the often excruciating—and punitive—nature of dream logic, a dream without a single moment's relief or respite. It is the noir dream carried to its predictable extreme: an unremitting, undeflectable, recurrent nightmare. The film's narrative becomes a kind of Möbius strip in which claustrophobia and agoraphobia merge and are rendered indistinguishable.

Twenty years after Hiroshima, that most defining event in American noir, *Brainstorm* reverberates with its aftershocks. For if *Kiss Me Deadly* closes the classic noir period with an atomic conflagration engulfing Los Angeles, *Brainstorm* offers up a brief, blinding glance at the aftermath, and at a particular resident who has turned out to be one of the last classic film noir heroes, shattered beyond repair and locked away in a padded cell—the absolute dead center of his labyrinth, itself at the epicenter of a decimated landscape.

From 1970 to the present day, noir, in both style and substance, manifests itself in many forms: high-tech, science-fiction futurism, *Blade Runner* (1982) and *The Terminator* (1984); the narcotics caper, *The French Connection* (1971); the hard-bitten *policier, Sudden Impact* (1983), *Dirty Harry* (1971) and *Hustle* (1975); the espionage puzzler, *The Kremlin Letter* (1970); the heist flick, *Johnny Handsome* (1989), yet another entry in that sub-category of "Johnny" titles; the confidence scam, *The Last Seduction* (1994); the surrealist fantasy, *Blue Velvet* (1986); and a distinguished string of that ever-faithful vehicle, the psychological thriller, *Klute* (1971), *Taxi Driver* (1976), *Blood Simple* (1984), *Jagged Edge* (1985), and *Black Widow* (1986), to name a few.

Nearly all of these films are set in cities and shot on location, which is now the norm for film noir: Los Angeles and New York (where more films were shot on location in 1995, for example, than ever before) remain favored settings, though even in the list above, Honolulu, Austin, Miami, New Orleans, and San Francisco are all represented. *Blue Velvet* takes place in a small, unnamed Midwestern city. And *The Last Seduction*, which begins and ends in New York City, is otherwise set in a nameless upstate New York town. However, the femme fatale manages in her way to take the city with her when she flees it. A rude, ruthless, sexually aggressive conwoman— a sort of low-end parody of a Manhattan yuppie—she bilks and extorts her drug-dealing husband, among other people. And like Leonardo da Vinci, she has a knack for writing backwards (another oblique homage to *Kiss Me Deadly* and its backward-running credits?), so when she decides to hide out in Smalltown U.S.A. and needs to change her name, she settles on "Wendy Kroy," which is "New York" backwards.

During the past twenty-five years there has also been a virtual renaissance of film noir remakes of productions from the classic noir cycle. Sometimes these films merely update the old scripts with regard to locale (Sun Belt cities, say, instead of Rust Belt cities), ambiance, or topicality. For example, George Stroud, the editor of *Crimeways* magazine in *The Big Clock*, who is simultaneously trapped in the Janoth Building and conducting the search for himself as the supposed murderer of his boss' mistress, in the remake entitled *No Way Out* (1987) becomes a Naval Commander, an attaché to the Secretary of Defense, who is trapped in the Pentagon leading the (now high-tech) search for himself as the supposed murderer of the Secretary's mistress. The translation of the setting is not difficult to understand: in 1948, the tycoon heading a magazine empire housed in his own skyscraper was a powerful figure in the public mind; in 1987, with a more diverse national communications industry, and after a massive military buildup to combat the "Evil Empire," a Secretary of Defense in a bellicose Administration was a far more potent (and potentially sinister) authority figure. And the Pentagon, a particularly mysterious labyrinth, symbolically and also physically, dwarfs any and all contemporary office buildings.

Other such remakes are *Against All Odds* (1984), based on *Out of the Past,* and *The Postman Always Rings Twice* (1981), *D.O.A.* (1989), *Cape Fear* (1991), *Night and the City* (1992), and *Kiss of Death* (1994), all based on older films with the same titles. Not one of these remakes is on a par with—much less superior to—its original film noir source. But as "noir" suddenly became a cultural catchword going into the 1990s—there is a noir cologne, a noir line of clothes, noir makeup kits, and a supposedly noir "taste" in everything from fountain pens to automobiles—it is no surprise that, along with the advertising hucksters who realize the word can sell a certain kind of product, the boardroom strategists in Hollywood have discovered that the classic films noirs are now highly marketable. First, of course, they must be "repackaged," in color, with contemporary movie stars, their plots watered down for an audience—benumbed by an onslaught of mindless television programs, thirty-second commercials, and three-minute music videos—with a short attention span and limited patience for digressive action. The results have been terrible: all the remakes have been artistic and critical failures with mediocre box-office receipts. Yet the studios, not for altruistic reasons but because the popular appetite for film noir is apparent, keep churning out these tepid remakes.

It is debatable whether or not the original, 1950 *D.O.A.* would have fared better in commercial movie emporia if some distributor had been audacious enough to screen it—with a short announcement of its clear superiority as an entertainment product—in place of the abysmal 1989 version. True, the original is in glorious black-and-white, and the star, Edmund O'Brien, was in 1989 approaching his eightieth birthday, retired, in failing health, and unable to hustle the film on the talk-show circuit, but *maybe* it would have been a lunatic gamble that panned out. Still, don't count on catching a showing of *Gilda* or *Phantom Lady* anywhere but in a revival house or a late-night television slot, where they will hopefully remain safely concealed from the remake and development boys who answer to the megacorporations that now run Hollywood.

With regard to production in general, I would add a word about B movies, a production category into which many classic films noirs fell. In the 1940s and 1950s, film distributors normally screened double-feature programs; they were a theater staple that have gone the way of bottled milk, the ten-cent hamburger, and Checker cabs. Because distributors could not afford to book two A films—that is, expensive mainline releases from the major studios—cheaper B films were produced in abundance, at first by smaller production companies, and then by the major studios themselves, who set up in-house production units. As Chris Hugo points out in his incisive essay on the production conditions involved in the making of Joseph H. Lewis' *The Big Combo,* ". . . the rental for A features was based on a percentage of box-office takings . . . whilst B films played for a fixed or rental fee and were thus not so reliant on audience figures. . . . These B films were formed not so much out of a desire to produce progressive texts, but rather as the direct result of a particular method of employing production capital . . . which ensured budgetary restraint but which also allowed for a certain amount of creative freedom. . . . This fact may go some way to explaining how a low-budget specialist such as Joseph H. Lewis could make a film like *Gun Crazy* which—to contemporary eyes—looks more like something out of French *nouvelle vague* than a product of mainstream Hollywood."

The lack of financial pressure on Lewis—not because of his studio's creative altruism but because of their marketing procedures—was critical to him and to other talented film noir directors; it resulted in their finding themselves far less fettered than the makers of conventional A films. The experimentation and innovation that occurred during the classic film noir era thus gained important impetus not just because of the various aesthetic schools that converged on Hollywood at that time, but also because of a unique set of business circumstances in the film industry. Hugo goes on to suggest—and I agree with him—"that the economic conditions obtaining today would cause a remake of a film such as *The Big Combo* to look completely different from the 1955 model. Low-budget mass-market films of this sort and the relative freedom that went with them are virtually a thing of the past." I would also say, though, that it is encouraging to note the proliferation, beginning in the late 1980s, of small, independent production companies who create from scratch, unfettered, more artistically adventurous films, some of which are then distributed by the large studios. These films may be as close as the studios will come to supporting feature films that are not blatantly commercial simply by getting them out of the arthouse and into the mainstream theaters, even for short runs. Many of these films, true to the B-film tradition, are films noirs.

Since 1970, the richest and most trenchant of the neo-noirs have been either new and original material or, interestingly enough, films based on never-before-adapted literary properties that date to the classic film noir era. In other words, someone will write a sceenplay after unearthing an obscure or long-neglected Cornell Woolrich story from the 1940s or a pulp novel by Horace McCoy or Jim Thompson from the early 1950s. The latter material, respectfully treated, textually updated without being inanely jazzed up or sanitized, is remarkably contemporary for the simple reason that the strongest, most urgent, and most undiluted aspects of noir are not going to disappear so long as its essential wellsprings—violence, power, fear, and angst, the glamour and depravity of the city, and the seductiveness of our darkest impulses—keep bubbling to the surface. Those wellsprings existed before 1940, and they won't be running dry with the coming of the millennium; that they became veritable gushers just after the Second World War and at the height of the Cold War does not lessen the impact of their steady flow ever since. Tap into them and you may produce a film noir; ignore them and you are simply dashing off a stylization of the form, a kind of fashion show with noir accoutrements and little or no substance. And there has been no shortage of such faux-noirs, produced with much flash and fanfare, over the past twenty years.

Style is a tricky subject when it comes to film noir. If style, as an ingredient, is not to be found within the nucleus of the internal noir structure, then certainly we must discover it revolving around that nucleus as the lone and prominent electron. Occasionally as a free-floating, or errant, electron, but never one that drifts far from the core that it helps to keep intact. So how and why are we to see stylization in the neo-noirs as a trivializing, rather than binding, force? Perhaps this can be answered by way of some simple semantical parallels: for example, the difference in any of the literary arts between characterization and caricature; or between a poem and a "poeticism"; or—in an entirely different vein—between practicing politics in the Aristotelian sense ("political society exists for the sake of noble actions") and politicizing, as in exploiting an issue for short-term gain. In each case, the more debased form has its uses within the context of the purer form; there are caricatures among the secondary figures in the finest novels; the occasional archaicism, in specialized circumstances, can serve even the most experimental poet; and politicizing something might at times actually help to bring about a noble result. All of this is quite clearly a matter of degree: stylization, as such, has its place in every film noir from *The Big Sleep* to *Touch of Evil;* but when it becomes the film's raison d'être, it effectively undercuts the very elements it was meant to bolster.

As I noted earlier, Paul Schrader proclaimed style to be the very cornerstone of the film noir. He argued in 1972 that film noir has "tried to make America accept a moral vision of life based on style. That very contradiction—promoting style in a culture which valued themes—forced film noir into artistically invigorating twists and turns. Film noir attacked and interpreted its sociological conditions, and, by the close of the [classic] noir period, created a new artistic world which went beyond a simple sociological reflection, a nightmarish world of American mannerism which was by far more a creation than a reflection."

To Schrader, noir is not a mirror held up to the society, but a prism that recreates by scrambling and reassembling a myriad of reflections. Which, in itself, is an exclusively stylistic take on the films. He goes on to say: "Because film noir was first of all a style, because it worked out its conflicts visually rather than thematically, because it was aware of its own identity, it was able to create artistic solutions to sociological problems. And for these reasons films like *Kiss Me Deadly, Kiss Tomorrow Goodbye* and *Gun Crazy* . . . [are] works of art. . . ."

And it is for those same reasons that the remakes I cited earlier, and the plethora of faux-noirs that have tumbled out of Hollywood in the nineties—*China Moon, Golden Gate, Deadfall,* and *Jade*—to name some produced in 1994 and 1995—are neither works of art, by a long shot, nor even interesting films on the most superficial level. Style is not serving art in the faux-noirs. And their paint-by-number stylization of authentic films noirs can be expected to produce little more than the occasional, and haphazard, cinematic frisson: something carelessly (or exploitatively) tossed off, comprised of serious elements that in other contexts might be sustained with lasting impact, but which in these films offers us only a quick and unsatisfactory whiff of the real thing. The real thing, when we encounter it, comes to us in the classic language of noir; as in this snippet about the neo-noir *The Usual Suspects* from David Denby's review in *New York Magazine* in the summer of 1995: "The movie is a labyrinth . . ." shot "in mysterious chiaroscuro, and with obsessive close-ups of objects—a Zippo lighter, a coffee cup—that play a talismanic role in the plot." A hard-edged romp like *Pulp Fiction* (1994), with its violent pop-eclecticism and colorful 1960s ambiance pays homage to countless classic films noirs, from *Kiss Me Deadly* to *Point Blank,* but itself is more gangland camp than neo-noir. Its obsessions remain inturned, self-indulgent, and seldom radiate—or resonate—outwardly. Most important, it does not occur in the dizzying context of the maze with the off-center center that constitutes the noir city, and it is not a quest into the heart of darkness that vitally links a film such as *The Usual Suspects* with its most electric and distinguished predecessors: *The Asphalt Jungle, Out of the Past,* or *The Brothers Rico.* Rather, *Pulp Fiction,* like many similarly plotted (though less pyrotechnically stylish) films of the fifties, uses noir accoutrements to adorn a conventional gangster story; the film's scrambling of chronology is cinematically dazzling, but when its interlocking vignettes are unscrambled, we see that they have carried us over a broad surface which they have barely penetrated.

So how do we differentiate the very stylish neo-noirs with backbone from the purely flashy imitations—especially when the ones with backbone can be quite flamboyant? Again, not to labor the point, but we do it in the same way we distinguish a vital poem from a piece of flaccid versification. The one stimulates, moves, and ultimately transforms us; the other has the lasting effect of a piece of chewing gum. Vladimir Nabokov, when asked how he knew when a poem was good, gave a nonacademic answer that serves succinctly with any art form: "It sends a tingle up my spine," he replied. The authentic neo-noir should do the same for the viewer.

A large and quite various group of films produced between 1970 and 1996 meet this standard, all building on the foundation of the classic films noirs and many carrying the noir sensibility into new terrain. Femmes fatales, for one, are more complex; they would have to be now that they are moving through a society where they are not the only women who are perceived to be (or, cinematically, *allowed* to be) powerful and sexually aggressive. And noir heroes, in league or at odds with these women, find themselves in ever more treacherous labyrinths than their predecessors. What most distinguishes them from earlier heroes is not that their epiphanies are any more piercingly dark, or their destructions necessarily more gruesome or spectacular (though they certainly can be in a world where technology has pushed weapons—scatterguns, armor-piercing bullets, and the like—into a realm reserved for science fiction in the 1950s), but that their circumstances and surroundings are so radically different. The cities in which they make their quests are hyperbolically more chaotic and violent; crime and its practitioners are infinitely more sophisticated; and social and cultural pressures, from illegal immigration and the cynical institutionalization of a black underclass to an erratic, often stagnant, post–Vietnam War economy, have in many places reached the breaking point.

Beginning with *Chinatown* in 1974, there is a terrific assortment of neo-noirs, filmed from original screenplays, which almost painfully reflect their times. Robert Towne's screenplay of *Chinatown* manages to do this while drawing from a broad variety of sources: Nathanael West's Hollywood novels, James Cain's mysteries, and Raymond Chandler's Philip Marlowe stories, as well as a whole menu of classic noir films to which he has paid homage in broad strokes or subtle asides. The director, Roman Polanski, richly offers up a Los Angeles so parched by drought that the entire film revolves around water. Water as the city's lifeblood, as a commodity, as a religious and metaphysical element, as a ramifying symbol of sexual potency and barrenness, of political power and public fraud, and ultimately, of who will reside among the living and who will be dispatched to the land of the dead. A place which we come to feel is increasingly close at hand.

As in *Brainstorm* ten years earlier, the Los Angeles of *Chinatown* is in danger of merging with the desert that is slowly encroaching upon it. The complete absence of water for an extended period, after all, is the primary requirement for a desert. In *Chinatown*'s Los Angeles, whoever controls the water controls the city, and that person, in the beginning and the end, is a corrupt and ruthless old man, a character appropriately named Noah Cross. Cross is wonderfully played by John Huston, a directorial noir icon, of course, who put forth some of the defining early films like *The Maltese Falcon* and *Key Largo,* as well as the eccentrically remarkable, generally unrecognized neo-noir, *The Kremlin Letter.* Cross controls the land through which the water must flow to reach the city's reservoirs; he controls the local political machine; he controls his fractured family through incest and outright murder, like Percy Shelley's Count Cenci in his play *The Cenci;* and, above all, he controls the water.

Here we have a neo-noir film dealing explicitly with incest. In *Chinatown,* one of the most important characters (though, significantly, she has not a single spoken line) is the teenage daughter of the heroine, Evelyn Mulwray, who also happens to be her sister because her father, Cross, raped Evelyn when she was about the same age. At the end of the film, the last we see of Cross he is dragging this hysterical daughter/granddaughter from the car in which Evelyn (with Cross' complicity) was just shot dead. From the way Cross lays his hands on the girl, embracing her, smothering her cries with his palms, it appears certain that she will suffer the same fate as her mother/sister in his bed.

None of this would have survived the Hays Office in the heyday of film noir, except through the manipulation of symbols and the most oblique of references. In fact, thematically, sex in all its forms is what most differentiates the neo-noirs and their predecessors. It is not so much that the neo-noirs are graphically explicit in the bedroom— few of them are—as the fact that they *could* be. There's no need anymore for those lingering kisses or cigarettes passed in a darkened room to denote sexual intercourse. The vast range of suppressed subject matter in the 1940s and 1950s is now on the table, to be dealt with as directly as one wishes. In one of the most popular of the classic films noirs, *The Big Sleep* (1946), still a staple on television and in revival houses, priapism (General Sternwood), homosexuality and sexual cultism (Geiger), rape and pornography (Carmen Sternwood), not to mention wholesale adultery and the promiscuity of the hero (Philip Marlowe), are essential plot elements, but they're often concealed just enough to be ambiguous. One has to look and listen pretty carefully the first time around, for example, to pick up that

Carmen has been raped and that Geiger is a homosexual. In the neo-noirs, whether the sex is straight or gay, consensual or criminal, kinky or over-the-top, we'll know it up front (unless ambiguity somehow serves the story) and we'll be able to spend our time looking at, and listening to, other things.

The year after *Chinatown* was released, Arthur Penn directed *Night Moves,* a neo-noir set in Los Angeles and the Florida Keys—locales both sun-baked and seamy to which the hero is dispatched in pursuit of a runaway nymphet from a wealthy family. Played by Gene Hackman, the hero is a former pro football star turned detective. He is separated from his wife, who is actively dating other men. He is spent and world weary. Close to the end of his rope. All of this comprises a set of circumstances that might have been lifted from the classic noir era. But in 1975 Penn turns it up a few notches. In keeping with his times, the hero is an information maven; he amasses enormous amounts of data during his quest, working round the clock, hoping thereby to get the bigger picture in focus—except that there is no bigger picture. He wants a map of the labyrinth he's entered, and there is no map. The more he learns, the less he knows—and, unlike earlier noir heroes, the less empowered he becomes. In fact, along with the nymphet, who is being manipulated sexually and emotionally by a host of unscrupulous adults—incest here is the starting point for all other abuse she suffers—the hero is seen to be one of the weakest and most displaced characters in the film.

The film concludes with the sight of him shot in the leg, lying unconscious in a powerboat far out at sea, moving in ever-increasing concentric circles around the site of a disaster—the crash of a seaplane, which has provided him the final piece of information he required to solve the case. But there is nothing he can do with this information. And nothing he could have done, even if he had not been incapacitated. He has solved a mystery that, ultimately, no one—not the principals, not the police, certainly not his wife (who mocks him) or his acquaintances—cares about. The clear implication is that he will bleed to death in the boat. For the entire film we have watched him circuiting the byways of his labyrinth in vain, unraveling one "secret" after another, but finding no meaningful revelation, and not even hoping any longer for the kind of personal illumination that might accompany such a revelation. In the end—

again echoing Dante—he is drifting in circles within circles, a vortex of infernal futility. Considering the rich history of the investigative formula in film noir, this is a cruel fate for a noir hero, and a particularly ironic one at the dawn of the so-called Information Age. Running a terrible gantlet, enduring countless difficulties, he's arrived at the same dead end he might have reached (as thousands of others in the noir city reach it after desperately living out their lives) with little effort, and without having learned anything at all.

The most significant neo-noir after *Night Moves* is *The Driver* (1978), directed by Walter Hill, which is a true pivot point for all subsequent films noirs, up to and beyond the present day. *The Driver* takes the alienation and urban detachment of all film noir, strips it to the bone, and reassembles it allegorically. In this film, none of the characters have names. They are known as the Driver, the Detective, the Player, the Connection, and even a pair of characters called Glasses and Teeth—a conceit of allegory, of course, with a proud tradition, from John Bunyan's *Pilgrim's Progress* to Beckett's *Play.* The Driver is a getaway driver in holdups. He is very good at it and he has never been caught. He is a loner, detached and self-contained. If he takes pleasure in anything, it's his work: driving at high speeds through a city in dead of night, eluding capture. He makes sure he is well paid for it, but he never seems to evince any subsequent interest in the money he receives; as far as we can tell, he barely spends any of it. And he mentions no overriding material objectives—jewels, beach house, high living—for which he might be stashing it away. He lives in a succession of anonymous downtown hotel rooms, moving from place to place at night, silently, with little baggage. He eats take-out food. He dresses simply, and much of the time conceals his eyes behind a pair of dark glasses.

The film begins and ends with high-speed chases, brilliantly choreographed. Hill is a neo-expressionist, a throwback in that he assembles each frame and sequence, light and shadow, action and backdrop, with a craftsman's precision. Though completely nocturnal, the Los Angeles he paints—structured in planes, with strong Cubist and Futurist overtones—is one of vibrant nocturnal colors evocatively balanced, a lot of yellows and oranges, purple and indigo. We never leave the city and we never leave the night. Much of the action—involving complicated rendezvous and the transferring of stolen cash—occurs in Union Station, a landmark of early films noirs. But it is the grid of late-night streets that Hill uses to present us with yet another vision of the post-apocalyptic city: a dizzying mix of modern high-rises, decaying office buildings, and cheap bars and clubs—all seen from the *outside* only—it is a silent and barren place, emptied of people, and even of other automobiles, a seemingly endless maze through which The Driver speeds from pursuers, invisible and otherwise.

It feels like an infinite labyrinth: the noir labyrinth expanded to the *n*th power. And the noir city carried to its logical extreme: an empty city in which a loner is chased at the highest possible speed by an obsessed pursuer. For the Detective is every bit as alienated a character as the Driver; because he is edgier, more hot-tempered, and outright sadistic, he is also a lot less likable. And this is saying a lot when one considers the coldly isolated persona of The Driver. The Driver, however, also possesses a high degree of mental clarity, which is surely his most redemptive quality. He may be self-absorbed, but he is also elementally self-aware; he may be engaged in activities that seem at any point ready to veer out of control (like a high-risk robbery, or driving ninety miles per hour down a narrow unlit street), but he seems to be curiously, unashamedly, in control of himself at all times. His self-possession—the flip side of his solipsism—is enticing, even reassuring, in an environment so blankly malevolent and physically vacant. He is a man presented to us (like all the other characters) devoid of an inner life; we are never privy to his fears or passions—if he has any—only his actions, in the purest sense. Yet we never leave off imagining what he is thinking and feeling and imagining himself. And this tension is not sustained because Hill engages in some sort of perverse narrative withholding, or in minimalist gamesmanship, but because the lack of information, in the end, plays right into the film's overall premise, as an allegory.

If the Driver is indeed a kind of Everyman, and the icily remote, almost abstract city he roams is indeed the apotheosis of the noir city, and his allegory is that of the noir hero condemned to run to and fro in the city, without alteration, without resolution, then there is not much more we need to know. For in the end, the Driver is not destroyed by the relentless Detective, as he would be in a 1940s film noir. He is not even captured. He gets away after the final frenetic chase, disappearing into the night, frustrating the Detective, whom he has outwitted and escaped, as—it's become clear—he always must. There may be a "next time," but the Driver will get away then, too. The catch is—and here we part from Bunyan and move much closer to Beckett—that he cannot possibly, by definition, escape a labyrinth that is infinite. He will always be out there, in another rundown hotel or another hopped-up car, in that city which stretches on forever, or turns in on itself, consisting of a million streets, or just a few. And he will always be alone. The noir hero in a deserted city which is the only city, wandering (at high speed) in the night which never ends.

In the 1990s, films drawn from the writings of the hard-boiled novelists McCoy, Cain, and especially Thompson, are updated accordingly—if not technologically, then often in terms of the intensity of their grittiness and despair. Again, the theme of incest is crucial to a film like *The Grifters,* but it's even more in the forefront of the film's plot—in fact, it's central to it—than it was in *Chinatown.* Directed by Stephen Frears and based on a 1950 novel by Thompson, *The Grifters* would surely have been infinitely less explicit with regard to the hero's incestuous relationship with his mother had the film been produced in the 1950s, under the constraints of the Hays Office, rather than in 1990. One has only to consider the perverse mother-son relationship between the psychotic train robber Cody Jarrett and his doting, but criminally savvy, mother, Ma Jarrett, in the 1949 film noir *White Heat* to get an idea of how the parallel relationship in *The Grifters* might have been handled in a film version shot during the same era. Cody suffers from blinding headaches that cause him to writhe in agony on the floor or in his bed: he can only be relieved by the ministrations (she massages his head) of Ma, and never by his stunning wife Verna. In fact, when Verna steps forward during one of Cody's attacks to help him, Ma elbows her aside, with Cody's acquiescence. The massages relieve Cody of his angst exactly as sexual relations would have relieved him of the sexual tensions he clearly experiences but never attends to.

In *The Grifters,* no bones are made about the fact that the young hero and his young mother (and Anjelica Huston plays her as a far more alluring woman than Ma Jarrett) share an incestuous past. When another woman, the hero's age, and just as fetching as Verna Jarrett, enters the scene, the triangle is complete; but unlike Verna (who betrays Cody because of her sexual frustration), this young woman played by Annette Bening, is every bit as wily and lethal a con-man as the hero and his mother. In the end, after they've all negoti-ated a maze of lies, betrayals, and double-dealing that more resembles a snakepit than a labyrinth, it is the mother who survives, murdering the younger woman and burning her body and, in a fit of rage (he finds her desperately rifling his apartment for getaway money), slug-ging her son with an attaché case so that a glass he's sipping from shatters and a shard pierces his jugular vein and kills him. His mother seems horrified at first when he's sprawled out before her, but mo-ments later, without tears, she recovers, slips out of his apartment building, and disappears into the Los Angeles night. Without forget-ting, however, to gather up his cache of money, some of it blood-spattered, in that same attaché case, which she tucks under her arm.

Another Jim Thompson novel adapted with equally raw and graphic energy is *After Dark, My Sweet,* also released in 1990. The ti-tle of this film obviously echoes the 1944 *Murder, My Sweet* (remade in 1975 as *Farewell, My Lovely,* which of course was Raymond Chan-dler's book title), a film with which *After Dark, My Sweet,* a desert noir built around a drifter and a dangerous woman, otherwise shares nothing in common. *Body Heat,* on the other hand, directed by Lawrence Kasdan in 1981, is based completely on *Double Indemnity,* with the locale, several plot elements, and the array of subplots al-tered and updated. Kathleen Turner's femme fatale is every bit as lethal as Barbara Stanwyck's was thirty-seven years earlier, but she's also a bit smarter: in *Body Heat,* the femme fatale not only has an-other man murder her husband, but by means of a doppelgänger and some tremendously complicated legal maneuvering she man-ages to escape with her life and her husband's considerable fortune; we last glimpse her reclining on a tropical beach being served a cool drink by a natty servant. In *Double Indemnity,* as we've seen, the femme fatale and her lover not only die violently, but living with un-bearable tension from the moment they commit murder, never have a chance to enjoy a penny of her dead husband's money.

Though film noir is rife with satanic figures, such as the psychi-atric and criminal masterminds and the omnipotent tycoons we have discussed, by 1987 Satan himself emerges as a character in the neo-noir *Angel Heart.* True, in 1949, John Farrow directed an unusual hybrid, a noir-fantasy entitled *Alias Nick Beal,* in which Ray Milland plays a suavely malevolent, sartorially splendid Mephistopheles named Nick Beal (his name conjuring up infernal associations to "Beelzebub," the angel Milton in *Paradise Lost* ranks "next to Satan in power and crime"), who leads his Faustus, a big-city politician, to perdition. But, alas, Satan never puts in an appearance. Forty years later, however, we're ready for the Man himself; no need now to fall back on the buffering device of imbuing a flesh-and-blood character with evil traits or tendencies: as in Goethe, Byron, and certainly Milton, simply have Satan come onto the scene in his own person, subtly developed and mythopoeically in sync with the times. That is, this Satan is not the sensationalistic grotesque of horror films, but a manifestation of numerous archetypes of evil—who manipulate, corrupt, pervert, and devour—very familiar to us at the end of this century.

In *Angel Heart,* written and directed by Alan Parker, Lucifer ("Louis Cyphre" is his earthly monicker) is played by Robert De Niro as a hard-edged dandy. Suave still, but more aggressive than Milland's ultra-smooth Mephistopheles, Cyphre possesses satanic physical characteristics immediately recognizable from folklore and fairy tales: pointed beard, slicked-back hair, penetrating, almost glowing, eyes, and long, sharp fingernails with which he can peel the shell from an egg in one long spiral. Cyphre plays his own Mephistopheles, but he has retainers to do the legwork for him; unlike the legions surrounding Lucifer in *Paradise Lost,* this Satan's fallen angels consist of particularly pliant and malignant lawyers, bankers, doctors, and other demons drawn strictly from the professional classes. In addition to his holdings in the underworld, he also controls a good deal of choice earthly (mostly urban) real estate, from Harlem churches to luxury apartment buildings, that serves his needs. His basic need, as always, is for human souls, for which he barters with all the gusto we expect of him. Primary among these is a gumshoe detective named Harold Love who shuttles between New York City and New Orleans after Cyphre seduces him into a world of voodooism, taboo miscegenation, and street-gritty supernaturalism, wherein Love is manipulated mercilessly—even unto committing multiple murders. The film's subject matter turns out to be no less than the transmigration of souls, for Love's body is inhabited by the soul of another man—a dead crooner named Johnny Fontaine—who sold it to Cyphre for transitory fame. Interestingly, despite the strong 1980s feel of its occultism, *Angel Heart* is set in 1955, in a meticulously evoked New York of that day (that is, of the classic noir era); the unsettling disjunction between the film's eighties' themes and fifties' atmosphere heightens the insidiousness of the action. In the end, we last see Love/Fontaine, his facial contortions worthy of a Hogarth print, on an eerie, flashingly lit freight elevator in the bowels of the city, clanging down through successive circles of the inferno.

If Satan himself is walking its streets, employing its citizens, and buying up its real estate, then surely as the neo-noirs develop, the city will logically be seen, too, not as a symbolic mirror-image, but as the site of Hell itself. That is exactly what happens eight years after *Angel Heart,* in the 1995 neo-noir *Seven,* directed by David Fincher. Two police detectives are pursuing, without much success, a particularly vicious and demonic serial killer who alleges that his seven victims have committed, respectively, the seven deadly sins, and whose murders he fashions after the sins themselves. That is, he forces an especially greedy lawyer to cut a pound of flesh, carefully weighed, from his own body; a glutton to eat himself to death; a vain fashion model to commit suicide because he has disfigured her, and so on. In the end, the killer gives up his own life in order to destroy the life of one of the detectives, heinously provoking the latter—a man whose greatest sin is wrath. This is a serial killer who zealously plays god, and the devil—claiming for himself a profound, even spiritual, logic where there is only insanity—with the city he terrorizes. And the insanity he imposes succeeds on some level in reconfiguring the human map. New York is thus presented as a city conflated with Hell to such a degree that it makes perfect sense when the older, more seasoned police detective calmly visits the rare-books section of the public library at Forty-second Street and photocopies a "Map of Dante's Inferno" to aid him in tracking down the killer.

It is also in 1995 that Satan makes his most textured, down-to-earth—and, frankly, satisfying—appearance to date in a neo-noir. This time it is not a killer playing the devil, but the Devil himself posing as a low-level criminal in order to manipulate the execution of a fantastic series of crimes that serve his purposes. This manipulation involves not just the masterminding of the crimes, but the stage-

managing of their aftermaths: confusing the police beyond compre-
hension by sending them in and out of one hypothetical maze of
events after another—but never the *right* maze. The film is *The
Usual Suspects,* one of the finest neo-noirs and by far the best of the
1990s to date. *The Usual Suspects* boasts an original and—a rarity in
film noir—Academy Award–winning screenplay, by Christopher Mc-
Quarrie, brilliant direction by Bryan Singer, and an ensemble cast
that meshes seamlessly in the service of the story. One of the latter,
Kevin Spacey, who played the role of the serial killer in *Seven,* also
received an Academy Award, for best supporting actor, for his work
in *The Usual Suspects.* Two such awards for a noir film, especially
one produced by a small independent studio, are highly unusual; in
the classic film noir era, it was inconceivable that an equivalent, low-
budget B-movie would receive such attention. And only a few A films
noirs from that era come to mind for having received even Academy
Award nominations: *Double Indemnity, Crossfire,* and *Panic in the
Streets. Double Indemnity* is an aesthetic masterpiece, but the other
two films were most certainly nominated because they were socially
topical films about, respectively, an antisemitic murder and the fear
of bubonic plague (a metaphorical stand-in for the Red Menace)
gripping an American city. In only one other neo-noir film, *Chinatown,* a big-studio, big-stars production, has the screenwriter actually won the Academy Award. In the case of *The Usual Suspects,*
these awards are especially heartening because, while sleek and
stylish, the film does not rely on stylistics or pyrotechnics to achieve
its effects, and the attention it garnered was due, not to a studio's
publicity machine, but to a strong critical reception and simple word-
of-mouth among buffs and general moviegoers alike.

　With appropriate symmetry, *The Usual Suspects* is set evenly in
those two epicenters of the noir world, New York and Los Angeles.
The story begins in the interrogation room of a Manhattan police
station and ends in the interrogation room of a Los Angeles police
station. It is a bicoastal tale of two cities, and many crimes, told in the
form of questions and answers—though the formal structure which
that implies is often bent beyond recognition. For on its deepest
level, *The Usual Suspects* is a story about the implication of telling
stories, and about the inherent ambiguities of the storyteller's role,
especially when his motives may be a story unto themselves, with

myriad roots: to convey a putative reality, to refashion events or make sense of them, to purge himself, to deceive. As with any narrator, what he amplifies or diminishes, includes or omits, and the infinite variations therein, are what make the story what it is. Thus in the best of film, as in literature, there is always the story behind the story, the word within the word, the revelations that come not only from content, but from seeing how and why a story is being told, and with what particular fusion of those disparate essential elements: memory and fantasy, truth and lies. In the case of *The Usual Suspects,* it is the story behind the story which gradually draws us in, since the storyteller turns out to be Satan wearing one of his innumerable human masks. In telling a story, he is skillful beyond measure, surely the greatest novelist of all, seeing that his subject matter includes every life in the miasma of human history—a dizzying, Borgesian notion—all of them as familiar to him as the back of his hand.

"People say I talk too much." Thus does Verbal Klint, our narrator, a small-time confidence man, introduce himself to us. He is a cripple with a gnarled-up left hand and a left leg so damaged he must drag it, at a right angle to his torso, when he walks. He is being interrogated by the police and a U.S. customs agent named Daniel Kujan in the San Pedro police station in connection with a freighter that burned and nearly sank in the harbor with twenty-eight dead men aboard. All of the men had been shot or stabbed to death, most of them members of a Hungarian criminal gang. Whatever debacle occured in the harbor, Verbal is one of only two survivors; the other is the ship's captain who, fished from the sea badly burned, begins ranting to the police that the men on the ship were killed by one Keyser Soze. The mere mention of this name makes an FBI agent who arrives at the hospital stop in his tracks. And who is Keyser Soze? The captain, like his crew, speaks only Hungarian. So the FBI agent brings in a Hungarian translator, and an artist. The translator begins relating what the captain is saying, and such is the latter's agitation that, despite his weakened condtion, he cannot stop talking. There are two simultaneous narratives in this film: all the while that Verbal is telling his tale to Agent Kujan, the captain is telling his to the translator. We hear all of Verbal's tale, but only a bit of the captain's.

"He saw the Devil, looked him in the eye," the translator says.

"Who's the Devil?" the FBI agent inquires.

"Keyser Soze. He was in the harbor killing many men."

From the first we understand that the captain is not talking about a man with devilish qualities; he's talking about the Devil. The FBI agent wants a description of Keyser Soze, and while the captain offers one up, feature by feature, the translator relays these details to the police artist, who begins sketching on a pad. All of them have first put on surgical gowns, gloves, and masks, to protect the captain from germs, so badly burned is he. Scalded, as if he was lifted, not from the San Pedro harbor, but from the burning lake in Hell where we first meet Milton's Lucifer. But who *is* Keyser Soze, and if he's the Devil, what does he look like?

First we return to Verbal, being grilled at the police station. Throughout the film, we always return to Verbal. His story is primary. The captain's story, while crucial, will become an appendix—or, better yet, a coda—to Verbal's. But without Verbal, it soon becomes clear, there is no story. Verbal is the man of words par excellence, the confidence man perhaps more gifted than his mediocre criminal record would indicate. He is supremely confident, honey-tongued, his speech artful and fluid, even while his body movements remain awkward and uncertain. Physically he is forever stumbling and fumbling. He sips coffee whose quality he disdains and smokes cigarettes which, with his maimed hand, he lights with difficulty as he unfurls that tale of which he is in complete control at all times.

Verbal's voice-over is what we hear from the first scene to the last, delineating and distilling "the facts," not only for the police, but for the film audience. Craving the bigger picture, demanding from Verbal the empirical truth about a set of circumstances of which they know little and he apparently knows everything, the police are predictably asking all the wrong questions. Even when they become aware that he may know a great deal more than he says, they never suspect that he is not merely the witness to the story they are eliciting from him, he is its creator, and beyond that—truly mind-boggling—he is the architect of the events that comprise the story. That is, if the story he is telling bears the slightest resemblance to what occurred in the harbor when those twenty-eight men died. The customs agent and the FBI man and the police will never know. Nor will we, though at film's end we may think we do.

Seen from one angle, *The Usual Suspects* is a classic film noir type, the heist movie—like Kubrick's *The Killing* or Huston's *The Asphalt Jungle*—in which several distinct personalities with varied talents join together to pull off a job. But in this film that model is carried into the realm of the surreal. The first layer of narrative with which Verbal provides us is concerned with the heist aspect of the story. Five men in Manhattan are pulled in for a police lineup around the investigation of a truck hijacking. Four of them have long criminal records, including one named Dean Keaton, a former cop. Actually, a fallen cop, despised and worked over by his police interrogators. The fifth man is Verbal, who has served time briefly for a confidence scam. These men are "the usual suspects" of the title. In his voice-over, as they take their places in the lineup, Verbal confides to us with a chuckle, "It was fun. I got to make like I was notorious." All five of them profess their innocence in the truck hijacking. But they are kept in a holding cell overnight. A kind of incubator, as Verbal sees it: "You don't put men like that in a room together for too long," he says, or they're sure to hatch a crime. He ought to know: he's the one who lays out the blueprint for another heist: the interception of a courier, protected by crooked cops, who is transporting stolen emeralds. "Mr. Verbal, the man with the plan," the others call him.

And despite Keaton's deep reluctance at first, he is drawn into the scheme. He is living with his lawyer, an attractive woman named Edie who not only is in love with him, but has been supporting him and trying to help him go straight. And Keaton himself has been trying hard to stay straight. But the indignity of being publically hauled in and physically roughed up pushes him over the edge. That and the very real fact that, in arresting him, the police exposed—and ruined—him before a group of potential (legitimate) business partners. Now, ironically, he will find himself with a very different set of partners. It is Verbal who provides the decisive push, drawing Keaton into the gang. Verbal explains in detail how he does this (even as we watch it happen in flashback), but at the same time claims that he wasn't really responsible for drawing Keaton in. And, incredibly, like Agent Kujan, we accept this statement from him; with us, as with Kujan, Verbal's contradictions can seem truer than the truth.

As for Edie, she is the only woman in the film with a speaking role. And her part is very small. In fact, except for the police artist, a nurse, and a woman who appears in a brief, out-of-focus flashback, Edie is literally the only woman in the film. A staggering notion for film noir. There is no femme fatale here: none is needed when you have the Devil himself doing her work for her, enticing men like Keaton into the labyrinth. Where it took Kathie Moffet, a beautiful and sexually alluring woman, to usher Jeff Bailey to his destruction in *Out of the Past,* in *The Usual Suspects* Keaton, a far more cold-blooded character than Bailey, is seduced by a crippled conman. The femme fatale has been internalized by the male seducer, who then employs both masculine and feminine wiles.

Initially, in pure macho style, Verbal plays on Keaton's raw pride—goading him with the fact that he's financially dependent on a woman—to involve him in the heist. Running his filling station in obscurity, Jeff Bailey required much stronger incentive than that to return to the noir underworld: namely, the raw threat of blackmail, and then his lust for Kathie, for whom he was willing to throw everything over. Bailey couldn't have cared less what the assorted tough guys he encountered threw his way, verbally or otherwise, and he could and did pick apart every nuance of their efforts in his voice-over; but with Kathie his blindspot was enormous. Like Bailey, then, Keaton leaves behind a "good" woman, Edie—not for a femme fatale, but for the company of four criminals embarked on a dubious enterprise. Nearly fifty years after *Out of the Past,* the population of this noir labyrinth is entirely male and its contours have become harder and blunter, without the sinuous progressions imparted by a female guide. The apogee of Edie's role is the brief moment in which she is an unwitting hostage to Keyser Soze's worldly ambassador, the lawyer Kobayashi, who threatens to murder her if Keaton doesn't back down on his threat to bolt the labyrinth. Keaton backs down.

Edie, a dim satellite to the story's central action, through no fault of her own hasn't a clue as to the danger she is in. It is her well-intentioned relationship with Keaton, and then her ignorance of his true situation and even his whereabouts—for he has disappeared without a word—that proves fatal to her. And we see that these circumstances are no anomaly in their relationship, which has been one of wishful thinking and confusing cross-purposes—a kind of high-wire balancing act set on conflicting planes. This is neatly symbolized by both Edie's apartment and her office. It is in her multileveled living room, with its platforms, stairs, and deep well, and its many prismatic and chromatic effects of light—a room of many shifting colors—where Verbal comes to enlist Keaton. Edie's office in the Cast Iron Building in Manhattan is also high-ceilinged and irregularly shaped; from a platform near the ceiling, reached by a stairway in the adjacent room and affording him a tortuous bird's-eye angle onto the room, Keaton gets his next-to-last look at her. His last look is in Kobayashi's offices, through a series of bluish glass doors, again from an oblique angle, so that she does not see him. In fact, despite Keaton's submission to blackmail, Edie is murdered, too, after he himself is, so he dies without knowing her fate. From a remark he makes to Verbal in the last hour of his life, we know that Keaton clearly expects her to survive him.

Verbal is a marvel of gender elasticity: masculine when he needs to be, and at other times effortlessly displaying the strongly feminine aspect of his nature. It is not only Keaton and the other members of the gang whom he seduces in the manner of a femme fatale, using words the way the latter might use them (Kathie Moffet, for one, is as glib as she is sexy), but also Agent Kujan. Sometimes in his asides to Kujan, Verbal is talkative in a female way, chatty or beguilingly contemplative: "A man can't change what he is," he purrs, "he can convince everyone else, but never himself"; and sometimes his asides are vintage machismo, as when he describes the aftermath of the first heist, which was engineered not only to steal the emeralds but to implicate the crooked cops: "Everybody got it right in the ass," he snaps, "from the chief on down. It was beautiful." But all the while, through his conversational feints and digressions, Verbal is coolly, unerringly, sending Kujan spinning into a unique variety of labyrinth, one created entirely in, and of, the stale air in the cluttered office which they share for an afternoon in the San Pedro police station: a labyrinth far more dangerous and invidious in its way than the city streets, that opens up, and closes down, completely within the confines of Kujan's mind. This mental labyrinth which Verbal constructs is the most elegant and advanced that we encounter in film noir: it remains vital and ever-shifting to the end, the more terrifying for its fluidity.

Put another way, Verbal is a master improviser in an utterly fluid situation: facts which he must continually digest and adapt are dribbling in to the police station all day; like an alchemist, he must keep the truth liquid at a high temperature so as to be able to refashion it, practically and semantically, at any moment. To accomplish this, in weaving his tale he deflects facts this way and that, digresses endlessly, changes key whenever the need arises, and under cover of making disclosures, tosses up obstacles for Kujan in the form of outright lies or—far more frequently and effectively—half-truths or extraneous information that confuses the issue at hand.

In *The Origin of Satan,* Elaine Pagels writes: "In biblical sources the Hebrew term the *satan* describes an adversarial role. It is not the name of a particular character. Although Hebrew storytellers as early as the sixth century B.C.E. occasionally introduced a supernatural character whom they called the *satan,* what they meant was any one of the angels sent by God for the specific purpose of blocking or obstructing human activity. The root *śtn* means 'one who opposes, obstructs, or acts as adversary.' (The Greek term *diabolos,* later translated 'devil,' literally means 'one who throws something across one's path.')" Which is exactly what Verbal does, first to Keaton and then to Kujan.

And who is Keyser Soze? A question to which we return repeatedly. We learn the answer, as does Kujan, from both the FBI agent and, far more extensively, from Verbal. It is significant, and astonishing, that Kujan has not previously heard of Soze, who he learns is, for starters, a premier international smuggler of drugs, jewels, and armaments, a murderer many times over, and a highly sophisticated extortionist and blackmailer: one would think Keyser Soze would be high on the U.S. Customs Agency's most-wanted list. But Agent Kujan is not alone in this respect. Verbal at first professes not to know who Soze is. And Keaton says he doesn't know, though the other three members of the gang, McManus, Fenster, and Hockney, all recognize Soze's name the moment Kobayashi mentions it to them. In fact, cool and breezy as we have seen these three tough guys remain in the face of harsh physical danger, at the mention of Soze they clam up and grow very unsettled. It's the first time we see them sweat. And it is interesting that, at the same time, the film's three principal characters are saying they have never heard of Soze; and two of them truly haven't.

Keyser Soze, Kujan learns from Verbal in bits and pieces, is the mastermind of a complex, far-flung international crime empire. His identity and whereabouts are unknown. There are no known photographs of him anywhere. No fingerprints. Nothing. He is literally a citizen of the world, and seems to live everywhere and nowhere, with no known haunts. His origins are murky: born in Turkey, his father possibly German, he began his professional life as a drug dealer and murderer. He has few enemies who would admit to the fact, outside of a Hungarian criminal gang with whom he tangled early on in Turkey. The criminals who work for him always operate in ignorance of one another. And serve very short tenures. That is, through intermediaries, many steps removed from himself, Soze hires freelancers or blackmails skilled criminals into working on his behalf, then moves on. He seldom uses the same underlings twice, Kobayashi says, describing Soze's methods to Keaton and the others. "One cannot be betrayed if he has no people," Kobayashi adds, omitting the fact that Soze frequently makes sure those in his temporary employ who are closest to him are betrayed themselves, turned against one another, or killed outright. Fenster confirms Kobayashi's words: "I knew a guy in New York," he says, "who knew a guy who said he once worked for Soze."

Some people say Soze is "a spook story criminals tell their kids," Verbal tells Kujan, who has begun to doubt that Soze exists. Kujan thinks he's "a shield," a convenient front for other, more pedestrian criminals. Kobayashi, on the other hand, ominously says to Keaton and the others in the gang, "I assure you Mr. Soze is very real, and very determined, gentlemen." And when Kujan asks Verbal if he believes Soze exists, Verbal offers up a surprising reply: "I believe in God," he says, "and the only thing that scares me is Keyser Soze."

One thing is clear: when Soze comes out ahead, which he always does, he is invariably alone. Far from the reach of the law, he enjoys the knowledge that his own reach has no limits. Anyone who crosses him pays swiftly for it; many cross him without even knowing that they are doing so. For example, the five members of Keaton's gang, who, according to Kobayashi, have individually committed crimes that in some way inconvenienced Soze or affected his interests. Having documented these and their other crimes—"everything I've done since I was eighteen," McManus mutters, examining a dossier Soze has sent him—Soze blackmails them into making a murderous assault on the ship that is later found burning in the San Pedro harbor. On that ship is a man whom the Hungarians are "purchasing" from another criminal gang, the one man alive, we are told, who can positively identify Keyser Soze. It is Keaton and the others who murder the Hungarians, and are themselves murdered. Picked off one by one on this ghost ship by Keyser Soze himself, whom the ship's captain places at the scene. Verbal, the lone survivor, also places Soze there. "A slender man in a business suit" is how he describes him. After shooting the contraband witness twice in the head, Soze shoots Keaton, too, according to Verbal, who, while hidden behind a coil of rope and tackle—a coil as tangled as his tale—witnesses Keaton's death. Or so he tells Kujan. Soze, Verbal concludes, has killed the one man who can identify him, taken the money with which the Hungarians were to purchase him, and disappeared. "My guess is you'll never see him again," Verbal says.

But Kujan will have none of it. "You say Keaton was your friend, Verbal," he taunts him. "You had a gun—why didn't you save him?"

Verbal leans forward, glassy-eyed. "I was afraid," he replies. "It was Keyser Soze, Agent Kujan. I mean, the Devil himself. How do you shoot the Devil in the back? What if you miss?"

Meawhile, we cut back to the hospital room a couple of times where the ship's captain, hooked up to intravenous fluids, half his face bandaged and tubes in his nostrils, continues to spit out his description of Keyser Soze in his gravelly voice. And the translator puts his words into English, and the police artist converts the words into an image with her pencil—an image to which we are not privy.

And Agent Kujan continues to be skeptical about the very existence of Keyser Soze, much less his purported role in the carnage on the ship. Keaton didn't believe in Soze, either, Verbal informs Kujan with a shrug. Like Kujan, he adds, Keaton was a cop, matter-of-fact and to the point, and he scoffed at the notion of some archcriminal pulling the strings somewhere; Keaton was certain Kobayashi himself was a conman playing them for suckers behind the spectre of Soze. Kujan agrees with a self-satisfied smile. "There is no Keyser Soze, Verbal," he says, sipping his coffee. "He's a spook story, just like you said."

And then Verbal delivers the speech that is the centerpiece of his rambling story, and of the film itself—the center of the enormous web he has spun. In such a web, the spider always sits immobile at the center, waiting. And what is a web, after all, but a fluid labyrinth.

"Nobody ever believed he was real," Verbal says of Keyser Soze. "Nobody ever knew him or saw anybody that worked directly for him. But to hear Kobayashi tell it, anybody could have worked for Soze. You never knew. That was his power. The greatest trick the Devil ever pulled was convincing the world he didn't exist." Raising his open palm, he blows across it, and whispers, "And—like that—he's gone."

But Kujan, who has already told Verbal that he is smarter than him and can't be fooled by him, merely shakes his head contemptuously. It's not Kobayashi or anybody else, he informs Verbal, who is behind these crimes: it is Keaton. Kujan's explanation is simple: after killing the witness and the rest of his gang, Keaton staged his own death and then disappeared with the Hungarians' money. Keaton the fallen cop, adept at manipulating both cops and criminals, he's the one behind everything—whatever the name he's using. Like the cops in New York, Kujan has it in for Keaton, and he doesn't plan to look any farther than Keaton for his answer.

And at this juncture, in looking back at the nuances of Verbal's story, we too see how all the facts, tilted just so, like a mirror, could appear as Kujan suggests. It could easily be Keaton.

Now Kujan is told he has to release Verbal Klint, for whom bail has been posted. Verbal has given his evidence after being granted immunity, and he will be on call for a trial, if there is one. Kujan is all for holding Verbal, but it's not possible; the San Pedro police chief informs him that there's been tremendous pressure "from above" to have Verbal sprung. The police commissioner, the mayor, even the governor have weighed in. This puzzles Kujan: why such heavy clout exerted for a small-time hood? The chief shakes his head in bewilderment, and says, "This guy is protected from on high by the Prince of Darkness."

Still, Kujan doesn't get it—though he thinks he does. It occurs to him suddenly that Keyser Soze—that is, Keaton—is exerting the pressure. He wants Verbal sprung so that he can finish him off, too. Kujan pleads with Verbal to remain in police custody, for his own protection. No thanks, Verbal says, collecting his personal effects—a gold watch, a gold cigarette lighter—he'll take his chances. And with his crippled leg dragging and his maimed hand dangling, he limps and shuffles out of the police station onto the sunlit street.

Meanwhile, across town at the hospital, the police artist has finished her sketch finally, and an FBI man slips it into a fax machine and sends it to the San Pedro police station. Inch by inch, the sketched face appears to us for the first time, and of course it is not Kobayashi or Keaton. It is Verbal.

Verbal is Keyser Soze. *The man with the plan.* And of course all the while the story he has been spinning—to manipulate Kujan—is the story within the story that is his manipulation not just of the narrative but of the action behind it. Keyser Soze, the hidden man of the film, is at the same time Verbal Klint, the man in the forefront of the action; the man who never speaks is the man who has not stopped speaking. A delicious and quintessential noir paradox. It is Keyser Soze himself who we have been hearing from the first, in the voice-over. He masterminded the crime and also the way the crime's particulars have been recorded. He has been pulling *all* the strings, concealed and otherwise—just as he himself told us he was. Again, his lies sound truer than the truth—as it would seem with the Devil himself. Whether what *really* happened and what he told Agent Kujan happened are one and the same, we'll never know. We know that twenty-eight dead men were found on the ship and Edie was found dead in a motel room. We know Kobayashi was an intermediary. And we know that Keyser Soze is about to disappear for good, as Verbal told us he would: "My guess is you'll never see him again."

Kujan rushes from the police station, in vain, to catch Verbal. But Verbal, far down the street, is undergoing a metamorphosis: his dragged foot, at right angles to his torso, gradually straightens itself out, his knee no longer falls inward, his limp fades away, and he is walking at a rapid stride now, putting the police station behind him. All the while, the voice-over has suddenly undergone its own metamorphosis; instead of Verbal's solitary voice, we hear an extraordinary auditory montage. A babble at first, which then comes stunningly clear as crucial bits of dialogue and voice-over from the film flow past us, assembled so as to demonstrate that all along, buried in the lines we heard throughout the story, was an inexorable line leading to the fact that Verbal was Keyser Soze. Poised at the center of his web. A film about storytelling on its deepest level after all had to be a film about language in the end. About Babel. Which of course is the Hebrew for Babylon, the city where in Genesis the Lord did "confound the language of all the earth" so that the people "may not understand one another's speech."

References to language in these terms are peppered through the entire film, around the central conceit of a character named "Verbal." In the lineup at the opening, Fenster, who speaks with a lilting, eccentric inflection, is told by the police (a booming voice on a loudspeaker belonging to an unseen interrogator) to "speak English," though he is clearly speaking English, inflection notwithstanding. In Keaton's first scene, in a restaurant, Edie is speaking French to the would-be business associates. Then there is the ship's captain and the Hungarian translator, and it's interesting to note that Hungarian is one of two languages whose origins cannot be ascertained. To this day, it remains a linguistic mystery, appearing full-blown apparently, in the center of Europe. The only other such language is Japanese, and one might think that would be Kobayashi's native tongue; but, no, despite the fact that his name is surely Japanese, we are told that he is "an Englishman." Physically—and in an amazing bit of casting—Kobayashi looks as if he could be either English or Japanese! Or he might be Eurasian. His accent, highly inflected, is indeterminate. He is an international lawyer, after all, and Keyser Soze is the most international of characters, for the Devil is at once everywhere and nowhere, inside all men yet capable of manifesting himself in a single man. And of course he is fluent in all languages. It is also interesting to note that in *Angel Heart* Lucifer's worldly surname is "Cyphre," as in "cipher," which of course means "a message in code," a trick of language—and he uses several of them to confound the hero—and in *Seven* the killer leaves an encoded message at each crime scene in order to lead on, and simultaneously confound, the police.

In *The Usual Suspects* Verbal was literally Soze's mouthpiece, ironically speaking on his own behalf, but now, as Agent Kujan stands frantically before the police station, Verbal down the street appears silently amid the rush of crowds and traffic. Stopping by the curb, no longer the cripple, "the gimp," the penny-ante conman with the questioning eyes, he is a man in full possession of himself, ramrod-straight, cold-eyed. With a shake and twist of the wrist, he straightens out his maimed hand, which felt as coiled as that tangle of rope, something that could never be straightened out—like his story. His story that is coming to an end now, at least as far as we'll follow it. Verbal has disappeared before our eyes, and Keyser Soze is about to follow suit. He lights a cigarette with a quick, fluid motion—no more fumbling—as a sleek black Jaguar pulls up beside him. Kobayashi, Keyser Soze's lawyer, is behind the wheel, and his client slips in on the passenger side and puffs on his cigarette as they exchange a long glance without a word. Nothing to say now, not a word, as Kobayashi turns the corner, weaving deftly through the traffic, and the babble of the voice-over slows down, distills itself into two final messages, which we've heard before, from Verbal: *My guess is you'll never hear from him again. . . . The greatest trick the Devil ever pulled was convincing the world he didn't exist.* Then, for a split-second, we see a flashback of Verbal, blowing across his upraised palm. *And—like that—he's gone.* And the screen goes black.

By giving us the noir city in pristinely allegorical terms—that is, in the realm of symbolic representation—Walter Hill in *The Driver* prepared us for *Angel Heart* and *Seven,* and, especially, *The Usual Suspects,* films in which an allegorical figure like Lucifer can appear effortlessly in the flesh, or a symbolic labyrinth can lock into place, superimposed on the city, as an enduring Hell. William Butler Yeats might well have been discussing symbolism and allegory in film, as well as painting and literature, when he wrote that "all art that is not mere story-telling, or mere portraiture, is symbolic, and has the purpose of those symbolic talismans which medieval magicians made with complex colors and forms. . . ." This is a symbolism that has fused with reality, and heightened it, in the magical frozen moment of a work of art which then serves as entry to the vast, cyclical world of illuminations—and epiphany. By the 1990s, the best of the neonoir films represent a form that aspires to this more highly evolved, sophisticated, and artistically secure platform. More than ever, film noir fulfills itself as a mythographic medium, so that, through its lens, ever-evolving, the American city will inevitably come clear to us as a mythological city—in the way of Blake's London, Dostoevsky's St. Petersburg, Balzac's Paris, and Joyce's Dublin—as firmly and luminously embedded in our imaginations, where the truly transformative moment may manifest itself, as is the actual city in our memories and experience.

It is axiomatic that the evolution of film noir entering the new millennium will be linked, as always, with what happens to, and in, the American city. If we continue, as seems certain, to become an ever more urbanized society, even as—paradoxically—our urban cores disintegrate, the material which defines noir will become that much more significant. If urban sprawl, with the ever-multiplying suburbs growing impossibly dense, is carried to its logical (and terrifying) extreme, will there be a linking up of megapolitan systems? For example, a merging from Boston to New York to Philadelphia to Washington to Atlanta to Miami, until the entire Eastern seaboard is a continuous city? So that, on a map, instead of a series of black dots connected by highways, there will be a thick black line rimming the continent. Fantastic—but no more so than the notion of a single megalopolis would have been a mere two centuries ago.

Noir continues to be one of the central cultural phenomena of the postwar American city, a cutting-edge form that inevitably appears in, and emblematizes, times of deep stress. Making a prophet of Thomas Jefferson, the word "city" itself at the close of our century invariably implies that which is darkly complex, chaotic, and corrupt. In film noir, a primary implication is that the city of tomorrow will be an apocalyptic city. That the climax set in motion by the darker forces of predatoriness, prodigality, and dread will surely manifest itself in biblical terms: the wave of fire (like the atomic fireball) that levels the cities of the plain. Despite myriad treaties, diplomatic niceties, and even the end of the Cold War, the fact remains that human society maintains the means of self-annihilation which it did not possess prior to 1945. Anyone born after that year has lived with that unalterable reality as if it were no less than a de facto appendage to the laws of nature. That an American city is now more likely to be devastated by the nuclear weapon which a terrorist can plant in a car trunk than the intercontinental ballistic missile that screams through the sky from eastern Russia is surely cause for more, not less, angst. That the terrorist may as easily be an American citizen—with far more lethal capabilities than the old Cold War saboteur—as a foreign national ought to be the source of even greater angst.

Alongside the constant of nuclear and biological terrorism, we now accept as givens the institutionalization of corporate crime and the internationalization of high-tech organized crime in which illicit capital can move between distant cities at the speed of a computer command. That sort of rarefied criminal ether, by its very rapidity and abstractness, and the fact that—like Keyser Soze—it is so many steps removed from its victims, feeds into one of the basic tenets of the noir ethos: that remote forces more powerful than ourselves, whom we will never confront, perhaps never even be aware of, and who are insulated from any accountability, can change our fate in a flash. The incomprehensible sizes of institutions private and public since the Second World War, from business conglomerates to governments overseeing enormously complex populations, has been a prime factor in the development of noir as a cultural force; for the individual faced with a physical and psychological labyrinth so fantastical in scope or design as to be unnegotiable, the quest may devolve from a goal of illumination with a slim chance of escape—as with earlier noir heroes—to one of bare survival while seeking out the least excruciating torment. At the same time, in an era in which we have absorbed the notion of computer criminals devising credit scams and instilling viruses, and detectives who, with laptops and cellular phones, track them down in cyberspace—yet another labyrinth of infinite rooms and corridors—we also have an everyday, street reality more barbaric than ever before, with battlefield weapons, semiautomatic rifles and pistols, in the hands of even low-level criminals like muggers and stickup men. So the apocalyptic city for which we seem hell-bent in film noir is one that will combust on many levels, from the political to the criminal, from virtual reality to the gutter.

Northrop Frye observes that in William Blake's work, "the struggle between good and evil conceals a genuine dialectic of eternal life and eternal death, the separation of which is achieved only in the apocalypse. Satan in Blake's visionary poems is the death-principle, including not only physical death but all the workings of the death-impulse in human life, the discouraging or prohibiting of free activity. . . ." Freud famously reaches a similar conclusion, and it is important to recall Lewis Mumford's definition of "civilization" ("the ability to live and thrive in cities") when we read it in this context: "And now, I think, the meaning of the evolution of civilization is no longer obscure to us. It must present the struggle between Eros and Death, between the instinct of life and the instinct of destruction. . . ." A struggle that is anything but black and white, both in the noir city and in the psychological terrain of the film noir: after all, it is the same Ariadne who has provided him with a route out of the labyrinth and with whom he has fallen in love, whom Theseus, in his haste to return to the city-state, later abandons on a paradisal island. Mumford, more pessimistic than Frye or Freud, might insist that Theseus' true mission, just begun by bringing the thalassocracy of Crete to Athens, is grimly to move his polis a few notches along the scale toward the necropolis it must eventually become. For, back home, Theseus becomes one of the first great city-builders: he abolishes the numerous towns and villages that constitute Attica and concentrates their inhabitants into a capital city. "In this way," according to Plutarch, "he transformed them into one people belonging to one city," where he built a "single town-hall and senate house" on the Acropolis and abolished, by force when necessary, all vestiges of the existing local governments; in short, he created a centralized metropolis. He then consolidated his power by executing fifty of his most formidable opponents, but also drew up the city's first rudimentary constitution and became the first Greek king to mint coinage. Ariadne was gone (having hanged herself), but not completely forgotten, for Theseus ordered that the city's inaugural coins be imprinted with the head of a bull, to celebrate his slaying the Minotaur and escaping the labyrinth.

Film is of course a twentieth-century phenomenon, its most direct antecedents photography and the theater. Films with sound have only been around for seventy years. With the technological free-for-all that has been set in motion by computer chips and fiber optics, who knows if film, as we understand the term, will retain any meaning seventy years from now. What will come over phone lines (or via satellite receivers) into our homes in the year 2100, visually, aurally, and perhaps tactilely and olfactorily, may be a noir experience akin to the "feelies" that Aldous Huxley foresaw in *Brave New World*. For the moment, however, we still have films, and a virtual renaissance of neo-noir films that are being shot today. Film noir retrospectives, like the one I stumbled on at The New Yorker cinema in Paris in the summer of 1973, and the many I have attended ever since on this side of the Atlantic, are still flourishing. Many are thematic, based on the films' respective femmes fatales, or on a subtext like the communist menace, or on the oeuvre of a director like Aldrich, Welles, or Wilder, or on the fact that the featured films were shot in a particular city. Others consist simply of a dozen films, shown in pairs, that share nothing more than the identification tag "film noir," which—a far cry from the early 1950s when it was known only to cineastes— has now become a familiar element in our cultural vocabularly, long since freed of its italics as a French borrowing.

Every so often in one of those darkened theaters, someone will for the first time watch Jane Greer as Kathie Moffet step from the sunlight into the deep shadows of that cantina where Robert Mitchum as Jeff Bailey is sitting alone. He is also watching her, in her white dress that suddenly turns luminous, gazing at her face as it comes into view for the first time, beautiful and wary and glowing, before she slips past him, and draws him with her, back into the darkness.

Appendix: A Brief Genealogy

Noir.
Black.
Black on black. Its own spectrum, with gradations.

According to Webster's, "black" derives from the Middle English *blak,* Old English *blœc,* Old High German *blah,* and "probably to the Latin *flagrare,* to burn, from the Greek *phlegein.*"

Black derives from burn. Black fire? Or the aftereffects of fire, as in: charred, cindered, reduced to ashes? Or are its origins in both fire and ashes?

In the Oxford English Dictionary, "black" commands two full pages. Its initial entry is preceded by the proviso that it is "a word of difficult history," and then defines it as "the absence or total absorption of light, as its opposite 'white' arises from the reflection of all the rays of light." In Old English, the entry continues, the word is also found with a long vowel, *blace, blacan,* and is thus confused with *blác*—shining, white: "as is shown by the fact that the latter also occurs with a short vowel, *blac, blacan;* so that in Middle English, then, black and white become "distinguishable only by the context, and sometimes not by that."

It is this that makes the word one "of difficult history."

Black blurring into white.

Which linguistically can be seen occurring, frozen in time, in the obsolete English word "blake." "Blake" originally meant "shining," as in white from excess of light. This usage strangely passed to that of "pale, that is, white from deficiency of color, dead white," which added to the formal confusion with black, since "dark" and "pale"

267

alike express deficiency or loss of color. Or, to conclude, as the OED does in a parenthetical footnote: "Many early instances of *blake* (white) may be examples of *blak* (black), with the final *e* inflexional or phonetic, the context leaving the sense uncertain."

As the context often leaves the sense uncertain in film noir.

In film noir, everything is in black and white, and at the same time is never quite what it seems.

Film noir: black film.

Black on a white screen, projected by white light.

Black and white.

Aesthetically pleasing. Morally blurred. All too often in the latter area drawing a blank.

Which is another word for "white," whose origins, however, according to the OED, are not just difficult, but "obscure," unknowable.

Blanc.

White.

Sources

Barthes, Roland. *Mythologies.* Hill and Wang, 1957

Borges, Jorge Luis. *Labyrinths.* New York: New Directions, 1964

Boyer, Paul. *By the Bomb's Early Light.* New York: Pantheon, 1985

Brown, Norman O. *Life Against Death.* New York: Vintage, 1959

Brown, Norman O. *Love's Body.* New York: Vintage, 1966

Cameron, Ian (editor). *The Book of Film Noir.* New York: Continuum, 1993

Campbell, Joseph. *The Hero With a Thousand Faces.* Princeton, N.J.: Princeton, 1972

Campbell, Joseph. *The Masks of God: Vol. I, Primitive Mythology; Vol. II, Oriental Mythology; Vol. III, Occidental Mythology.* New York: Penguin, 1976

Céline, Louis-Ferdinand. *Journey to the End of the Night.* New York: New Directions, 1960

Céline, Louis-Ferdinand. *Castle to Castle.* New York: Penguin, 1968

Céline, Louis-Ferdinand. *North.* New York: Penguin, 1972

Copjec, Joan (editor). *Shades of Noir.* London: Verso, 1993

Defoe, Daniel (with an afterword by Kenneth Rexroth). *Moll Flanders.* New York: Signet, 1964

Deming, Barbara. *Running Away from Myself.* New York: Grossman Publishers, 1969

Freud, Sigmund. *The Basic Writings of Sigmund Freud.* Trans. & ed. by A.A. Brill. New York: Random House, 1938

Freud, Sigmund. *Civilization and its Discontents.* Trans. & ed. by James Strachey. New York: W.W. Norton, 1961

Frye, Northrop. *Anatomy of Criticism.* Princeton: Princeton University Press, 1962

Frye, Northrop. *Fables of Identity.* New York: Harcourt, Brace & World, 1963

Gay, Peter. *Freud: A Life.* New York: Anchor Books, 1990

Goldberger, Paul. *The Skyscraper.* New York: Alfred A. Knopf, 1981

Higham, Charles, and Greenberg, Joel. *Hollywood in the Forties.* Cranbury, N.J.: A.S. Barnes, 1968

Hillman, James. *The Dream and the Underworld.* New York: Harper & Row, 1979

Hirsch, Foster. *The Dark Side of the Screen: Film Noir.* New York: Da Capo Press, 1981

Huizinga, Johan. *Homo Ludens.* Boston: Beacon Press, 1955

Kaplan, Ann E. *Women in Film Noir.* London: British Film Institute, 1978

Karimi, A.M. *Toward a Definition of the American Film Noir (1941–1949).* New York: Arno Press, 1976

Katz, Ephraim. *The Film Encyclopedia.* New York: Perigee, 1979

Knight, W.F. Jackson. *Roman Vergil.* London: Faber & Faber, 1944

Krutnik, Frank. *In a Lonely Street.* London: Routledge, 1991

Leaming, Barbara. *Orson Welles.* New York: Viking, 1985

Leaming, Barbara. *If This Was Happiness: A Biography of Rita Hayworth.* New York: Viking, 1989

Leff, Leonard J., and Simmons, Jerold L. *The Dame in the Kimono.* New York: Anchor, 1990

Levy, Gertrude. *The Gate of Horn.* London: Faber & Faber, 1948

McArthur, Colin. *Underworld U.S.A.* New York: Viking Press, 1972

McCarthy, Todd, and Flynn, Charles. *Kings of the Bs: Working Within the Hollywood System.* New York: Dutton, 1972

McLuhan, Marshall. *Understanding Media: The Extensions of Man.* New York: Signet, 1964

Mumford, Lewis. *The City in History.* New York: Harcourt, Brace & World, 1961

Ottoson, Robert. *A Reference Guide to the American Film Noir: 1940–1958.* Metuchen: The Scarecrow Press, 1981

Pagels, Elaine. *The Origin of Satan.* New York: Random House, 1995

Paglia, Camille. *Sexual Personae.* New York: Vintage, 1991

Plutarch. *The Rise and Fall of Athens: Nine Greek Lives.* Trans. by Ian Scott-Kilvert. London: Penguin, 1960

Roheim, Geza. *Magic and Schizophrenia.* New York: International Universities Press, 1955

Schrader, Paul. "Notes on *Film Noir,*" from *Awake in the Dark,* ed. by David Denby. New York: Vintage, 1977

Shadoian, Jack. *Dreams and Deadends: The American Gangster/Crime Film.* Cambridge: MIT, 1977

Silver, Alain, and Ward, Elizabeth. *Film Noir: An Encyclopedic Reference to the American Style.* Woodstock: The Overlook Press, 1979

Spengler, Oswald. *The Decline of the West: Volumes I & II.* New York: Alfred A. Knopf, 1928

Telotte, J.P. *Voices in the Dark.* Urbana and Champaign: The University of Illinois Press, 1989

de Tocqueville, Alexis. *Democracy in America.* Trans. by George Lawrence. New York: Harper & Row, 1966

Tolstoy, Leo. *Resurrection.* Trans. by Rosemary Edmonds. New York: Penguin, 1966

Trefil, James. *The Scientist in the City.* New York: Doubleday, 1994

Tuska, Jon. *Dark Cinema.* Westport: Greenwood Press, 1984

Veblen, Thorstein. *The Portable Veblen.* Ed. by Max Lerner. New York: Viking, 1948

Wood, Michael. *America in the Movies.* New York: Basic Books, 1975

Yeats, William Butler. *Essays and Introductions.* New York: Collier Books, 1968

The Accused (Paramount) 1949, d. William Dieterle

Act of Violence (MGM) 1949, d. Fred Zinnemann

Angel Face (RKO) 1953, d. Otto Preminger

Appointment with Danger (Paramount) 1950, d. Lewis Allen

Armored Car Robbery (RKO) 1950, d. Richard Fleischer

The Asphalt Jungle (MGM) 1950, d. John Huston

Berlin Express (RKO) 1948, d. Jacques Tourneur

Beware, My Lovely (RKO) 1952, d. Fritz Lang

The Big Carnival (Ace in the Hole) (Paramount) 1951, d. Billy Wilder

The Big Clock (Paramount) 1948, d. John Farrow

The Big Combo (Allied Artists) 1955, d. Joseph H. Lewis

The Big Heat (Columbia) 1953, d. Fritz Lang

The Big Knife (United Artists) 1955, d. Robert Aldrich

The Big Sleep (Warner) 1946, d. Howard Hawks

Black Angel (Universal) 1946, d. Roy William Neill

The Blue Dahlia (Paramount) 1946, d. George Marshall

The Blue Gardenia (Warner) 1953, d. Fritz Lang

Body and Soul (United Artists) 1947, d. Robert Rossen

Boomerang (20th Century-Fox) 1947, d. Elia Kazan

Border Incident (MGM) 1949, d. Anthony Mann

Born to Kill (RKO) 1947, d. Robert Wise

The Brasher Doubloon (20th Century-Fox) 1947, d. John Brahm

The Breaking Point (Warner Bros.) 1950, d. Michael Curtiz

The Brothers Rico (Columbia) 1957, d. Phil Karlson

Brute Force (Universal-International) 1947, d. Jules Dassin

Caged (Warner Bros.) 1950, d. John Cromwell

Call Northside 777 (20th Century-Fox) 1948, d. Henry Hathaway

The Captive City (United Artists) 1952, d. Robert Wise

Caught (MGM) 1949, d. Max Ophuls

Champion (United Artists) 1949, d. Mark Robson

Christmas Holiday (Universal) 1944, d. Robert Siodmak
The City That Never Sleeps (Republic) 1953, d. John H. Auer
Clash by Night (RKO) 1952, d. Fritz Lang
Conflict (Warner Bros.) 1945, d. Curtis Bernhardt
Cornered (RKO) 1945, d. Edward Dmytryk
Crack-Up (RKO) 1946, d. Irving Reis
The Crimson Kimono (Columbia) 1959, d. Samuel Fuller
Criss Cross (Universal-International) 1949, Robert Siodmak
Crossfire (RKO) 1947, d. Edward Dmytryk
Cry Danger (RKO) 1951, d. Robert Parrish
Cry of the City (20th Century-Fox) 1948, d. Robert Siodmak
D.O.A. (United Artists) 1950, d. Rudolph Maté
The Dark Corner (20th Century-Fox) 1946, d. Henry Hathaway
The Dark Mirror (Universal-International) 1946, d. Robert Siodmak
Dark Passage (Warner Bros.) 1947, d. Delmer Daves
The Dark Past (Columbia) 1948, d. Rudolph Maté
Dead Reckoning (Columbia) 1947, d. John Cromwell
Deadline at Dawn (RKO) 1946, d. Harold Clurman
Decoy (Monogram) 1947, d. Jack Bernhard
Desperate (RKO) 1947, d. Anthony Mann
Detective Story (Paramount) 1951, d. William Wyler
Detour (PRC) 1945, d. Edgar G. Ulmer
Double Indemnity (Paramount) 1944, d. Billy Wilder
Edge of Doom (RKO) 1950, d. Mark Robson
The Enforcer (Warner Bros.) 1951, d. Bretaigne Windust
Fallen Angel (20th Century-Fox) 1946, d. Otto Preminger
The Fallen Sparrow (RKO) 1943, d. Richard Wallace
Fear in the Night (Paramount) 1947, d. Maxwell Shane
The File on Thelma Jordan (Paramount) 1950, d. Robert Siodmak
Follow Me Quietly (RKO) 1949, d. Richard Fleischer
Force of Evil (MGM) 1948, d. Abraham Polonsky
Framed (Columbia) 1947, d. Richard Wallace
Gilda (Columbia) 1946, d. Charles Vidor
The Glass Key (Paramount) 1942, d. Stuart Heisler
Guilty Bystander (Film Classics) 1950, d. Joseph Lerner
Gun Crazy (United Artists) 1950, d. Joseph H. Lewis
He Ran All the Way (United Artists) 1951, d. John Berry
He Walked by Night (Eagle-Lion) 1949, d. Alfred Werker
The High Wall (MGM) 1947, d. Curtis Bernhardt
His Kind of Woman (RKO) 1951, d. John Farrow
The Hitch-Hiker (RKO) 1953, d. Ida Lupino
Hollow Triumph (Eagle-Lion) 1948, d. Steve Sekely
House of Strangers (20th Century-Fox) 1949, d. Joseph L. Mankiewicz
The House on 92nd Street (20th Century-Fox) 1945, d. Henry Hathaway

The House on Telegraph Hill (20th Century-Fox) 1951, d. Robert Wise
Human Desire (Columbia) 1954, d. Fritz Lang
I, The Jury (United Artists) 1953, d. Harry Essex
I Wake Up Screaming (20th Century-Fox) 1941, d. H. Bruce Humberstone
I Was a Communist for the F.B.I. (Warner Bros.) 1951, d. Gordon Douglas
In a Lonely Place (Columbia) 1950, d. Nicholas Ray
Jeopardy (MGM) 1952, d. John Sturges
Johnny Angel (RKO) 1945, d. Edwin L. Marin
Johnny Eager (MGM) 1942, d. Mervyn LeRoy
Johnny O'Clock (Columbia) 1947, d. Robert Rossen
Journey into Fear (RKO) 1943, d. Norman Foster
Kansas City Confidential (United Artists) 1952, d. Phil Karlson
Key Largo (Warner Bros.) 1948, d. John Huston
The Killers (Universal) 1946, d. Robert Siodmak
Killer's Kiss (United Artists) 1955, d. Stanley Kubrick
The Killing (United Artists) 1956, d. Stanley Kubrick
A Kiss Before Dying (United Artists) 1957, d. Gerd Oswald
Kiss Me Deadly (United Artists) 1955, d. Robert Aldrich
Kiss Of Death (20th Century-Fox) 1947, d. Henry Hathaway
Kiss the Blood off My Hands (Universal-International) 1948, d. Norman Foster
Kiss Tomorrow Goodbye (Warner Bros.) 1950, d. Gordon Douglas
The Lady from Shanghai (Columbia) 1948, d. Orson Welles
The Lady in the Lake (MGM) 1946, d. Robert Montgomery
Laura (20th Century-Fox) 1944, d. Otto Preminger
Leave Her to Heaven (20th Century-Fox) 1945, d. John M. Stahl
The Lineup (Columbia) 1958, d. Don Siegel
The Locket (RKO) 1947, d. John Brahm
The Long Night (RKO) 1947, d. Anatole Litvak
Macao (RKO) 1952, d. Josef von Sternberg
The Maltese Falcon (Warner Bros.) 1941, d. John Huston
The Mask of Dimitrios (Warner Bros.) 1944, d. Jean Negulesco
Mildred Pierce (Warner Bros.) 1945, d. Michael Curtiz
Ministry of Fear (Paramount) 1944, d. Fritz Lang
Mr. Arkadin (M & A Alexander Prods.) 1955, d. Orson Welles
The Mob (Columbia) 1951, d. Robert Parrish
Murder, My Sweet (RKO) 1944, d. Edward Dmytryk
My Name Is Julia Ross (Columbia) 1945, d. Joseph H. Lewis
Mystery Street (MGM) 1950, d. John Sturges
The Naked City (Universal-International) 1948, d. Jules Dassin
The Narrow Margin (RKO) 1952, d. Richard Fleischer
New York Confidential (Warner Bros.) 1955, d. Russell Rouse
Niagara (20th Century-Fox) 1952, d. Henry Hathaway
Night and the City (20th Century-Fox) 1950, d. Jules Dassin
Night Editor (Columbia) 1946, d. Henry Levin

Night Has a Thousand Eyes (Paramount) 1948, d. John Farrow
Nightfall (Columbia) 1957, d. Jacques Tourneur
Nightmare (United Artists) 1956, d. Maxwell Shane
Nightmare Alley (20th Century-Fox) 1947, d. Edmund Goulding
99 River Street (United Artists) 1953, d. Phil Karlson
Nobody Lives Forever (Warner Bros.) 1946, d. Jean Negulesco
Nocturne (RKO) 1946, d. Edwin L. Marin
Nora Prentiss (Warner Bros.) 1947, d. Vincent Sherman
Notorious (RKO) 1946, d. Alfred Hitchcock
Odds Against Tomorrow (United Artists) 1959, d. Robert Wise
On Dangerous Ground (RKO) 1952, d. John Houseman
One Way Street (Universal-International) 1950, d. Hugo Fregonese
Out of the Past (RKO) 1947, d. Jacques Tourneur
Panic in the Streets (20th Century-Fox) 1950, d. Elia Kazan
Party Girl (MGM) 1958, d. Nicholas Ray
The People Against O'Hara (MGM) 1951, d. John Sturges
Phantom Lady (Universal) 1944, d. Robert Siodmak
The Phenix City Story (Allied Artists) 1955, d. Phil Karlson
Pickup on South Street (20th Century-Fox) 1953, d. Samuel Fuller
Pitfall (United Artists) 1948, d. André de Toth
Port of New York (Eagle-Lion) 1949, d. Laslo Benedek
Possessed (Warner Bros.) 1947, d. Curtis Bernhardt
The Postman Always Rings Twice (MGM) 1946, d. Tay Garnett
Private Hell 36 (Filmakers) 1954, d. Don Siegel
The Prowler (United Artists) 1951, d. Joseph Losey
Pushover (Columbia) 1954, d. Richard Quine
The Racket (RKO) 1951, d. John Cromwell
Raw Deal (Eagle-Lion) 1948, d. Anthony Mann
The Reckless Moment (Columbia) 1949, d. Max Ophuls
Ride the Pink Horse (Universal-International) 1947, d. Robert Montgomery
Roadblock (RKO) 1951, d. Harold Daniels
Road House (20th Century-Fox) 1948, d. Jean Negulesco
Rogue Cop (MGM) 1954, d. Roy Rowland
Rope (Warner Bros.) 1948, d. Alfred Hitchcock
Scandal Sheet (Columbia) 1952, d. Phil Karlson
Scarlet Street (Universal) 1945, d. Fritz Lang
The Second Woman (United Artists) 1951, d. James V. Kern
Secret Beyond the Door (Universal-International) 1948, d. Fritz Lang
The Set-Up (RKO) 1949, d. Robert Wise
711 Ocean Drive (Columbia) 1950, d. Joseph M. Newman
Shadow of a Doubt (Universal) 1943, d. Alfred Hitchcock
The Shanghai Gesture (United Artists) 1941, d. Josef von Sternberg
Shock (20th Century-Fox) 1946, d. Alfred Werker
Side Street (MGM) 1950, d. Anthony Mann

The Sleeping City (Universal-International) 1950, d. George Sherman
Slightly Scarlet (RKO) 1956, d. Allan Dwan
The Sniper (Columbia) 1952, d. Edward Dmytryk
So Dark the Night (Columbia) 1946, d. Joseph H. Lewis
Somewhere in the Night (20th Century-Fox) 1946, d. Joseph L. Mankiewicz
Sorry, Wrong Number (Paramount) 1948, d. Anatole Litvak
Southside 1-1000 (Allied Artists) 1950, d. Boris Ingster
The Spiritualist (Eagle-Lion) 1948, d. Bernard Vorhaus
The Strange Love of Martha Ivers (Paramount) 1946, d. Lewis Milestone
The Stranger (RKO) 1946, d. Orson Welles
Stranger on the Third Floor (RKO) 1940, d. Boris Ingster
Strangers on a Train (Warner Bros.) 1951, d. Alfred Hitchcock
Street of Chance (Paramount) 1942, d. Jack Hively
The Street With No Name (20th Century-Fox) 1948, d. William Keighley
Sudden Fear (RKO) 1952, d. David Miller
Suddenly (United Artists) 1954, d. Lewis Allen
Sunset Boulevard (Paramount) 1950, d. Billy Wilder
Suspense (Monogram) 1946, d. Frank Tuttle
Sweet Smell of Success (United Artists) 1957, d. Alexander Mackendrick
T-Men (Eagle-Lion) 1947, d. Anthony Mann
The Tattered Dress (Universal-International) 1957, d. Jack Arnold
Tension (MGM) 1950, d. John Berry
They Live by Night (RKO) 1949, d. Nicholas Ray
They Won't Believe Me (RKO) 1947, d. Irving Pichel
The Thief (United Artists) 1952, d. Russell Rouse
Thieves' Highway (20th Century-Fox) 1949, d. Jules Dassin
The Third Man (British-Lion) 1949, d. Carol Reed
This Gun for Hire (Paramount) 1942, d. Frank Tuttle
Three Strangers (Warner Bros.) 1946, d. Jean Negulesco
Too Late for Tears (United Artists) 1949, d. Byron Haskin
Touch of Evil (Universal-International) 1958, d. Orson Welles
The Turning Point (Paramount) 1952, d. William Dieterle
The Undercover Man (Columbia) 1949, d. Joseph H. Lewis
Undercurrent (MGM) 1946, d. Vincente Minnelli
Union Station (Paramount) 1950, d. Rudolph Maté
The Unknown Man (MGM) 1951, d. Richard Thorpe
The Unsuspected (Warner Bros.) 1947, d. Michael Curtiz
Vicki (20th Century-Fox) 1953, d. Harry Horner
Walk East on Beacon (Columbia) 1952, d. Alfred Werker
The Web (Universal-International) 1947, d. Michael Gordon
When Strangers Marry (Monogram) 1944, d. William Castle
Where Danger Lives (RKO) 1950, d. John Farrow
Where the Sidewalk Ends (20th Century-Fox) 1950, d. Otto Preminger
While the City Sleeps (RKO) 1956, d. Fritz Lang

Whirlpool (20th Century-Fox) 1949, d. Otto Preminger

White Heat (Warner Bros.) 1949, d. Raoul Walsh

The Window (RKO) 1949, d. Ted Tetzlaff

The Woman in the Window (RKO) 1944, d. Fritz Lang

The Woman on Pier 13 (RKO) 1949, d. Robert Stevenson

Woman on the Run (Universal-International) 1950, d. Norman Foster

World for Ransom (Allied Artists) 1954, d. Robert Aldrich

The Wrong Man (Warner Bros.) 1956, d. Alfred Hitchcock

Selected Neo-Noirs: 1960–1997

After Dark, My Sweet (Avenue) 1990, d. James Foley

Angel Heart (Tri-Star) 1987, d. Alan Parker

Black Rain (Paramount) 1989, d. Ridley Scott

Black Widow (20th Century-Fox) 1986, d. Bob Rafelson

Blade Runner (Warner Bros.) 1982, d. Ridley Scott

Blast of Silence (Malda) 1961, d. Allen Baron

Blood Simple (Circle) 1984, d. Joel Coen

Blue Velvet (DEG) 1986, d. David Lynch

Body Heat (Warner Bros.) 1981, d. Lawrence Kasdan

Brainstorm (Warner Bros.) 1965, d. William Conrad

Cape Fear (Universal-International) 1962, d. J. Lee Thompson

Chinatown (Paramount) 1974, d. Roman Polanski

Dirty Harry (Warner Bros.) 1971, d. Don Siegel

The Driver (20th Century-Fox) 1978, d. Walter Hill

Farewell, My Lovely (Avco Embassy) 1975, Dick Richards

Frantic (Warner Bros.) 1988, d. Roman Polanski

The French Connection (20th Century-Fox) 1971, d. William Friedkin

The French Connection II (20th Century-Fox) 1975, d. John Frankenheimer

The Grifters (Miramax) 1990, d. Stephen Frears

Hustle (Paramount) 1975, d. Robert Aldrich

Jagged Edge (Columbia) 1985, d. Richard Marquand

Johnny Handsome (Tri-Star) 1989, d. Walter Hill

Klute (Warner Bros.) 1971, d. Alan J. Pakula

The Kremlin Letter (20th Century-Fox) 1970, d. John Huston

The Last Seduction (October) 1994, d. John Dahl

The Manchurian Candidate (United Artists) 1962, d. John Frankenheimer

Mickey One (Columbia) 1965, d. Arthur Penn

Mirage (Universal-International) 1965, d. Edward Dmytryk

Night Moves (Warner Bros.) 1975, d. Arthur Penn

Point Blank (MGM) 1967, d. John Boorman

Seven (New Line) 1995, d. David Fincher
Someone to Watch Over Me (Columbia) 1987, d. Ridley Scott
Sudden Impact (Warner Bros.) 1983, d. Clint Eastwood
Taxi Driver (Columbia) 1976, d. Martin Scorcese
Terminator (Cannon) 1984, d. James Cameron
Tightrope (Warner Bros.) 1984, d. Richard Tuggle
Underworld U.S.A. (Columbia) 1961, d. Samuel Fuller
The Usual Suspects (Polygram) 1995, d. Bryan Singer

Index

281